KU-605-074

Explorers

Desmond Wilcox Explorers

Book Club Associates, London

This edition published 1975
by Book Club Associates
By arrangement with
the British Broadcasting Corporation

© Desmond Wilcox 1975

Printed in England
by Jolly & Barber Ltd, Rugby

I would like to acknowledge the help of the
production team of the television series *Explorers*,
particularly Michael Latham, the producer; Gordon
Watkins, the script editor; and researchers John
Dollar and Tristan Allsop; and Patsy,
whose own journey and achievements
match any in this book, and Cassandra, Adam,
and Claire whose voyages of discovery
are all ahead.

                                                    D.W.

Preface

Explorers. Some travelled with an ideal. Others searched in greed. Some were map-makers; or travellers in search of trade; others went to spread their own form of religion; some simply to claim new lands for their country – with the promise of wealth and personal honour.

For many explorers, curiosity itself was sufficient reason to travel to the unknown, to risk their lives in searching. For them, just to survive the experience, and later to tell of it, was enough.

Whatever their varied reasons, they all shared a single fundamental experience. They all endured that particular brand of fear and discomfort, that special kind of homesickness and weariness, even the acceptance of death – and, just occasionally, that rare, ecstatic arrival that made it all worthwhile.

This book doesn't set out, in any way, to be a history of exploration. It echoes – and expands on – the stories of the nine men and one woman who were the subjects of the BBC Television series, *Explorers*. Their lives and travels occurred during roughly five hundred years of time and were spread around the world. As people, they reflect only some of the backgrounds, motives, pressures and fears that have driven explorers always.

Ten people who made journeys, and chronicled them, and were then remembered. From their stories the rest of the world learned, and benefited.

And they are exciting stories.

The first tale in this book is also the most recent: an epic, fearsome journey within the memory of many still living today; an exploration that set out from a background, a society and times that, also, are not too different from those we know today.

Roald Amundsen 1872–1928

Roald Amundsen, a Norwegian, was a man hungry for success. He planned, calculated and worked with only that end in mind. In 1909, he was completing his plans to drift to the North Pole in the icepack when an American, Commander Peary, reached it by dog sledge.

There was one glittering prize left: the South Pole – and the explorers of two nations, Great Britain and Norway, began urgently to compete for it. Amundsen was already famous for sailing through the North-west Passage, from the Canadian Arctic to the Pacific. It was a voyage great explorers had attempted – and failed to complete. It was not enough for Amundsen. He had a greater ambition – to be the first man to reach the South Pole – and he achieved that too. But he was to learn how sour triumph can taste when the methods he used were condemned, labelled unsporting and inhuman.

There was one final bitter irony. The man Amundsen beat to the Pole, Captain Scott, by tragically failing to survive the return journey, became, posthumously, the real hero of the South Pole. Amundsen's achievement was swamped. He had calculated, planned, and worked for success. He was a man with great qualities of organisation, imagination and leadership. He achieved what he set out to do. But somehow, unfairly, he also failed.

ogs were the key to everything. Nansen had recommended them, and to Amundsen, Nansen was the most revered figure in the world. Amundsen had already used them himself, in 1905, on his discovery of the North-west Passage.

Greenland eskimo dogs, little more than half-tamed wolves, able to withstand the most terrible conditions of ice and snow; not the Siberian huskies that Scott was using. Six of them could pull a loaded sledge over the snow-covered wastes of Antarctica twenty miles a day. Six of them also represented 300 lbs of fresh meat.

That was how Amundsen saw them now: 'Twenty-four of our brave and faithful companions were marked out for death.'

He bent and pumped the primus – hoping the noise would drown the sound of the shots.

They called the place 'Butchers'.

It lay 85° 36′ south of the equator, at the top of the Axel Heiberg glacier.

Amundsen had chosen it with typical, cold logic, two years earlier, sitting in his study in Oslo planning every meticulous detail of this expedition never before achieved by any man.

'Butchers.'

He had never seen the place – though he knew exactly what was going to happen there. Twenty-four of the weakest animals were to be slaughtered to provide fresh meat for the remainder – and for the five men. Everyone agreed to it. But there wasn't a man who wasn't sickened by the prospect of shooting the dogs.

Men and dogs had been together more than a year. The dogs had names: Colonel, Ring, Arne. Helmer Hanssen, an expert dog-handler who had been with Amundsen through the North-west Passage, regarded his dog Helge as the best friend he had.

At Butchers he put a pistol to her head, shot her – then prepared to eat her.

'We had agreed to shrink from nothing,' said Amundsen, 'in order to reach our goal. Shot now followed upon shot – they had an uncanny sound over the great plain. A trusty servant lost his life each time. In everybody's view, there was no other way.'

Butchers cost Amundsen most of the acclaim he deserved. To many people, the idea of

The dogs on board the *Fram* before departure. It was the last idle time they were to have.

slaughtering dogs, in the calculated manner that he did, was unsporting. To eat them was revolting. To enjoy the experience was horrific.

The British, in particular, were outraged by Amundsen's remarks:

'The next day we treated ourselves to dog cutlets. . . . It was excellent, absolutely excellent.'

And the British had a vested interest in the affair, for Scott was also on his way to the South Pole.

mundsen had been planning a polar expedition for years. The North and South Poles were the two main plums left to explorers. Amundsen already knew the Arctic. His successful North-west Passage expedition which started in 1903, went on after several years to relocate the magnetic North Pole. As early as 1907, he had been to see Nansen to ask if he might borrow *Fram*, the ship that Nansen had taken into the Arctic. He wanted it for another journey to the north. Then, in the autumn of 1909, the American explorer Peary reached the North Pole by dog sledge, even while Amundsen

was planning to drift there in the icepack, and the scheme had to be scrapped. At once he switched targets, began to plan for a trip south, though he told no one except two or three of his closest associates. Even Nansen wasn't told, and Nansen was an idol to him, a father figure who represented all that was noble in human exploration.

Nansen wasn't the first idol. That was Sir John Franklin, the English explorer who had died in 1847 attempting to discover the Northwest Passage. As a boy, Amundsen conceived the idea of emulating him. But the sea itself also influenced him, as well as the men who sailed it.

He was born near Oslo on 16 July 1872, the fourth son of a prosperous shipping businessman who died when Roald was fourteen. He was a normal healthy child, reasonably adventurous, not particularly academic. Like many young men, he had something of a fetish about his physique. He slept with his windows open as part of a deliberate programme to toughen himself. He skied and played football, and exercised to build his muscles. He did so with that tenacity and determination with which he did everything, and was to do everything throughout his life. When he enrolled for National Service the Army doctors who examined him were impressed by his physical condition. His only recorded physical weakness was a degree of shortsightedness, though it never seems to have inconvenienced him.

His relationship with his mother was close. He was, after all, the baby of the family, and she turned to him increasingly after the death of her husband. Although he conceived the ambition of being an Arctic explorer early in his teens, he accepted his mother's wish that he should become a doctor and for two years dutifully studied medicine at university. Then, when he was twenty-one, his mother died. He had never found any particular appeal in academic life, or in medicine. Now there was no longer any reason for him to stay at university. He left – and turned to the sea.

His reading in the field of Arctic exploration had already convinced him that one reason for the failure of some previous expeditions had been divided leadership. A seaman was necessary to take the party through the pack-ice, a land explorer to take it to its final objective. Disagreements between the two commands led to endless difficulties. Amundsen was convinced that any expedition should have one undisputed leader, whose authority was never to be challenged. The ideal leader – he looked to Nansen's example – would discuss his plans with his team and listen to their opinions. But in the end his decision would always be final and his team would accept it as such. It was this concept of leadership, this understanding of command, that decided him on a career at sea. His interest in land exploration, backed by a sea captain's qualifications, would, he believed, equip him for sole command of his own expeditions.

In 1894, he signed on as a sailor with a sailing ship bound for the Arctic. It says much for his hard work, tenacity and single-mindedness, that only three years later he sailed as first mate on the *Belgica*, becoming a member of the Belgian Antarctic Expedition that went to study the South Magnetic Pole. The experience was invaluable. It gave him his first contact with the Antarctic continent. It also gave him more insight into the nature of leadership.

9

The idea was that he should be put ashore, with three others, to spend the winter in south Victoria Land, while the ship returned to civilisation. But, largely due to the captain's carelessness, the ship was trapped in the winter ice and had to lie there for thirteen months. Two of the crew went mad. The entire ship's company went down with scurvy, including the captain. Suddenly Amundsen found himself in command, as the senior ranking officer still on his feet. It is characteristic of him that he should already have had a plan at his fingertips. One of the causes of the scurvy outbreak, as he saw it, was the absence of fresh meat. He turned to the medical officer for specialist advice, and promptly added penguin and seal meat to everyone's diet. Recovery was dramatic. Little wonder that in his future planning Amundsen attached such importance to fresh meat.

He achieved his Master's ticket when he returned from the Antarctic. At last he could begin to plan his own expedition to the Arctic. Nansen was there as an example before him. Franklin still caught his imagination. 'What appealed to me most strongly was the suffering he endured. A strange ambition burned within me to share those same sufferings.'

He planned to force the North-west Passage that had taken Franklin's life, and at the same time relocate the north magnetic pole. With this in mind he bought a fishing smack, built the year he was born, renamed her *Gjoa* and set out to equip her. It took him three years. He tried to anticipate every situation he was likely to encounter, and then plan for it in meticulous detail. It was his nature to do so. His whole way of life was orderly and neat, obsessed with logistics: 'I can do twice the amount of work when I see tidiness and comfort around me,' he said. This meticulousness was even apparent in his dress. There was something of the dandy in him; he was often described as 'the best man to go exploring with – and the best-dressed explorer too!'

There was, however, one aspect of the preparation with which he had trouble. (He was always to do so.) The question of money. Perhaps his well-to-do, middle-class back-

Roald Amundsen. 'The best-dressed explorer.'

THE ADVENTUROUS VOYAGE OF THE TERRA NOVA TO THE ICY WASTES OF THE ANTARCTIC.

CAPTAIN SCOTT AND HIS COMPANIONS HELD UP BY AN ICE-PACK IN POLAR SEAS.

Mrs. Scott, who is a well-known sculptor, and her little son.

Captain Scott and the men who took part in the expedition in the ward room of the Terra Nova while the vessel was held up by an ice-pack.

Captain Scott, wearing naval uniform.—(Thomson.)

Master Scott, who is not yet two and a half, among his crocuses.

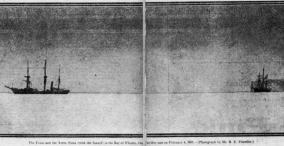

The Fram and the Terra Nova (with the funnel) in the Bay of Whales, where they met on February 4, 1911.—(Photograph by Mr. R. E. Priestley.)

Captain Amundsen and his dog. In the background is his ship, the Fram.

The photographs of Mrs. Scott and her little boy by *The Daily Mirror*, the one showing them together having been taken this week. That of Captain Scott and the other members of the expedition is by Mr. H. G. Ponting, camera artist to the British Antarctic Expedition. It is copyright in U.S.A. and Europe.

The Daily Mirror, 8 March 1912, showing Scott, his family, his polar party, and his ship. Amundsen and his pet dog in front of *Fram* receive second billing. It was a nationalistic age.

---

ground made him regard the financing of an expedition as of secondary importance. Perhaps his zeal in working out the details of route and equipment made him overlook it. But more likely he hoped that time would help him to sort out the problem. Whatever the reason, Amundsen was so plagued by creditors that by June 1903 he was forced to slip his berth secretly under cover of darkness to avoid being arrested for non-payment of debts. It taught him a great deal, and unquestionably later influenced his decision to go south after Peary had reached the North Pole.

The present voyage, in any case, was a success. Amundsen did, after all, become the first man to navigate the North-west Passage. That achievement brought him fame, and a good deal of money from his writings and lecture tours. But it followed that if he was to continue to mount expeditions they had to be equally successful. Success brought money. Money allowed him to buy the stores and equipment that he saw as essential. 'Truly', Nansen had said, 'the whole secret lies in arranging things as well as possible.'

There were other reasons for wanting success. He loved his mother – and later the memory of her. Success would make him feel that, had she lived, she would have had cause to be proud of him, despite the fact that he hadn't followed the path of medicine that she had chosen for him. Success would bring him esteem in the eyes of his peers: men like Nansen, Peary, Shackleton, Scott. Perhaps most important, success would bring prestige to his country. It was a nationalistic age, in which a man might do things for his country without risk of being labelled just jingoistic. Scott wanted the South Pole for Britain; Peary took the North Pole in the name of America. So why shouldn't Norway bask in the glory of Amundsen's achievements?

There was this difference between Norway and the rest: when Amundsen turned south from Madeira in the summer of 1910 (after Peary's success), Norway was only five years old. For a hundred years she had been a reluctant part of the Swedish kingdom, and for four hundred years before that she had been part of Denmark. As a newly-born independent sovereign state, she had more need than any other country in Europe to make her mark. There was a new feeling of national euphoria, and it needed great achievements to feed on.

What Amundsen had in mind in 1907, when he persuaded Nansen to let him use *Fram*, was an attack on the North Pole. For two years after Nansen's reluctant agreement, Amundsen planned with that goal in mind. Then, in September, 1909, news reached him of Peary's success. The

Fram, built for polar exploration

whole complicated, carefully planned, immensely considered edifice that he had been constructing was destroyed in half a dozen words. What was the point in going north now? If he reached the North Pole, there would be no achievement, no reward, in coming second. Norway's reputation would hardly be advanced. The book he was planning about the journey and the lecture tours he intended to give would arouse little interest now, and without the money he was expecting to earn how could he pay the debts that he had already incurred?

It was there and then that he decided to go south instead. It was a secret he had to keep almost entirely to himself. The strain must have been considerable, even for so single-minded a man. If he told his backers, would there be time to persuade them of the need for such a change of plan before someone reached the South Pole ahead of him? Shackleton had managed within a hundred miles of it the year before; Scott was preparing for another attempt. The urge to tell Nansen must have been great. But suppose he

refused to lend *Fram* for a journey that he had in mind himself?

Amundsen decided not to take the risk.

Now he had to undertake a complete rethinking of the expedition. He recalled his own experiences in Antarctica in 1907. He read Shackleton and Scott again with a new sense of involvement. He wondered whether the dogs he had been planning to use in the Arctic would stand up to conditions in the Antarctic. Scott, it was widely known, was using ponies and mechanical sledges as his principal means of transport. Amundsen tried to imagine every detail of the situation, based on what he knew already and what he had read, and with a magnificent self-assurance that only faltered once during the entire expedition, he made the most important decision of his life:

'Although I had never seen this part of the Antarctic regions, I was not long in forming an opinion diametrically opposed to that of Shackleton and Scott, for the conditions both of going and surface were precisely what one would desire for sledging with Eskimo dogs, to judge from the descriptions of these explorers. If Peary could make a record trip on the Arctic ice with dogs, one ought, surely, with equally good tackle, to be able to beat Peary's record on the splendidly even surface of the Barrier.'

Dogs had another advantage besides speed over the ponies that Scott was taking. Beyond the flat shelf of the Ross Ice Barrier was a range of mountains rising more than 10,000 feet to the central plateau of Antarctica. Dogs could climb such mountains, taking sledges with them. And even Shackleton had said it would be out of the question to get ponies up. 'Not only can one get the dogs up over the huge glaciers that lead to the plateau, but one can make full use of them the whole way,' Amundsen wrote later. 'Ponies, on the other hand, have to be left at the foot of the glacier, while the men themselves have the doubtful pleasure of acting as ponies.'

Dogs had yet another advantage. Each of them was in fact a fully mobile store of fresh meat, to be killed and eaten when necessary. Each dog represented fifty pounds of food less to be carried on the sledges. The concept of dogs as mobile food depots as well as beasts of burden must have opened a whole range of new possibilities for Amundsen, the logician, the planner: 'The greatest difference between Scott's and my equipment lay undoubtedly in our choice of draught animals,' he says. The truth of that statement, in view of the vastly different outcomes of the rival expeditions, can hardly be denied.

The dogs that Amundsen chose were from Greenland. The Royal Greenland Trading Company agreed to deliver a hundred of them to Norway in July 1910. They were square-set creatures, never really tame, with thick dense coats full of natural oils that even the most bitter polar winds failed to penetrate. Their legs were sturdy and well-muscled, their feet round and comparatively large with thick pads, well-insulated against the frozen ground. Properly controlled, they were able to pull a half-ton sledge up to fifty miles a day. Amundsen understood the need for such control if the dogs were to justify their keep. In the Arctic, he had taken the trouble to learn how to work with these animals. It was to prove a crucial factor in his race south.

The plan was to take the *Fram* into the Pacific, then south into the Bay of Whales. There the shore party would disembark on the Ross Ice Barrier, whilst the *Fram* withdrew to Buenos Aires for the winter. The shore party – nine, including Amundsen – were to make the assault on the South Pole the following summer.

That party was handpicked by Amundsen. He wanted men of experience, men with skill in working out of doors in the cold. Equally important, he wanted men with experience in handling dogs, since each would be responsible for looking after his own team.

Frederick Hjalmar Johansen was forty-four, a native of Skien. He was a captain in the army, a magnificent athlete, and a particularly fine skier. He had been with Nansen's 1893 expedition to the Arctic in *Fram*. Nansen had been impressed by him and chose him to be his only companion on a long overland journey into the ice field. 'A fine fellow physically and mentally,' he had said, in recommending him to Amundsen.

Frederick Johansen, athlete and skier

Johansen proved to be good with his dogs, and one of his special responsibilities was the packing of the sledge cases. But he had one drawback from Amundsen's point of view. He was fond of drink. It had amused Nansen to find that Johansen had been sufficiently inventive in the Arctic to set up a still. Amundsen, less immediate than Nansen, more circumspect, would have viewed such a discovery with suspicion.

Kristian Prestrud was thirty, a lieutenant in the navy. He was an outgoing personality, good-humoured, with wide travel experience. He even had a musical ability useful on occasions such as Christmas. Amundsen gave him the general scientific responsibility of drawing up charts, copying tables, and making astronomical readings and calculations.

Adolf Henrik Lindström was the cook, a Hammarfest man of forty-six, generous, good-natured and amusing. He had been with Amundsen on the three-year trip to the North-west Passage and Amundsen liked him. He had that orderliness and sense of method that always

(*Left to right*) **Lindström, the cook, with buckwheat cakes. His inventiveness in the galley was constantly admired. Prestrud in winter dress; Bjaaland in winter dress.**

commended itself to Amundsen. As a cook he was first class. He also acted as librarian for the party, but it was his inventiveness that made him particularly valuable. He managed in the end to produce from provisions that had been brought half round the world, a series of meals that were almost in the gourmet class. 'To the end of my days,' said Helmer Hanssen of him, 'I shall see before me Lindström standing at the end of the table, comfortable and round, while four of us at each side of the table sat expectant like hungry young birds in a nest, waiting for the hot cakes he dealt to each from the tower in front of him.'

Olav Olavson Bjaaland was a ski-maker and carpenter of thirty-eight, from Norgedal in Telemark. He was an athlete and, like Johansen, a brilliant skier. His major contribution to the success of the expedition was to be his carpentry skills.

Helmer Hanssen was from northern Norway. He had been at sea from the age of eleven. Now,

at forty-one, he was a Master Mariner with vast experience. He too had been part of the North-west Passage expedition, when Amundsen had seen his work with dogs and decided that Hanssen was to be chief dog man and lead sledge on all the polar journeys. Hanssen and Johansen had known each other for years and were friends.

Sverre Hassel, another Oslo man, was thirty-five, and had been at sea since he was a boy. He was now a Master Mariner with Arctic experience, during which he had met Johansen. He was a man of wit, charm and vivacity – and Amundsen put him in charge of the expedition's fuel supplies.

Oskar Wisting was a married man of forty from Larvik. He was a trained navigator and a sergeant in the marines. A solid, reliable man whom Amundsen made responsible for out-fitting during the long winter wait before the final polar thrust. He was inventive, skilful with his hands, and particularly good with dogs.

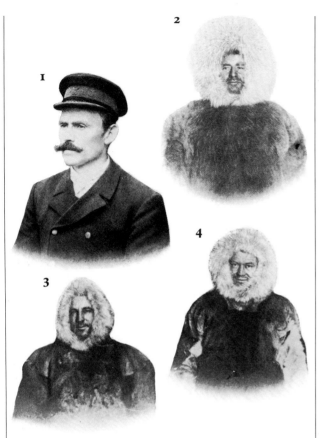

1. Helmer Hanssen, 2. Sverre Hassel, 3. Oskar Wisting, 4. Jörgen Stubberud

Jörgen Stubberud, an Oslo man, was twenty-eight, the youngest member of the expedition. Stubberud's major contribution began long before *Fram* left Oslo. With his brother he constructed the prefabricated hut – to be called *Framheim* – in which the party wintered on the Ross Ice Barrier.

Fram left Oslo fjord on 7 June 1910. The King and Queen visited her before she sailed, carrying so many Norwegian hopes with her. Nansen himself saw his beloved ship pull clear of the quay with Amundsen on the bridge. Despite his natural generosity, it was he said, 'the bitterest hour of my life'.

As far as everyone knew, they were witnessing the start of another Arctic expedition. *Fram* was to go south beyond the equator, turn north round Cape Horn into the Pacific, and come into the Arctic Ocean through the Bering Straits.

Only four men on board knew the truth: Amundsen himself, his second-in-command Captain Nilsen, and the two first officers, one of whom was Lieutenant Prestrud.

In Madeira, Amundsen revealed his true intentions. He was going south, not north. His objective was the South Pole.

He even sent a terse cable to Captain Scott in Melbourne.

With a handful of exceptions, the world was taken aback. One of Amundsen's brothers in Oslo even went to see the King to tell him of the changed plan. Helland-Hansen went to see Nansen. Nansen's reaction was one of total shock. He had lent *Fram* on the understanding that she was to go north. For years he had been planning an Antarctic expedition of his own. But, he was too great a man to complain that he had been misled. All he said was: 'If only he had told me, I could have helped in so many ways.' But to Frederick Johansen on board the detoured *Fram* it seemed underhanded. He was deeply attached to Nansen and felt it a betrayal of the great man.

In October, Scott sailed into Melbourne with his own expedition bound for the Pole. Amundsen's cable was waiting for him. 'Am going south. Amundsen.' What had seemed to Scott a serious scientific voyage of discovery had become a race.

Scott wrote to Nansen, whom he knew and trusted: '. . . it is evident that Amundsen has left everyone in ignorance of his intentions and if that is so, I am sure you will agree with me in deploring the fact. I do not believe the report that he is going to McMurdo Sound – the idea seems to me preposterous in view of his record – but the fact that he departs with so much mystery leaves one with an uncomfortable feeling that he contemplates something which he imagines we should not approve.

'However, it's no use discussing the matter till more is known. I hope to sail on the 25th and to be in the ice early in December. Everything has worked out well and the spirit of enthusiasm in my party is very fine – as you know, this expedition is on a very big scale. We may have made a mistake in having such an extensive organisation, but I am most anxious to get really good scientific results and for that one ought to have a number of experts. As to the travelling, we might have improved matters by having more dogs and fewer ponies. It is difficult to say – the animals we have are splendid and all in good condition.'

Amundsen was perfectly frank with his team. In view of the change of plan, any who wished could withdraw and he would pay their way home. Whatever their secret doubts might have been, no one left.

And in January 1911 the *Fram* set them down on the Ross Ice Barrier, 788 miles from the South Pole.

In this, Amundsen was taking perhaps the biggest calculated risk of the whole venture. He had chosen an untried route. Scott was heading along a known route, already attempted by Shackleton. Amundsen planned to win by beating the unknown.

The Ross Ice Barrier, now called the Ross Ice Shelf, is the largest known floating ice shelf in the world – a wilderness of ice approximately the size of France. It supports virtually no life, animal or vegetable. On the landward side its base is set on rock, but towards the open sea it floats freely. Huge slabs of the shelf ice are constantly breaking off – 'calving' – and drifting into the open sea. Shackleton's description of the conditions at the time of his visit seemed far from promising. Mile after mile of ice had broken away, and he 'thanked God he had not made his camp there.' The idea of erecting the prefabricated hut *Framheim* on the edge of the shelf, and finding one morning that the whole area had become detached and was drifting into the South Pacific, was disturbing. Yet against all previous evidence, Amundsen backed his own judgement: 'I knew that this plan of wintering on the Barrier itself would be exposed to severe criticism as recklessness, foolhardiness, and so forth. . . . I had devoted special study to this peculiar formation in the Barrier. For 70 years, this formation – with the exception of the pieces that had broken away – had persisted in the same place. I therefore concluded that it could be no accidental formation. . . . I therefore had no misgivings in placing our station on this part of the Barrier.'

The problem was, where on the Barrier was *Framheim* to be erected? The nearer to the sea it

1. Roald Amundsen, played in the film by Per Theodor Haugen.

2. The base camp, *Framheim*, being erected. It was to be their home as well as their base; their survival depended on it.

3. The ice tunnels and workshops which extended around *Framheim* from the cooking area. The workshop for the sledges. Amundsen ordered the sledges to be lightened from 165 lb to 53 lb.

4. Their first attempt at the Pole was defeated by the weather. Five days out. It was far too cold. Even the compass froze. All they could do was huddle in igloos.

5. After killing 24 of the dogs at the place they called 'Butchers', one sledge was abandoned. The carcasses became food for the men and the rest of the dogs. The remaining 18 dogs were divided into three teams of six. This calculated act was, later, to shock the world and cost Amundsen much of the true credit for his achievement.

6. The final dash for the Pole, with three dog teams, started in a blizzard. Amundsen wrote in his journal: 'It was sheer madness, we were running blind over unknown ground.'

7. 'For us humans driving to the south pole regions was just like play, but it was no fun for the dogs. They had to

(*continued p.17*)

16

be driven hard and whipped if we were ever to get there in fact. If there is any truth in the doctrine of transmigration of the souls I sincerely hope my next incarnation will not take the form of a dog on a Polar expedition.'

8. This was the Pole. Amundsen checked the meters, took sextant readings. They had beaten Scott by 35 days. They each put a hand on a pole made of ski sticks and pushed the flag into the snow. Amundsen named the place King Haakon the Seventh's Land.

The film was directed by David Cobham and shot on locations beyond the arctic circle in Norway.

was, the more quickly could supplies be unloaded from *Fram* and placed in permanent store. But how close to the sea could one go without risking 'calving'? Amundsen's punctilious mind had examined the question long ago in that study of his in Oslo.

'My idea had been to get everything – equipment and provisions – conveyed far enough into the Barrier to secure us against the unpleasant possibility of drifting out into the Pacific in case the Barrier should be inclined to calve. I had therefore fixed upon ten miles as a suitable distance from the edge of the Barrier. But even our first impression of the conditions seemed to show that we should be spared a great part of this long troublesome transport.'

Again, his judgement was to be proved right. The final site decided on for *Framheim* was two miles from the Barrier edge. He observed later: 'My hypothesis of the solidity of the Barrier . . . seems to be confirmed at all points by our observations during our twelve months' stay on it. . . . During our whole stay we never heard a sound or felt a movement on this spot.'

Framheim was assembled under the direction of Stubberud, who had made it, and the dogs set to work to haul the mountain of supplies up from the cliff face. It was the height of the Antarctic summer, with temperatures around zero centigrade. Amundsen's plan was to spend the remaining six weeks of daylight in organising the stores and laying down depots at 80°, 81° and 82° South. When the polar night began in March and temperatures fell to −30°C., he wanted to be quite sure that everything was secure for the long winter siege. He intended to make the attack on the Pole in September, as soon as spring came. There was no danger that Scott could move before that.

Six hundred yards to the west of *Framheim*, the main stores were set down. In this way the distance they had to be carried from *Fram* was reduced, and the ship could be unloaded more quickly. Even at the height of summer there was a chance that the ship might be iced in, and Amundsen's experience with the *Belgica* had taught him what that meant. Five marker flags were placed between *Framheim* and the stores depot, and a further row between there and the

sea. The track beaten by the sledges and the feet of the dogs from the sea to the depot and on to the hut 'resembled a good Norwegian country road'. Nine hundred cases of provisions had to be unloaded from *Fram* and hauled over the ice. The dogs – six to a sledge – could haul six of them at a time, a weight of about 660 pounds. Each case was marked with a distinguishing number and stacked according to its contents: coal, oil, wood, food, clothing and the like.

The erection of *Framheim* posed problems. By some incredible oversight, only two shovels had been brought with the expedition, and Stubberud and Bjaaland almost wore them out in chopping through the solid ice of the Barrier to provide some level foundation on which to put up the hut. Pickaxes – fortunately! – were avail-able for the deeper foundation work. Every piece of wood had been numbered when the hut was dismantled in Norway, but the reassemblage was nevertheless slow work, and until the roof was on and the walls were high enough to give some protection from the wind, the work was bitterly cold. 'At that time their job was undoubtedly the worst of any.'

At night, during the process of unloading, the dogs were tethered to wire ropes fifty yards long, arranged in a square. Initially they had given some trouble. For six months they had been doing nothing, lying in their quarters in *Fram*, warm and well-fed. They found it hard to re-acclimatise themselves to the harsh realities of life in the Antarctic. They refused to work and sat in their traces, snapping at one another. 'The

(*Left*) The formidable Ross Ice Barrier. (*Below*) Digging the ice corridors around *Framheim*.

most undisguised astonishment could be read in their faces,' says Amundsen. 'When at last we had succeeded, with another dose of the whip, in making them understand that we really asked them to work, instead of doing as they were told they flew at each other in a furious scrimmage.' Their days of growing fat were over for ever. From now until the end, they were to know little else but work and hardship. 'For us humans driving to the South Pole regions was just like play, but it was no fun for the dogs,' said Helmer Hanssen. 'They had to be driven hard and whipped if we were ever to get there in fact. If there is any truth in the doctrine of transmigration of souls I sincerely hope my next incarnation will not take the form of a dog on a Polar expedition.'

On 10 February the laying of depots began. These were intended to be used as sources of food and equipment on the journey to the Pole in September. The weather was warm, with temperatures on the second day rising to –10°C. Men took off their clothes and dropped them on the sledges; Amundsen christened one ascent Singlet Hill. It was hazy and there was a temptation to push up their goggles to get a better view. But they were too well-trained. The risk of snow-blindness is as great in overcast conditions as in full sunlight.

There were four of them – with three sledges. Prestrud had the worst job as forerunner. He had to ski alone ahead of the others, trying to steer as straight a course as possible, without any landmarks to guide him. If he veered to right or left, one of the men behind him with a compass called out the necessary correction. He was there to mark the crevasses and potholes and prevent the sledges falling into them. If he fell in himself, he had to hope the others could get him out. Amundsen was on the rear sledge on this first trip. It was his responsibility to make sure that nothing dropped off the sledges ahead.

Each sledge carried some 550 pounds of provisions to be left at the depot. There was a good deal of pemmican both for dogs and men, together with seal-meat steaks, blubber, dried fish, chocolate, margarine and biscuits. There were ten long bamboo poles with dark marker flags to mark the depots and the lines of approach to them. Additionally there were the supplies necessary for the trip to and from the depot: tents, more clothes, sleeping bags, stove, thermos flasks, sextant, artificial horizon, oil for the stove, matches, lanterns, and the like.

The depots, when they were completed, were no more than a collection of stores set down on the ice floor of the Barrier, surrounded by 12ft walls made of snow blocks. Each depot was topped by a flag, dark-coloured so as to stand out against the background of blue-white ice. The flag-topped bamboo poles marking the approach routes were set at distances of fifteen kilometres, and at right angles to the depots were additional flags. Each flag was numbered so it could be immediately identified. What Amundsen wanted to guard against was the possibility of bad weather on the journey in September making it difficult to find his essential supplies.

As summer drifted into autumn, the last of the three depots was completed. In all, some three and a half tons of stores had been set down at sixty-mile intervals on the Ross Ice Barrier, on Amundsen's projected route to the Pole.

Everything he had planned had been done.

The first depot (latitude 80° S.) held 4200 pounds, made up of seal meat, pemmican for the dogs, biscuits, butter, milk powder, chocolate, matches and paraffin. The second depot (latitude 81° S.) held half a ton of dogs' pemmican, and the third depot (82° S.) held 1366 pounds of supplies: pemmican for men and dogs, biscuits, milk powder, chocolate and paraffin.

Near *Framheim*, preparations for the long dark winter were complete. Fourteen of the sixteen-man tents that had been brought from Norway were erected on the ice. Snow was already drifting against their walls, increasing their insulation against the wind and cold. Some were used for food and other provisions; one stored coal and wood; eight, their floors sunk six feet below the Barrier surface, were used to house the dogs. One was used as a dog maternity home, where 'the pups waddle about like geese'. Additionally, there were two ice huts in use as dog hospitals. As winter finally settled on the place and there was no prospect of the dogs wandering off after seals, they were left unchained during the day.

The first supply depot. Built at latitude 80°S. it held 4200 lb of supplies.

Hassel in the ice corridor oil store. Most of the supplies were kept in these tunnels.

The dogs caused a problem for Lindström in the kitchen. There was no shortage of water for cooking, in the form of snow and ice, but 120 huskies fouled the area round the tents and *Framheim* and the snow became unusable. It occurred to him that he might burrow into the snow now drifted against the hut walls, and supply the kitchen from there. In time he excavated a passage round the hut that he used as a store from which the kitchen was supplied. He went further and built snow shelves along both walls of the passage. Along them he stored the incredible variety of food that Amundsen had brought with them. There were enough steaks of seal-meat for their entire stay at the base. There were tinned goods, salted meat and bacon. There were caramel puddings, Dutch cheeses, butter, sweets. There was tea and coffee and sugar, and a great range of wines and spirits that had been given by a large Oslo store: schnapps, gin, Benedictine, punch, aquavit. There were potatoes, cabbages, carrots, peas, celery, apples, turnips and prunes.

Amundsen attached perhaps the greatest importance to food. Scurvy had been the scourge of previous polar expeditions. He was determined to avoid it. Fresh meat was therefore something of the utmost importance in his eyes: he had sixty tons of it stored in the tent at *Framheim*. His team must have marvelled at his organising genius when they saw the vast range of provisions available to them that winter.

There was one additional food that he regarded as valuable for both men and dogs: pemmican. He had come across it first in the Arctic, and he still felt a debt of gratitude to the Indians who had first invented this particular method of drying meat. But, characteristically he wasn't satisfied with the traditional mixture of dried meat and lard. He experimented until he found a way of adding vegetables and oatmeal to it. The result had good flavour, could be eaten raw or cooked, and was particularly convenient for use when on the move. 'A more stimulating, nourishing and appetising food, it would be impossible to find.' For the dogs, he produced two types: one fish, the other meat.

Amundsen had that capacity for infinite attention to detail that so frequently marks the difference between success and failure. Not only had he thought out in advance what types and quantities of food would be necessary: he had also imagined how they might be used most conveniently. Under the cramped conditions that are an inescapable part of any expedition, one doesn't want the additional burden of having to weigh out rations if it can be avoided. Amundsen found a way of avoiding it. The pemmican, for example, was moulded into cylinders measuring two inches in height by four and three-quarter inches in diameter. Each weighed half a kilogramme, sufficient for one man for one day. Biscuits, dried milk and chocolate, which with the pemmican were the four main provisions when on the move, were packed in such a way that the weight was immediately known. Everything could then be counted, rather than weighed.

The winter was long: six months of darkness with temperatures outside down to as low as —50°C. (—59°C. on 13 August). But there was plenty to do. Lindström's excavations into the snow bank surrounding *Framheim* had opened up possibilities for increasing the size of the working space. Other cavities were excavated. In one of them Bjaaland set up a carpenter's shop. During the setting up of the depots it had become clear that the sledges were too heavy for the dogs to pull easily. Amundsen wanted them reduced from their present weight of 165 pounds to 48 pounds. Bjaaland and Stubberud, planing here and cutting away there, managed to get them down to 53 pounds. Other work was done on the tents. They were dyed with ink to cut down the glare that came through the walls. Wisting then converted four of the three-man tents into two, because Amundsen had decided that a larger number of men in a single tent would add to mutual warmth and comfort. Such 'neat-fingered fellows' as Wisting were invaluable on expeditions of this sort, Amundsen observed.

This inventiveness was a feature of the whole team Amundsen had picked. It proved to be invaluable both for its own sake and also as a means of fully occupying the time. Hassel invented a nose-protector; Bjaaland devised a new opening to his double sleeping bag of reindeer skin, as well as a new form of snow goggles. Lindström invented instruments, even, on one occasion, adapting an old meat tin still bearing

The party in *Framheim* during the long polar night, at work on their tents and clothing

the label 'Stavanger Preserving Co.'s Finest Rissoles'.

With Amundsen, nothing was left to chance, and if his team was able to amuse itself with inventions whilst waiting for the interminable polar winter to ease, then the credit is entirely Amundsen's. They were, without doubt, remarkable men, but it was Amundsen who brought them together – and held them without conflict. How did he manage to do it? Perhaps because they were caught within sight of their goal. They had already come a distance of 12,000 miles. There were only 788 more miles to cover, before the South Pole.

They must have felt, in the splendid visibility of clear weather, that they could almost see their goal.

Yet they were held in check for six whole months by cold and wind and darkness. That frustration must have brought them close to breaking point at times, cooped up together in that wooden shed, playing darts or whist to while away the interminable night. But they never broke. If there were bitter feelings and deep irritations, they never showed. As if by some indefinable magic, Amundsen held together this tiny human community on the very edge of the world throughout a whole polar winter, and brought them out of it physically and psychologically intact. Only later, when they were back in action, did any flaws in the group that he had himself picked begin to show.

By 27 August they were ready to start on the last 788 miles of the long journey. The men were fit. Rations had been packed and loaded on to the sledges. They stood, now, seven of them, waiting to be hauled through a hole in the clothing store by block and tackle. But mean temperatures in the afternoon were still little higher than −40°C. It was still too cold. The strain began to show in Amundsen. He hated the delay. He wondered if Scott had started to move. There were debts waiting for him back home, creditors screaming to be paid off. He had to explain his change of plan to Nansen, the King, and Norway.

But if he got to the Pole first, no one would press him over such trivialities.

Johansen said that if the temperature rose it was only likely to be temporary. It was still not the end of winter. Johansen had been to 86°14′N., closer to the North Pole than Amundsen had ever been. He had been there with Nansen. No doubt it caused Amundsen's confidence in his own judgment to waver, having this voice of the great Nansen warning him.

On 7 September the temperature showed a sudden rise of 8°C. Johansen said it was the false start of spring that he had been expecting; in a day or two it would drop again. Amundsen overruled him. Johansen was older and it could be argued that he was also more experienced. Certainly Nansen had had absolute confidence in his judgment. But Amundsen was the leader and, ultimately, it was his judgment that mattered. He decided that they would leave for the Pole – the very next day. Lindström didn't like the idea. The next day was Friday; it wasn't lucky to go on a Friday. The doubts that Lindström cast only increased Amundsen's determination.

Johansen was right. By 11 September, the tempertaure had fallen to −49°C. Johansen wrote in his diary: 'Travelled 15·2 miles. . . . The breath of men and dogs freezes the moment it hits the air.' Fortunately there was no wind. As far as Amundsen could see, no one was feeling the cold. He had to admit that there had been truth in Johansen's warning. The weight of responsibility on his shoulders was very heavy. The next day the temperature fell to −53°C. 'Only four miles today,' Johansen wrote. 'All the compasses frozen. We therefore stopped and built two igloos for shelter.' Bitterly, it became clear to Amundsen that the attempt was going to fail. There was no sign of better weather. The dogs were suffering badly. The attempt had to be called off. He would press on as quickly as possible until they reached the depot at 80°S. The sledges could be unloaded there, and they would return to *Framheim* and wait for better weather.

They reached the depot on 14 September and turned for the base. The dogs were in a poor state; the weight of the sledges and the savage cold had sapped their strength. Some of them were bleeding from the feet. It was little comfort to Johansen that he had been proved so right. This wasn't the kind of leadership he had known with Nansen. Scott must have been pressing on Amundsen's mind as an obsession.

23

The temperature was down to —56°C.

There was no relief from the cold, no improvement in the weather, that day or the next. On 16 September Amundsen was in the lead. After twelve miles, Johansen and Prestrud were so far behind it seemed they would never catch up. Prestrud was on skis, his heels severely frostbitten. The meter wheel for recording mileage had broken on his sledge and Hassel had taken it in tow. They passed one of Stubberud's dogs that had dropped dead in the snow. It was a warning. They were the last of the party. If they didn't keep going, there was no one behind to help.

They reached *Framheim* at midnight in a state of near collapse. Johansen by now had the most serious doubts about Amundsen's behaviour. It seemed to him that Amundsen had tried to abandon them. He should have been in the rear in case he was needed, not racing ahead. There was some flaw in that calm, controlled personality that had caused him to panic. It was an extraordinary conclusion to have come to, but, he felt, what other explanation was there? In Johansen's view, the whole experience had created 'a sad drop of poison'.

Most of the men had frostbite. Toes, fingers, chins, noses. Prestrud's feet were very bad. The big blisters had to be lanced, the fluid inside painfully squeezed out. After that they were treated with boracic compresses night and morning. Gradually the old skin came away exposing the new healthy skin underneath. It was an appalling, painful process.

When Johansen got up the next day, the others were at breakfast. Some had reached *Framheim* as early as the previous afternoon. Amundsen had been the first; then Wisting and Hanssen, then Hassel and Stubberud and Bjaaland.

Johansen, angry, resentful, wanted some explanation for what had happened. Before he could say anything, Amundsen angrily asked – as the commander – why it was he had got back so late. To Johansen, it seemed an extraordinary, insulting, unfeeling, thing to ask. It was Amundsen who should be answering questions, not Johansen. Johansen said as much: This was no way to lead an expedition; what Amundsen had done on the way back, virtually abandoning his companions, was nothing but sheer panic.

'I was astounded,' wrote Amundsen. 'That he saw fit to question both our method of travel and my position as leader was outrageous. To make matters worse, he had spoken so that all could hear. On a polar journey, the leadership must not be challenged – especially by an experienced polar traveller like Johansen. For them it is doubly dangerous.'

The matter couldn't rest. Amundsen knew his men. He had picked them himself. But he felt, nevertheless, that they must be left in no doubt concerning the leadership. It had to be made quite clear, and quite public, that there was only one leader of the expedition – Roald Amundsen.

He announced that in view of what Johansen had said, he wouldn't now be included in the next party attempting to reach the Pole. He would be sent instead with Lieutenant Prestrud on a small scientific expedition to King Edward VII's Land.

Johansen was appalled. He refused to accept Amundsen's decision unless it was confirmed in writing. He turned to the others for support. He knew Amundsen was being manifestly unfair. For a moment it looked as if Bjaaland might support him – as ex-ski champions they had views in common. But in the end no one spoke, and Johansen had to bow before Amundsen's authority. It was over, the conflict between them. Never again was anyone to challenge Amundsen's leadership. Whether he knew it or not at the time, Johansen was broken. He felt disgraced and humiliated at being excluded from the polar party. He had stood alone with Nansen in the Arctic; but now he was being denied the chance of what he believed to be ultimate glory.

For all that, his loyalty can hardly be questioned. Interviewed later in Hobart, Tasmania, he said: 'Amundsen is a great leader – something of the same kind of man as Nansen, whom I know as well as one man can know another.' It was a generous attitude, but Johansen had been changed deeply. When he got back to Norway he started drinking heavily. Fifteen months later – on 3 January 1913 – he killed himself.

Amundsen waited a month after the aborted trek. Then on 20 October he left *Framheim* with a reduced party. He took with him Bjaaland, Hassel, Wisting and Hanssen, together with four sledges. Within two days, the weather deteriorated. The temperature dropped and they were blinded by continuous snow. To make matters worse, they hit an area of deep crevasses. Many seemed bottomless, and were narrow enough for falling snow to bridge them and turn them into pitfall traps. Bjaaland found himself slithering into one of them, as the snow gave way under the weight of the sledge which dropped out of sight into the dark cleft. It was vital to recover it. Amundsen had calculated the party's needs to the last slab of pemmican. Without the supplies they wouldn't reach the Pole. Worse, one of the two vital primuses was dangling from the bottom of the sledge on a lead, and without it they would be hard put to melt enough water from the snow. One at a time they took the supplies off the sledge and brought them to the surface, and finally the sledge itself was hauled back.

Beyond the depot at 81°S. the temperature dropped to −34°C. It began to look as if the summer in Antarctica was indistinguishable from the winter, except for the long hours of daylight. Then on 1 November they passed the last of the crevasses and began to make the kind of progress that Amundsen had hoped for – an average of twenty miles a day. The last of the depots lay behind them. The only supplies were those on the sledges – together with the fresh meat represented by the dogs themselves.

By 12 November – twenty-five days out from *Framheim* – they had reached 84°S., and the great mountainous mass of the central Antarctic plateau came into view. Amundsen decided to make a depot and leave thirty days' supplies at the foot of the ascent, 85°S. That would leave sixty days' supplies to get to the Pole and back, a distance now of about 700 miles. On 17 November they began to climb towards the Axel Heiberg glacier. It was hard going. It was even hot going. The sun came out strongly enough to force them to take off some of their clothes. On the steeper slopes it was necessary to put two dog teams to a sledge, and even then manpower was necessary too. Amundsen wondered how Scott would manage it, with, by that stage of the arduous trek, only men to do the hauling. He wondered, too, if Scott, further to the west, on

Shackleton's old route, had already climbed the Beardmore glacier and was now somewhere on the plateau ahead.

The dogs were magnificent, 'twisting and turning their way through the mountains, across a maze of crevasses. There were steep descents to negotiate as well as climbs. The drops were sometimes terrifying.' The first day they covered 2000 feet, and the second day a further 3000. The third day, desperately hard, they climbed only 750 feet. But on the fourth they reached the polar plateau – after a climb of 5000 feet in a single day. In four days Amundsen had brought the whole expedition – sledges, dogs and men – up 11,000 feet of frozen rock and ice. They now believed they were six days ahead of schedule. They felt they must have a chance of beating Scott now! On 20 November they made camp.

This was the place that Amundsen called 'Butchers'.

This was where the dogs were to die.

After shooting the twenty-four weakest dogs, one of the sledges was abandoned. The remaining eighteen dogs were divided into three teams of six. But before they could move off the weather broke. The wind turned the snow into a solid blinding wall. There was no hope of getting through. For four days they sat in the tent that Wisting's 'nimble fingers' had converted during the long winter at *Framheim*.

On the fifth day the delay became unbearable. They decided that it was better to make what progress they could through the blizzard, rather than put up with the inaction. The wind howled and lanced into skin and through cracks in clothing; the dogs were loath to move, covered with snow; the tent was so stiff with ice that it would have broken if it hadn't been handled and folded with extreme care. When they did move, the whole plain ahead was a mass of drifting snow that covered everything. 'It was sheer madness,' said Amundsen. 'We were running blind over unknown ground. . . . I was afraid we might fall into a chasm before we could pull up.' There was nothing for it but to stop and wait for better weather. They stopped, without knowing it, only feet from the edge of a cliff.

The improvement, when it came, was only slight. Nevertheless, for the next ten days they averaged fifteen miles a day, ascending first the Devil's Glacier – named because of its lethal chasms and abysses – then crossing the Devil's Ballroom, a frightening glacial formation of several hollow floors of ice through which the dogs and men fell time after time, saved mainly by their ropes.

They reached the final plateau on 4 December 1911. Two days later snow still fell. There was no horizon. Ground ran into sky. Every step had to be taken by compass. But still, that day, according to the sledge meters, they covered twenty-five miles. Unless there was some disaster ahead, they should reach the Pole by the 15th. Their faces were raw where the wind cut, covered with sores and open wounds. Dogs and men were reaching the limits of endurance. But they

Hell's Gate on the Devil's Glacier, aptly named, cruelly discovered

The Pole. And now the Norwegian flag flies above it. They had beaten Scott by 35 days.

had made good time, better than they could have dreamed.

But . . . there was still Scott, somewhere beyond the drifting veil of snow. At one point, Bjaaland thought he had made out sledges and men some way ahead. It proved to be nothing but his imagination.

On 8 December they reached 88°23'S., the farthest point reached by Shackleton three years earlier. Beyond that, no man had ever been. 'No other moment on the whole journey moved me as much as this,' said Amundsen. It was the final turning point. The weather changed dramatically, with brilliant sunshine and clear skies that gave a distant view – even, it seemed, as far as the Pole. Everything suddenly seemed to have been worth it. The open sores on the faces, the blistered feet; what did they matter compared with the immense achievement that lay now within their reach? 'It was like being a boy again,' said Amundsen.

On the 13th they took out the Norwegian flag and with swollen, chapped fingers tied it to a couple of ski sticks in readiness. They were fifteen miles from the Pole.

The next morning, the weather was perfect. The sledge meters were reset at zero, the 'bicycle' wheels dropped into position. They advanced steadily across the flat expanse of snow and ice ahead. There was nothing so far to indicate that Scott had beaten them. No cairn of snow, no flag. Steadily, mile after mile, they moved forward. They were more confident now, no longer desperately hurrying. One after the

other, the sledge meters ticked off the miles: nine, ten, eleven, twelve. Finally fifteen. They stopped and looked at one another. The dogs panted, their breath freezing as it hit the air. Amundsen checked the meters, took sextant readings. It was true. This was the Pole. They had beaten Scott by thirty-five days. Amundsen insisted on a solemn sharing ceremony. They each put a hand on the flagpole made of ski sticks and pushed it into the ground.

Amundsen named the place King Haakon VII's plateau, after the reigning King of Norway. Further observations were taken on the two following days, and they travelled a further nine kilometers as near true south as they could. Their final camp, 'Polheim', was reckoned to be as near to the Pole as was humanly possible. Amundsen left a note for Scott asking him to pass a message to the King in case he didn't

survive the return journey. He put the note, together with letters from his companions, a spare sextant and a pair of mittens, in a bag hung inside the little spare silk tent that they had brought with them.

They were left for Scott to find. They must have known how bitter that moment would be.

They stood together for a moment, bareheaded, looking up at the red flag with the white cross and the blue cross super-imposed on the white. Then they turned north again for *Framheim*. They had conquered the South Pole for Norway; perhaps even a little for themselves.

A month later, on 18 January 1912, Captain Scott's party reached the Pole – to find the Norwegian flag already flying there. Few explorers in history could ever have faced a more painful disappointment.

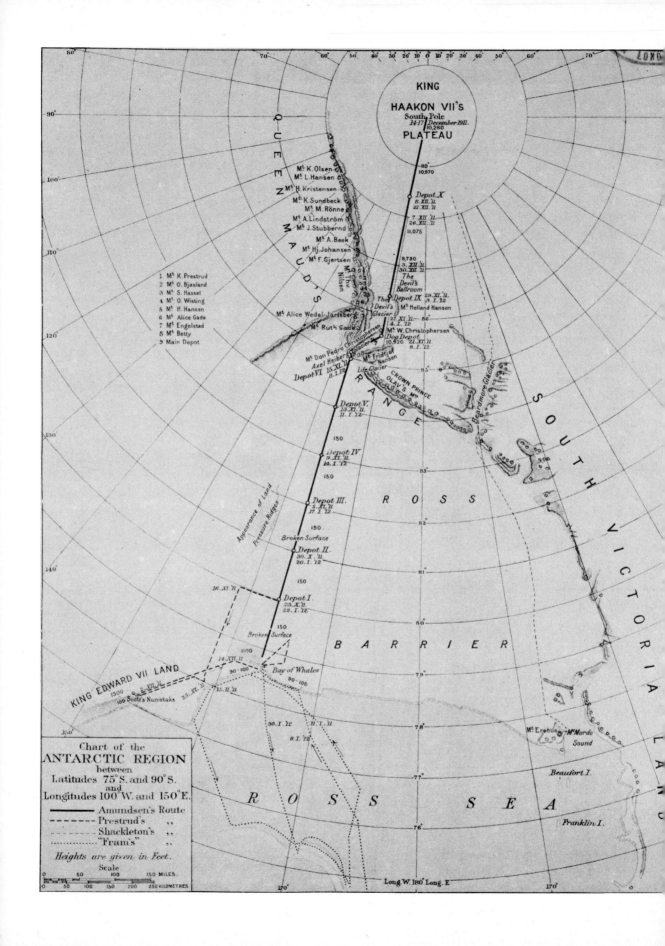

KING
HAAKON VII'S
South Pole
14-17 December 1911.
10,260
PLATEAU

QUEEN

MAUD'S

89
10,970

Mt K.Olsen
Mt L.Hansen

Mt H.Kristensen
Mt K.Sundbeck
Mt M.Rönne
Mt A.Lindström
Mt J.Stubberud

Depot X
8.XII.'11.
21.XII.'11.
7 XII.'11.
26.XII.'11.
11,075

Mt A.Beck
Mt Hj.Johansen
Mt F.Gjertsen

9,730
3.XII.'11.
30.XII.'11.
The
Devil's
Ballroom

Depot IX   29.XI.'11
3.I.'12

Mt Alice Wedel-Jarlsberg
The
Devil's
Glacier
Mt Ruth Gade

Mt Helland Hansen
27.XI.'11
4.I.'12
86

Mt W.Christophersen

Mt Don Pedro Christophersen
Axel Heiberg Glacier
Depot VI   15.XI.'11
8.I.'12

Mt Fridtjof
Nansen
Life Glacier
CROWN PRINCE
OLAV'S Mts

Dog Depot
10,920   21.XI.'11.
8.I.'12

85

RANGE

Beardmore Glacier

Depot V.
13.XI.'11.
11.I.'12.

1 Mt K.Prestrud
2 Mt O.Bjaaland
3 Mt S.Hassel
4 Mt O.Wisting
5 Mt H.Hansen
6 Mt Alice Gade
7 Mt Engelstad
8 Mt Betty
9 Main Depot

150

84

Depot IV.
9.XI.'11.
14.I.'12.

150

83

R   O   S   S

Depot III.
5.XI.'11.
17.I.'12.

82

150

Broken Surface
Depot II.
30.X.'11.
20.I.'12.

81

150

Appearance of Land
Pressure Ridges

16.XI.'11

Depot I.
23.X.'11.
22.I.'12.

80

S   O   U   T   H   V   I   C   T   O   R   I   A   L   A   N   D

150

1100
14.XII.'11

Broken Surface

B   A   R   R   I   E   R

90-100
90-100

79

KING EDWARD VII LAND

1300
2.XII.'11
106 Scott's Nunataks
23.XI.'11   15.II.'11

Bay of Whales

30.I.'12   11.II.'12
8.I.'12

78

Mt Erebus   McMurdo
Sound

Chart of the
ANTARCTIC REGION
between
Latitudes 75°S. and 90°S.
and
Longitudes 100°W. and 150°E.

———— Amundsen's Route
— — —   „   „
– – – – Shackleton's „
· · · · · · "Fram's"   „

Heights are given in Feet.

Scale
0   50   100   150 MILES.

0   50 100 150 200 250 KILOMETRES

R   O   S   S   S   E   A

77

Beaufort I.

76

Franklin I.

Long.W. 180 Long.E.

170°

Amundsen and his party arrived back at *Framheim* uneventfully, on the very day he had planned.

He returned to Norway in 1913, after a stay in South America where he wrote 'The South Pole', his account of the expedition. With the income that his writings now brought him – together with the money he made by lecturing – he began to plan another expedition to the North Pole. The Great War forced him to set it aside.

In 1918, he began to consider the project again, and finally set sail in the *Maud* in an attempt to drift across the Pole from the North Siberian Islands. But the currents were unpredictable and he abandoned the attempt in favour of a flight over the Pole. Using a dirigible, the 'Norge', built in Italy, he flew from Spitsbergen to Point Barrow, Alaska, in May 1926.

On 24 May 1928, General Nobile's airship, the 'Italia', was wrecked in the Arctic. Amundsen offered to go to look for him. On 17 June he left Bergen to fly to Spitsbergen in an aeroplane, and was never heard of again.

Amundsen never received the acclaim he deserved. His achievement in reaching the Pole as he did is monumental. He lacked the resources that were given to Scott. His own government could do no more for him than lend him £4000 in cash. Whatever else he needed, he had to raise himself. Yet his success has always been overshadowed by the tragedy of Scott's expedition.

But there are other reasons besides Scott's martyrdom. The British voice in the field of exploration at the beginning of the twentieth century was a powerful one. Scott was British, representing, in the eyes of most people, the Navy and the largest Empire on earth. Amundsen represented no one but himself, and a country that had only been in independent existence for five years.

His treatment of the dogs, again particularly in British eyes, was offensive. At best it was unsporting, at worst barbarous. He might have been forgiven if circumstances had forced him to kill and eat the dogs, but to do so as part of a coldly calculated plan put him beyond the pale.

The Daily Mirror headlines Roald Amundsen's achievement – and asks where Scott is.

March 9, 1912

CAPT. AMUNDSEN AT THE SOUTH POLE.

How the Explorer Planted His Flag on King Haakon Plateau.

STIRRING NARRATIVE

Sir E. Shackleton Expects News from Terra Nova by To-morrow.

By exclusive arrangement with the *Daily Chronicle*, which publishes the full story this morning, we are able to reproduce a portion of the long message in which Captain Roald Amundsen, the Norwegian explorer, describes how he reached the South Pole.

Captain Amundsen gives a graphic account of the wonderful southward journey of the five men (who had with them four sledges and fifty-two dogs, and provisions for four months) who set out on October 20 last from the depot where they had wintered on the dash to the Pole.

They encountered terrible hardships. Towards the end of November they had to kill twenty-four of the dogs, keeping the remainder for the sledges. Blizzards detained them for four days at a height of 10,600 feet.

A terrible three days were spent in surmounting Devil's Glacier. At last, on December 8, they passed 88deg. 73min., Sir E. Shackleton's farthest point.

From 88deg. 23min. the plateau commenced to slope down very slowly and smoothly towards the other side.

"We reached 88deg. 39min. on December 9. On December 10, 88deg. 56min.; December 11, 89deg. 15min.; on December 12, 89deg. 30min.; on December 13, 89deg. 45min.

RAISING THE FLAG AT THE POLE.

Captain Amundsen thus describes the actual discovery of the Pole:—

Up to this time observations and dead reckoning agreed remarkably well, and we made out that we ought to be on the Pole on December 14.

The afternoon of that day was a beautiful one; there was a light breeze from the south-east with a temperature of minus 23deg. Celsius. The ground and the sledging were perfect.

The day went on without incident, and at 3 p.m. we made a halt. According to our reckoning we had reached our destination.

All of us gathered round the colours, a beautiful silken flag. All hands took hold of it, and, planting it on the spot, gave the vast plateau on which the Pole is situate the name of "the King Haakon VII. Plateau."

It was a vast plain, alike in all directions, mile after mile.

During the night we encircled the camp in a radius of 18 kilometres.

The following day, in fine weather, we took a series of observations which lasted from 6 a.m. to 7 p.m. The result gave us 89deg. 55min.

In order to observe the position of the Pole as close as possible we travelled as near true South as we could for the remaining 9 kilometres.

THE POLE AT LAST.

On December 16 there we camped. It was an excellent opportunity. There was a brilliant sun. Four of us took observations every hour of the day's 24. The exact result will be a matter for expert examination.

This much is certain; we observed the position of the Pole as close as it is in human power to do with the instruments we had—sextant and artificial horizon. The place circles in with a radius of 8 kilometres.

On December 17 everything was in order on the spot. We fastened to the ground a little tent, which we had brought along, and fastened on top of it the Norwegian flag and the Fram pennant.

The Norwegian home on the South Pole was given the name "Polheim."

The distance from our winter quarters to the Pole was about 1,400 kilometres, so that on an average we had marched 25 kilometres a day.

The return trip was started on December 17, and as the weather proved unusually favourable, the journey home was made more easily than the march to the Pole, at a speed averaging about twenty-two miles a day.

DID SCOTT REACH THE POLE?

The world is still without news of Captain Scott, the English explorer.

Perhaps he also reached the Pole. Perhaps he reached it before the Norwegian.

One thing is certain, that Captain Amundsen has performed a glorious feat of fortitude and tenacity in reaching the hitherto unattained goal of every Southern explorer.

Yet the question still remains: Who won the international race? Sir E. Shackleton, who reached within ninety-seven miles of the Pole, expects that England will know what Captain Scott has done within a day or two.

"IF HE SAYS HE HAS, HE HAS."

According to the calculations of Polar experts, to-morrow should bring us news of Captain Scott, and the mystery of the "race" will be solved.

That is the opinion of Sir Ernest Shackleton, who thinks that on or about the 10th of this month, if

Captain Scott has kept to his programme, he should be back in civilisation.

"It is quite possible that both Amundsen and Scott have reached the Pole," Sir Ernest Shackleton said yesterday, in discussing with *The Daily Mirror* the news that has come through.

"There is no reason to assume that Scott has not reached the Pole, but supposing Amundsen had reached it first and had gone a different route he would not know anything about Scott. If he went by the same route he has.

"If both have done it, they both used great energy and perseverance. There is the same amount of those qualities wanted whether you are five or 200 miles of the Pole, but neither of them is likely to be daunted by obstacles.

"I am just like the rest of you. I am quite in the dark as to what has taken place, except that Amundsen has reached the Pole. I feel certain he has. If he says he has, he has.

WAS AMUNDSEN THERE FIRST?

With regard to Amundsen's statement (says Reuter) it is taken for granted that his telegram is meant to imply that he was the first to reach the Pole.

At the same time, it is not impossible that the two explorers—Captain Amundsen and Captain Scott—may have been within a mile of each other without knowing it.

Now that the date is known on which Amundsen attained the Pole, it is seen to be more than probable (says the Central News) that the parties in the great race were within sight of each other during the struggle.

Scott expressed the opinion that December 22 would be the ideal day on which to reach the goal; but this was before he knew of Amundsen's Antarctic plans, and it has been thought that, to lessen the risk of being forestalled, he might have started on his last dash a fortnight earlier than he had planned.

FROM POLE TO POLE.

Captain Amundsen will not rest until he has reached the North Pole.

A personal friend of the Norwegian explorer, Mr. C. A. Bang, manager to Mr. Heinemann, the publisher, told *The Daily Mirror* of Amundsen's expressed intention.

"Directly he has finished his book and his lecture tour he will set off again for the Arctic," said Mr. Bang. "He is not going to be satisfied until he has definitely reached both Poles."

Amundsen was born in July, 1852, in the little town of Borge, near Christiania. His father is a well-known shipowner, and, after leaving school, young Amundsen was sent to study shipping. He also went to Christiania University, and obtained his degree at the early age of seventeen.

Even in those early days, almost his whole conversation was round Polar expeditions.

In 1893, when he was twenty-one, Amundsen went to sea, and there he stayed for a few years until, with industry and application, he rapidly rose to the rank of captain.

It was in 1897 that he joined the Belgian South Pole expedition, under the leadership of Adrian de Gerlache de Gomern, as first officer.

When they got back, Amundsen set off, as soon as he could, on his own expedition to the North Pole. This was the expedition of 1901, in which the east coast of Greenland was thoroughly explored.

NO TIME FOR MARRIAGE.

Back once more, he only waited a little while before setting off again North Polewards. This time he was away three years, during which he reached the magnetic North Pole.

All his ambitions and energies are so centred in exploring that Amundsen has not had any time to get married, or even engaged. But he is a charming companion socially, and the most entertaining person to meet.

Mr. Bang, who furnished the above particulars, added some interesting details as to how Amundsen raised the necessary funds for his South Pole dash.

It had been his original intention to go North again, but he suddenly decided that the South Pole offered greater possibilities. And it had not been reached.

In order to get funds, said Mr. Bang, Amundsen mortgaged his house and raised money on everything that he had. His father also did what he could, and Nansen, who is a great believer in him, helped him as well.

The fact that Scott ate his ponies as part of a similar plan was for some reason a different matter, yet an entry in Scott's own Journals shows thinking very much akin to Amundsen's: 'Hunger and fear are the only realities in dog life. . . . It is such stern facts that resign one to the sacrifice of animal life in the effort to advance such human projects as this.'

It was unfair, of course, that Amundsen should be criticised for his behaviour over the dogs. But Amundsen himself used to tell the story – perhaps apocryphal – of a dinner given in his honour by the Royal Geographical Society in London: a distinguished occasion, to mark a singular achievement, by a famous man. After the meal, the chairman proposed a toast: 'To the dogs'.

More seriously, the fact that Amundsen had misled the world about his destination still rankled. It was felt to be, in some way, underhand, though under the circumstances it is difficult to see what else Amundsen could have done. Nevertheless, even in Norway there was a sense that Nansen himself had been betrayed. He had agreed to lend *Fram* on the clear understanding that the goal was to be the Arctic, and he was only told the truth when it was too late to do anything about it.

Perhaps the real reason lies in the character of Amundsen himself. He seemed somehow too successful, too much the calculating professional to catch the imagination. A brilliant machine that never made a miscalculation or gave a wrong answer. Hardly the stuff to fire the popular imagination as Scott could and Nansen had been able to. The public demands romance with exploration, a sense of mystery. But Amundsen's greatest contribution was just this – to strip exploration of its mystery, to show it as something susceptible to human intelligence and planning, able to be conquered in advance. 'Victory awaits him who has everything in order,' he said. 'Defeat is certain for him who has neglected to take the necessary precautions in time.'

He *was* a great planner, but he *was* a great leader too, able to live equally with his men, to sustain their spirits through the months-long midnight of an Antarctic winter, and at the same time retain an authority that with only one exception was never questioned. And he was generous towards the men he led, despite his clash with Johansen.

'Honour where honour is due,' he says. 'Honour to my faithful comrades; who, by their patience, perseverance and experience, brought our equipment to the limit of perfection, and thereby rendered our victory possible.'

Charles M. Doughty 1843–1926

Charles Montagu Doughty never intended to be an explorer at all. He was an amateur geologist and archaeologist; a Victorian Englishman with a passionate interest in the English language, which he believed had degenerated since Elizabethan times. His life's ambition was to write an epic poem on the origins of the British people. It drove him to become a discoverer and an explorer.

Thinking of his poem, he journeyed through Europe as a young man, and then, in Syria, he first heard of distant ruins in the Arabian desert, never before seen by anybody from the West. Other Europeans had ventured into the desert—but only by pretending to be Muslims. Doughty, a clumsy, stiff, obdurate man was the explorer who hated deception, wouldn't compromise, refused to pretend to be anything he wasn't. Nobody gave him permission to travel. Everybody warned him of the dangers—especially about the fierce nomads of the desert, the Bedouin. Stubbornly, he went; without permission, in 1876; and reached the ruins, and made sketches of them; and returned, after nearly two years, to write about it: a self-confessed Christian, at large and at risk, in the Arab world, a Nasrani—alone in a fanatic Muslim land.

He was an outlaw. He had broken every code of the country. He stood alone in the desert with his last few possessions at his feet.

The camel driver who had been paid to take him to Aneyza was already disappearing over the crest of a dune. Then there was nothing in sight, just an endless sea of rolling sand under the burning sun.

It was then, also, that the last grains of his hope ran out.

There had been difficulties, even dangers ever since he joined the Haj pilgrims more than a year ago. But nothing like this. Even two nights earlier, when he had been beaten and stripped to his underwear by the servants of the Emir of Boreyda, he believed he still had the protection of at least one friend. Now there was no one.

He was a Christian in the heart of Islam, without any letter of safe conduct; despised, feared, ridiculed. His sight had almost gone. His body was covered in sores. The bilharzia he had contracted earlier through drinking contaminated water gave him constant abdominal pain.

He turned eastwards and crossed the wady-er-Rumma, the longest dried-up water course in Arabia, and walked stumbling and barefoot into the deep shifting sands that he had come to know as 'nefud'. The sand scorched his feet, seared him. He carried what was left of his belongings – two German books on Arabia, an aneroid barometer, a tin of tea, pens, paper, a change of clothes – in two camel-bags. His notebooks were wrapped in a fold of the gown he wore. The corner of his headscarf was pulled across his mouth and nose to keep out the desert dust and protect his skin from the sun.

Later he was to write, 'He is a free man that may carry all his worldly possessions upon one of his shoulders'.

He walked on for a mile, his face screwed up against the glare in that 'incessant dog-like grinning' of the Bedouin nomad that he had come to know so well. Sky and sand, nothing else. No vegetation. No animals. No birds. Beyond the crest of each rolling dune lay another.

And beyond that another.

Imperceptibly, a shadow broke the haze above the horizon. A mirage? The kind of optical il-

The Nefud Desert, Arabia, north of Nejd, scorched, barren and forbidding

lusion that drives the desert traveller to despair by holding out hope where none exists? It was real – a line of black palm trees a little to his right. Where there were palms there was food, and water. But there were also people. And people, most recently, had been the cause of all his troubles. Might soon cause his death. Perhaps they hadn't heard of him here. It seemed unlikely. This was Aneyza and it seemed the whole of Arabia had heard of him by now. Khalil the Engleysi, the infidel, the Nasrani, the man who sold medicine, and wrote on paper.

There were tents in front of the palms, the low black tents of the Bedouin, made by the hareem women from woven goat and camel hair. He shuffled forward, paused, wiped the discharge from his eyes. Slowly he brought the encampment into focus. He put a hand inside his gown,

the inflamed eyes and the henna-coloured beard, then gave him some water. He drank it. It was warm and foul. But it established the necessary obligation on the Arab. And, for the moment at least, Khalil was safe.

Khalil was the name the Bedouin gave him. He was christened Charles. . . .

He was born on 19 August 1843, the second son of the Rev. Charles Montagu Doughty, Squire of Theberton in Suffolk, England. At birth he was, in his own words, 'so apparently a dying infant that I was christened by my own father almost immediately'. Fortunately for our knowledge of the interior of the Arabian peninsular, he survived. His mother died when he was a few months old, and when he was six his father died. He and his brother, orphaned, came into the care of their uncle, Frederick Goodwin Doughty of Martlesham Hall.

Doughty's mother's family were landed gentry with strong seafaring connections, and at an early age Doughty set his heart on a naval career. His aunt encouraged him, and with a future at sea in mind he was sent at the age of seven to Laleham School and later to Elstree. At neither place was he particularly happy. He was shy by nature. But his considerable size and incredible clumsiness made it impossible for him to retire into obscurity. He was never the kind who could disappear into the crowd – as he later found out, to his cost, in Arabia. Perhaps his lack of sociability made it necessary for him to defend himself, because he was remembered at both schools as a formidable fighter. It was also characteristic of his physical awkwardness that in a game of cricket he was struck in the face by the ball with sufficient force to crack a cheekbone and leave him scarred for life.

When he was eleven or twelve, he was sent to Beach House School in Southsea. This was a naval school, much more to his liking. He left two years later, and his headmaster said of him, 'He is the very best boy we have met with'. Yet within a year of arriving at Beach House he suffered one of the most bitter disappointments of his life. He failed to pass the medical examination necessary for a career at sea. One can

checked the revolver that hung loaded on the end of the lanyard round his neck. So far he hadn't used it in any of the towns he had visited. But Aneyza might prove the exception. Even if his reputation hadn't gone ahead of him, he was coming from Boreyda, the traditional enemy of the Emir of Aneyza.

He knew it was necessary to invoke the law of Islam before anyone knew who he was. Certainly before honesty compelled him to admit to being a Christian. 'Thou shalt not turn away a guest,' said the unwritten code of the Bedouin. 'If bread and salt have passed between you, thou shalt respect the person and property of thy guest.' True, the code was flexible. True, it didn't necessarily apply to an unbeliever. But it was the only hope.

A man was watering a little patch of garden. He went to him and asked if he might drink. The man looked slowly at the tall, gaunt figure with imagine his feelings, the youthful bitterness. From the earliest he had seen the navy as his natural career, considered nothing else. His aunt had encouraged him in his desires. He was immensely patriotic, also, in the tradition of his family. So, he had always seen the navy as offering exactly that opportunity for patriotic service that he so much wanted. Now at last in a naval school, his dream was about to be destroyed by some wretched defect of speech.

There is no doubt the experience had a profound effect on him. He drew increasingly into himself, becoming even more isolated from his contemporaries, spent much of his time in long solitary walks. The speech defect was never specified, but it seems to have been one of articulation rather than fluency. In later years he complained that his Arabic was 'imperfect and unready', but a perceptive Arab comment refers to neither grammatical imperfection nor unreadiness, rather to an inflexibility of the speech mechanism itself:

'These Franks labour in the Arabic utterance, for they have not a supple tongue: the Arab's tongue is running and returning like a wheel, and in the Arabs all parts alike of the mouth and gullet are organs of speech; but your words are born crippled and fall half dead out of your mouths.'

Whatever the exact nature of the problem it did not prevent Doughty lecturing successfully to the British Association in 1862 on 'Flint Implements from Hoxne'.

By the time he went to Cambridge in October 1861 geology had become his principal interest. He read classics at Caius, where his father and grandfather had been before him, but his real devotion was to natural sciences. The classics lectures he was compelled to attend failed to seize his imagination, and whenever he could he spent his time in geological pursuits.

Doughty's contemporaries thought him shy, nervous, very polite, but with no literary tastes whatever – and definitely no sense of humour. They were wrong, as it turned out. He became highly regarded as a poet in later life, and certainly he could not have survived his Arabian experiences without at least some sense of humour.

Doughty at Caius, Cambridge, already thinking of transferring to Downing College

There was a dogged individualism about him, a moral inflexibility to the point of obduracy. In Arabia it was to cause him one difficulty after another, even put his life at risk. It showed already at Cambridge. Lectures at Caius were compulsory; geology was frowned on, thought hardly to constitute a serious academic discipline. Doughty found the situation so irksome that he transferred to Downing. Here at least he could stay away – without being disciplined – from what he saw as irrelevant lectures.

The change was probably beneficial for both Caius and Doughty. Caius lost a grave and serious young man, absorbed, aloof, self-sufficient. A rather dull young man, significant only because he was convinced that he not only knew what truth was, but always insisted on telling it in its entirety.

Doughty now saw geology as his life's work. He secured dispensation to postpone his tripos until the end of 1865 and went to Norway to make a study of glaciers and glaciation. As a youngster he had spent a short time in France with a private tutor, but this was the first time he had come into close contact with a country other than his own.

He lodged with farmers and gamekeepers, and slept in log huts in the mountains when he was out on hunting trips. Whether he was aware of it or not at the time, the kind of austere travel he experienced in Norway was to become one of the main pillars in his life. Thirteen years later, on the road to Mecca, he was to remember with nostalgia the fjords and glaciers of Norway.

Norway also made him dissatisfied with the narrowness of his studies at Cambridge, a dissatisfaction that was compounded when he gained only a second-class degree. He was disappointed. Even his examining professor was disappointed. He would have given him a first if it hadn't been for his 'dishevelled mind'. 'If you asked him for a collar', the comment went, 'he upset the whole wardrobe at your feet.'

Doughty, of course, was clumsy. But it was really a lack of selectivity that shows throughout his life. It would be churlish, faced with the scholarship of *Arabia Deserta*, to believe that there was a grasshopper quality to his mind. Nevertheless one cannot completely escape such an impression. He was the antithesis of the single-minded Amundsen. He could never have said, as did Amundsen, 'What they call good luck, I call good planning'. Over the years, Doughty's centre of interest moved and shifted: from the sea to geology, to linguistics, to archaeology, to geography, to ethnology, to history, and finally to Arabian studies.

Yet he was not without self-discipline. Sitting long hours alone in the Bodleian Library, Oxford, he made a thorough study of early English literature. That study was to influence the rest of his life. In 1923, at the age of eighty, he could say: 'Nearly sixty years indeed in all I have given to the tradition of noble Chaucer and beloved Spenser.'

And out of this study arose his passion to write a 'patriotic work', to imbue readers with the same fervour he himself felt for his native land. The fact that he managed to do exactly that, almost fifty years later, says something for his determination.

In his reading, he came across Erasmus. In time the Dutchman assumed a position in Doughty's regard and affections comparable to that held by some of the early English writers he had already read. It was really Erasmus that led him to Holland. And Holland became the gateway to all his eventual wanderings.

He had only the vaguest of plans. For five years he drifted through France, Italy, Malta, Algeria, Spain and Greece. He had, in fact, already turned for home when a curiosity to visit 'the Bible-lands' struck him. Despite his patriotism, he was in no hurry to return to the damp English climate that didn't agree with his constitution. In any case, his family investments had dwindled to nothing between 1865 and 1870, and life in England was likely to be unpleasant. So, he records, he 'went forward to the Bible-lands where I remained and in the winter rode down to Cairo and thence to the Sinai Peninsular where I remained three months and then rode upward to Maan. There I heard of Medain Salih.'

The famous and awe-inspiring inscriptions and rock carvings at Petra were already well known. Those at Medain Salih were not. The idea of being the first to see and record them seized Doughty's imagination. It appealed both to his interest in geology and his growing interest in archaeology. It also appealed to the heroic in him. He had already conceived the idea of writing monumental works of travel literature. If that had meant journeying to the steppes of Russia or the jungles of Africa, it may well have been less appealing to him. But now he saw it as journeying into Arabia. And, for certain types of Englishmen, Arabia had – and still has – always held an irresistible attraction.

There were problems, of course, but once the decision had been taken, they faded into insignificance for Doughty. To begin with, Medain Salih lay in territory sacred to Islam. It was forbidden to the Christian, and Doughty, the son of a Church of England clergyman, was unshakeably Christian. But he believed he had discovered a way round the problem. If he were to join the Haj, the caravan of pilgrims on their way to the holy city of Mecca, he could reach Medain Salih unmolested.

Money was another problem. If he did succeed in joining the Haj, he would need equip-

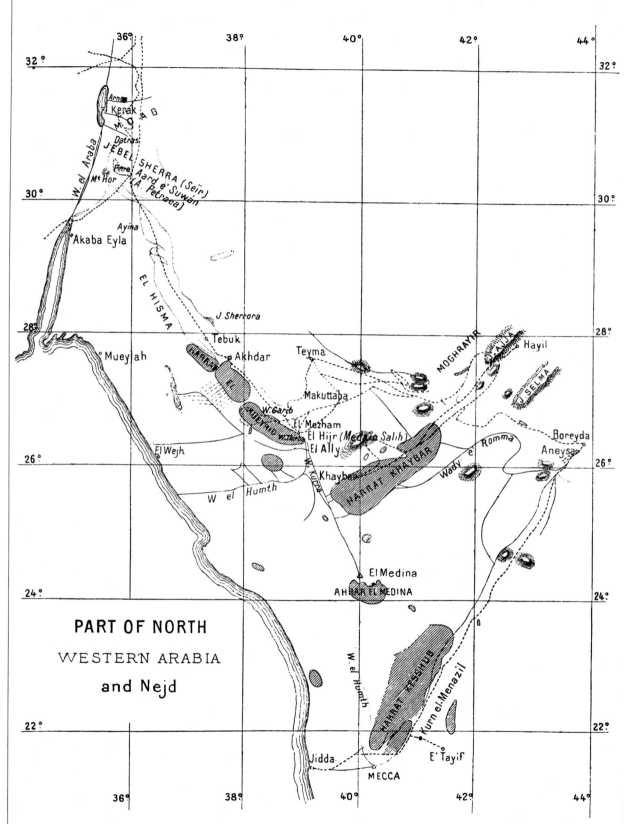

36 | **Map from 'Documents epigraphiques . . . dans le Nord de l'Arabie' by Charles M. Doughty, 1884**

ment – a camel, waterskins, Arab clothing. He wrote to the Council of the British Association, an organisation he had joined in 1863 when he was still at Cambridge, and asked for financial help. His optimism, in Arabia, was misplaced. The Governor of Maan, hearing of his plan to join the Haj, forbade 'anyone in the obedience of the Dowla' to help him. He went to Damascus to protest to a higher authority, without success. He was so determined by now to get to Medain Salih, that he went to Vienna and wrote for help to the Royal Geographical Society. But unfortunately the Society wasn't to meet for months. And, finally, they turned down his application.

Back in Damascus, he found the Haj had already left. There were ten months to wait for the next pilgrim caravan, and he had almost nothing in his pocket. He was broke. But he was quite clear now what he was going to do. He would get to Medain Salih, whatever the opposition, then stay on in Arabia, supporting himself by practising medicine.

Without realising it, he had committed himself to one of the most extraordinary journeys in the world.

It is characteristic of Doughty that he put the long wait for the Haj to good use. He settled in Damascus, dressed himself as a Christian Arab, and set out to learn the language. Whatever the Bedouin thought of his Arabic later, his tutor in Damascus, Abdu Kahil, said that in eight months he picked up conversational Arabic faster than any of his previous European pupils. This was no doubt true. When Doughty became determined about a subject, he didn't let go until it was mastered to his satisfaction. Though he never claimed, himself, to have any particular skill in the language – 'I could never speak their difficult language without solecisms' – his ability to handle the language competently made it possible for him to establish contact with people around him. It was here in Damascus that Charles Doughty became known as 'Khalil'.

As well as language preparation for the journey, Doughty put himself through a process of physical training. He went to Bakrina in the mountains of anti-Lebanon. There he lived on a diet of dry bread, raisins and dates. It is possible that this training saved his life later.

Doughty in Arab dress, painted on his return

But it could never begin to match the reality of what lay ahead.

Damascus, when he returned towards the year end, was already full of pilgrims waiting for the Haj. The weather was delightful, the worst of the heat past, the evenings still pleasantly warm. His spirits rose. He now felt physically prepared for the journey, and he knew sufficient of the language to convey his needs to his fellow travellers.

But at the last moment he was again refused permission to travel. The Haj left without him. The disappointment was almost beyond endurance. He had absolutely made up his mind to get to Medain Salih, and once more he had been stopped.

But in the morning his luck changed. The leader of a group of 700 Persian pilgrims said that he could join them. They intended to live off the land. And, in the barren tracts of the Arabian peninsula, that is much the same as saying one is going to live off the air.

When they set off, in the early evening of Thursday 10 November 1876, Doughty's one fear was that he would be discovered and turned back. A 'Nasrani' – an infidel – joining the Haj

37

to Mecca? It was sacrilege. He minimised the chances as best he could, wore Arab costume to look like 'a man of simple fortune'. He rode a mule, and with the exception of a small tent carried all his possessions in two camel-bags. His light colouring and red beard weren't out of place in cosmopolitan Damascus. He might have passed for a Persian, or an Arab who had dyed his beard with henna. His luggage was large by Bedouin standards, though by European it was minimal, containing only what Doughty regarded as essentials:

A tin of tea, comb, watch, brass reel tape measure, Cavalry carbine, pistol, ammunition and powder.

Books: Die alte Geographie Arabiens, *Zehme's* Arabian seit hundert Jahren, *works by Spenser and Chaucer,* The Koran, *and Arabic Psalter.*

Reed pen, cheque book, passport, brass Arab inkhorn, white blotting paper and brush for making pressings of inscriptions.

Aneroid barometer, thermometer, pocket sextant, telescope, square compass, penknife.

Gold coins.

Change of Arab clothes.

Medicine box containing croton oil, officinal nitre, smallpox vaccine, pills, laudanum powder, eye-wash, magnesia, morphia, ivory vaccination pens, medicine cups, scales.

It took the Persian pilgrims eighteen hours to catch up with the main body of the Haj, an enormous train moving steadily south on the road to Maan and Medain Salih. There were 6000 pilgrims and 12,000 camels.

By the time he reached the little garrison at Medain Salih, Doughty had learned a great deal about the country and the people. In the first place, he discovered, the Christian principles of love and helpfulness to one's neighbours didn't apply. 'They are wolves to each other,' he observed. And an acquaintance said to him 'Khalil! the stronger eat the weaker in this miserable soil, where men only live by devouring one another.'

'There is no ambulance service with the barbarous pilgrim army,' wrote Doughty, 'and all charity is cold in the great and terrible wilderness of that wayworn suffering multitude . . . the lonely indigent man, without succour, who falls in the empty wilderness, is desolate indeed.

When the great convoy is passed from him, and he is forsaken of all mankind, if any Beduw find him fainting, it is but likely they will strip him, seeing he is not yet dead. The dead corpses unburied are devoured by hyenas which follow the ill odour of the caravan. There is little mercy in those Ageyl [followers] which ride after; none upon the road will do a gentle deed "but for silver".'

The hyena was not the only scavenger to follow the Haj south. Wild dogs and foxes unearthed the bodies of the dead – more than twenty people had died before the Haj reached Medain Salih, to say nothing of mules and camels – and took what the hyenas left. Buzzards and brown and white carrion eagles wheeled every day over the miserable collection of animals and humanity making their weary journey in obeisance to the Prophet.

The land itself was cruelly inhospitable. From the limestone platform of Northern Arabia – the 'brow of Syria', as Doughty called it – the Haj wound down into a narrow defile. The floor was of sand, with walls of red sandstone on either side.

The wall to the east was 'crushed with a blackish shale-stone'. 'Belly of the Ogre' or 'strangling place', the Bedouins called it.

To Doughty it was 'a sink of desolation amongst these rusty ruins of sandstone droughty mountains, full of eternal silence and where we see not anything that bears life'.

Near Maan, the defile opened into a barren plain where the wind carried the loose sand, shuffling, over the hard surface beneath. To the west, the 'strange wasted ranges' of the Hisma mountains rose in the distance, disappearing south of Tebuk to be replaced by the forbidding black platform of the volcanic Harra et-Areyud.

Doughty reached his goal of Medain Salih on 4 December 1876 and left the Haj. The journey had taken twenty-six days. For the first week in Medain Salih he was a virtual prisoner in the garrison. The place consisted of a few palms, a square stone tower with a courtyard inside, and a well with a bucket-pump worked by a mule. The guard commander, Mohammed Ali el-Mahjub –

Rock-cut tomb, Medain Salih. To record these was the goal Doughty had set himself.

'a fiend dim with the leprosy of the soul and half fond' – screamed at him and demanded money to show him the inscriptions that he had come so far to see. Zeyd, a leader of the local Fukara tribe of Bedouin, suggested 1000 piastres. The figure was out of the question. Doughty had about 900 piastres (£9) left to finance his return to Damascus. It took him ten days to beat the two men down, to 300 piastres.

Between 14 and 22 December Doughty recorded three-quarters of the monuments around Medain Salih, making notes and sketches of them and also taking pressings.

Pressing was a tedious and often inaccurate method of recording the inscriptions. Water had to be carried in which to soak the blotting paper sheets used. The inscription itself then had to be soaked with a brush loaded with water. The blotting paper had to be forced as closely into the inscription as possible, then left to dry in the sun. The wind was a problem, it would lift the sheets clear of the inscriptions before

Tombs in Khraiba Saudi Arabia. Doughty made pressings of all the inscriptions.

they were dry and cause the result to be distorted. At a later site, Doughty used a notched well-beam, eighteen feet in length, to reach the higher inscriptions. It was a precarious activity, hanging on to the beam with one hand and pressing in the blotting paper with the other, whilst the wind plucked at his long gown, tried to twist him off.

Doughty was extraordinarily lucky to have come so far without serious mishap. He hadn't been robbed or injured. He hadn't suffered

---

A drawing from the Medain Salih inscriptions

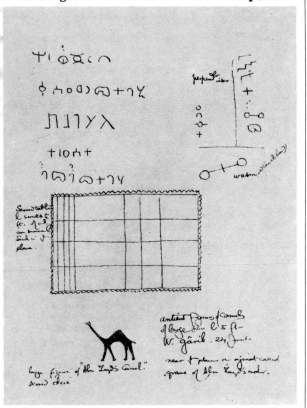

serious illness. But as the year turned so did his situation become more complex, as he experienced another side of the Arab character. He was, by then, very short of money. He spent ten days in the nearby settlement of el-Ala practising medicine in the hope of earning a few *reals*. It was an attractive place, a stone-built modern village surrounded by a wall and bordered by palms. The streets were narrow but clean, sweet smelling, with a clay bench outside every doorway. The floors of the houses were of beaten earth, the internal woodwork tamarisk, the doors

of rough palm boards. Above many doors was a curious triangular symbol in red ochre, that no one would explain to Doughty. It may well have been this persistent inquisitiveness that turned people against him, as much as the fact that he was a Nasrani. The children jeered at him, reviled him. He knew he had touched that herd instinct that made so many groups in Arabia band against him and force him out. It distressed him profoundly. It was to happen again and again.

Back at the garrison in Medain Salih, Doughty discovered that he could also arouse in the Arab something more extreme than a self-protective herd instinct. He had given Mohammed Ali his cavalry carbine as payment for escorting him again to the monuments. Mohammed Ali refused to keep his part of the bargain, and handed back the carbine. Doughty was adamant and pressed the gun on him again. Mohammed Ali lost his temper. He pushed Doughty, struck him and – the profoundest of Arab insults – pulled his beard. Doughty was shattered. What had he done? He turned to the others, appealing to them to witness how he was being treated, but he refrained from fighting back or losing his temper. Mohammed Ali was incensed. He beat Doughty with an old clouted shoe until he drew blood, then turned Doughty out of his room and put him in another overlooking the cesspool.

What, in fact, had incensed Mohammed Ali most was the indifference Doughty showed to this ill-treatment. To suffer uncomplainingly is not to be a man.

The Haj returned from Mecca on 5 February 1877, bringing a letter for Doughty from the British Consulate; also some money, and three pens of vaccine. He dispensed the vaccine at once; the Haj was carrying smallpox. He had already decided not to go with the pilgrims to Damascus. But for him, it was too soon to leave Arabia. Zeyd had already agreed that he could join the Fukara Bedouins and travel with them for a time. On 12 February, with £14 in his purse and riding an old female camel he had bought, he left the protection of the garrison at Medain Salih and rode into the desert:

'In the company of the great annual caravan, which travels from Damascus to the holy cities of

Mecca and Medina, I had entered the desert. I had intended to return among the pilgrims; but instead I sent my drawings with them, and myself remained in the desert with the Bedouin.'

Doughty stayed with the Fukara until the beginning of May, living independently, sleeping in his own tent. All their time was spent roaming the desert to the north-east of Medain Salih, searching for food for the camels and goats, making occasional visits to the oasis at Teyma. The area was a waterless desolation.

through the thin air stand far round about us. Herds of the weak nomad camels waver dispersedly, seeking pasture in the midst of this hollow fainting country. This silent air burning about us, we endure breathless till the lingering day draws down to the sun-setting. The herdsmen come again with the cattle to taste the first sweetness of mirth and repose. The day is done.

A camp on the edge of the Arafat Plain. Doughty joined just such a group of Pilgrims.

Salih, searching for food for the camels and goats, making occasional visits to the oasis at Teyma. The area was a waterless desolation.

Every day was the same. The sun exploded each morning on endless tracts of desert. Doughty recorded shade temperatures, in April, of 95°F at a height of 4000 feet above sea-level:

'It is March; already the summer enters. The night at end, the sun stands up as a crown of hostile flames from the huge covert of inhospitable sandstone bergs. Entering as a tyrant upon the waste landscape it darts upon us a torment of fiery beams. Grave is that giddy heat upon the crown of the head; the ears tingle with a flickering shrillness, a subtle crepitation it seems, in the glassiness of this sun-stricken nature; the hot sand-blink is in the eyes, and there is little refreshment to find in the tents' shelter; the worsted booths leak to the rain of sunny light. Mountains looming like dry bones

'The moon rises ruddy from that solemn obscurity like a mighty beacon: and the morrow will be as this day, days deadly drowned in the sun of the summer wilderness.'

Doughty was curious about everything he encountered, recording it all at length in his notebooks and summarising his experiences at a later date. It caused him trouble at times. He was thought at first to be a spy, or to be gaining some kind of power over the people by committing them in symbolic form to paper.

He was – inevitably – uncompromising. He refused to prostrate himself towards Mecca. When *he* prayed it was to the Christian God.

Life was hard enough for the Bedouin, scratching a living out of such natural desolation. The presence of such an extraordinary figure amongst them became a source of constant irritation. It says a great deal for them, with no knowledge of the world beyond the desert, that they put up with him at all:

In Bedouin encampments the men sat around and the women waited on them

'The presence of the Nasrani in the land of the Arab was an enigma to them: they put me to the question with a thousand sudden demands. At what distance, they enquired, and in what part, lay my country? I said a camel rider might alight among my neighbours a little before the year's end. They had not thought the world was so large. So they said, can it be that you have passed all that great way only to visit the Arab? Now what can this mean? Tell us, by Allah, art thou not come to spy out the country? Art thou not some banished man? Comest thou of thine own free will, or have other sent thee hither?'

Women, he discovered, even more than camels, were the beasts of burden. They cooked, they set up the tents, they packed when it was time to move. The tents were made out of material woven by the women from the hair and wool of the flock. They were spread out on the ground and pegged, then pushed up by the poles against protective pads of cloth. Even the guy ropes were made by the women. When the tent was up, side cloths were hung along three sides, the front usually left open. Inside, the tent was divided into two parts by a hanging cloth, to separate men from women. The women stored all the household goods in their part of the tent; corn, rice, rock-salt, utensils like leather watering buckets and bags of camel hides. And, during the whole process, the men took no part at all.

Doughty's relationship with the desert women was gentle, Victorian. (What would they know of Victorians?) But he showed a humane interest in them that none of them had experienced from a man before. He even helped them from time to time with particularly heavy work. The men looked on with amusement. 'The woman is in bondage,' he recorded. 'Her heart has little refreshment.'

From time to time one of the men would offer him a woman, on condition that he become a Moslem:

43

'I rode with a sheik called Zeyd and his son and their attendants, in a waste land of gravel and sand, full of rocky crags.

'"This is the land of the Bedu," Zeyd had said. "So thou will live here with us, we will give thee a maiden wife; if any children are born to thee, they shall be as mine own, by Allah."'

Sometimes, even, a woman offered herself, in the hope that he would take her away from a life of hardship and misery. He refused every offer and never took a woman during the whole of his travels in Arabia. He was not only a Christian but took pride in being a chaste one. However, the position and treatment of women in Arab society distressed him:

'The women's lot is here an unequal concubinage and in this necessitous life a weary servitude. They are few or nearly none that continue in their first husband's household. He will pass to new bride-beds; the cast housewife may pass to the servitude of some poorer person. Thus light are they in their marriages, and nearly all unhappy. Sometimes, as we ride, a husband has hailed me cheerfully and called: "Ho there, Khalil! O man, what is thy will? Hast thou any liking to wed? Is not this a fair woman? If this like you, I will let her go; only Khalil thou wilt pay me five camels." I have said: "What should she do in my country? Can she forget her language and her people?" Incredible it seems to the hareem, the women, that any man should choose to dwell alone.'

Food and drink formed the focus of the Bedouin's life. The day began with coffee. The beans were roasted and ground in a pestle, then thrown into the water that was boiling over a fire of twigs and dried camel dung. Cinnamon or cloves were sometimes added. When the infusion was ready, men were served according to the position they occupied in relation to the host. At such ceremonies, the only woman who might be present was the host's wife, and her function was simply to wait on the men. Smoking accompanied the coffee drinking, and both activities took place repeatedly throughout the day.

Food was usually girdle bread and leban, a type of sour milk. Water was drunk sparingly. Dates were a staple food when they were available, though Doughty had little time for them as a complete diet: 'where the date is eaten alone . . . human nature decays.' Locusts were eaten, roasted on the fire before having their heads broken off. There was goat's milk and clarified butter, buttered rice and grain. For meat there was camel, goat and mutton, less frequently gazelle and hedgehog. Some sheiks, Doughty discovered, kept falcons for hunting hares. Nothing was allowed to go to waste. Even coffee grounds were saved to be used again. And an injured animal was always killed and eaten.

Water was the most precious, almost sacred, commodity to the Bedouin. Doughty's habit of washing in it was regarded as wickedly anti-social. The Bedouin washed infrequently and then only in camel urine, even using it to wash their hair. In conditions of prolonged drought, they drank it. 'Their camels' excrements are pure in the sight of the nomads.'

Water was built into the Arab code. It could never be refused to a stranger if it was asked for. It was withheld from Doughty on one occasion, but Doughty was a Nasrani and outside the code.

At each waterhole the caravan came to, every available waterbag was filled. At times the water was so foul Doughty found it undrinkable. At one place where the waterhole had been used as a cesspit, even the Bedouin found it undrinkable.

It was from such water that Doughty contracted the bilharzia that was to cause him stomach pains for the remainder of his stay in Arabia.

Towards the end of April it became clear to Doughty that he must leave the Fukara. The code of hospitality required the Bedouin to accept a guest for three days. After that hospitality became 'like the back of a carpet'. Doughty had been accepted by the Fukara for three months. He was having an increasing number of quarrels with Zeyd, and the atmosphere in the camp was more unfriendly every day. Zeyd was a trim, strong man of middle years with near-black skin; he was greedy and mean, but he had one abiding virtue as far as Doughty was concerned. He lacked that fanaticism of so many Bedouin that was making Doughty's position almost untenable. When, on 1 May, Zeyd announced his intention of revisiting the garrison at Medain Salih, Doughty decided to go with him.

What he had now determined was to leave Arabia altogether. He planned to get a boat from Wejh on the Red Sea, a distance of 150 miles. 'No more than a sick camel now remained to me, and a little gold in my purse,' he wrote, 'and I began to think of quitting this tedious coil, where henceforth without a pretext, I must needs appear as a spy intruded among them; and – since it were impossible for me to conform to their barbaric religion – where my neck would be for every lawless and fanatic wretch's knife; and in what part soever I should pass, with great extremities, every soul would curse me.'

Seventeen days later, he heard of a small merchant caravan of Fukara tribesmen that was going to Wejh to fetch rice. He rode all night to join them. Understandably they weren't pleased to see him so soon after they had got rid of him. He rode the whole day without food or water in a temperature of almost 100°F, then the whole of the next day as well. That evening when he dismounted on the black volcanic Harra, he was broken. He had travelled fifty miles and another hundred was impossible for him. For the second time he had failed to get clear of the area. And it bound him to Arabia for more than another year.

His resilience was amazing. On 20 May, so weak that he was quite incapable of mounting his camel and joining them, he watched the Fukara caravan leave for the coast. Yet by the 30th of that month he was on his way to join the Moahib tribe of Bedouin and spend the four months of high summer under canvas with them.

Their territory centred in the 'iron wilderness' of the Harra, less barren than the country of the Fukara, and – comparatively speaking – 'good Bedouin ground suitable for rearing stock'.

'Green stems of wormwood and southernwood, shaeh, springing on the sharp lava shelves, give up a resinous sweetness under this withering broad sunshine: the last is gathered and dried by the hareem, for the hot cordial savour; they mix a little with their cold leban and mereesy. In all the deeper volcanic bottoms are tamarisks, and by the stony dry seyl-bed sides I saw woody green groves of the desert acacia. . . . The long-necked camels snatch as we ride at these thorny boughs of sweet mimosa-like leaves. It is a wonder that the hard finger-long sharp spines should not stab the great soft pharynx! – thorns which will strike at once through their horny soles, and wound so cruelly the nomads' feet that I have known men long bedridden by such accidents.'

The Moahib seemed less prone to the kind of fanatic behaviour he had found in some of the Fukara and experienced in the streets of el-Ala. During his stay with them he was shown no violence. Their leader, Tollog, was extremely old – no one, in fact, could remember him when he was young. On the whole he seemed to like Doughty, and showed a curiosity about Western inventions – balloons, submarines, telescopes. For a time he was wary, suspecting Doughty of spying, but in the end he stood up for him in his occasional quarrels with other members of the tribe. He knew something of the English – 'good Arabs', he called them.

The worst danger during this period was famine. For some time Doughty had survived on a daily ration of thin gruel and a small crust of bread. By 3 August 1877 he was almost at the end of his strength. He wasn't alone. The whole tribe was showing signs of starvation, and Tollog's hospitality was growing ever sparser. Even though Doughty was more or less independent of the tribe, sleeping in his own tent and feeding himself, he felt it politic to move. Besides he had heard of Kheybar, a town lying deep in the wilderness to the south-east, and increasingly he wanted to go there. Two days later he left the Moahib and returned to Medain Salih to join a mixed caravan of Fukara and Welad Aly tribesmen moving eastwards.

During all his encounters with Arab communities, Doughty's real passport was his practice of medicine. He wasn't a doctor, he had had no medical training. He relied on his general scientific knowledge, his commonsense and a copy of *Tanners Practice of Medicine*, a diminutive handbook only four inches by two, and already twenty years out of date. He could use the vaccine that was sent to him from Damascus to provide protection against smallpox. He could heal simple cuts that had festered in the heat. He carried eye-washes against the eye diseases that were the commonest ailments of the region, and from which he suffered himself. For cases of abdominal pain he might prescribe magnesia or laudanum.

He wrote: 'My croton oil, a drastic purgative, was in favour among them. Two drops is an ordinary dose. I gave six; nor might this always move the Arab ironsides. Finally, to some of this human brood I gave eight. "Ye ruin me with the expense," I complained. But "Give," they said, "give; it is a strong people the Beduw."'

He also saw the pitiful truth of his 'medical' situation: 'Only the most hopeless cases were brought to the physician; everywhere they brought me to help some whose eyes were perished. But, "I will pay for no medicines," they said, "I will pay only for the cure." They would catch after charms, and philters of dishonest love. The outlandish Nasrani, they imagined might write them a quick spell; and they thought it a marvel, poor as they saw me, that I denied them, when with a written word or two I might have enriched myself.'

Financially, his medical activities brought him just £2 during the whole twenty-two months of his journeyings in Arabia. But they did allow him access to communities which might otherwise have been completely closed to him. And he did receive some payment in kind. He was able to witness a circumcision ritual, for example, which wouldn't have been possible if he hadn't gone as a 'medical' man. The surgeon was a local blacksmith – a 'sany'. A sheep, a goat and a kid were slaughtered, and the child placed on a large metal dish with powdered horse dung under him. The sany brought his razor to a fine edge by honing it on his arm.

'He drew then the foreskin through a pierced stone shard, and there tied with a thread. "Look thou cut not over much," said the mother. Holding her child, with the other hand she blinded his eyes, and encouraged him with the mother's voice and promises of sweet milk and fat things. The sany, with a light stroke, severed the skin at the knot; then he powdered the wound with charcoal, and gave up the child, which had not felt a pain, to his mother; and she comforting him in her bosom, bade him be glad that he was now entered into the religion of Islam.'

The Arab attitude, which saw medicine as something that should be given free, is perhaps understandable. Life was full of diseases. They were part of the majestic design of Allah. They may try to buy a cure but if they were cured, then surely it was Allah who cured them, not medicine. 'The life and the death are in the hands of Ullah! There can nothing happen but by the appointment of Ullah!'

Doughty had paid a brief visit to the town of Teyma when he was travelling with the Fukara in the spring. He arrived back on the afternoon of 2 September, the first day of Ramadan, the period when the whole of Islam fasts during the hours of daylight. He was, quite characteristically, unaware of the fact, and betrayed himself as an infidel by asking openly for dates and water. Even if he had been aware of it, he might not have modified his behaviour very much. His obdurate sense of honesty would probably have led him to declare himself a Nasrani, rather than deceive anyone. He made no compromise, ever, with Islam. All summer he had suffered from lumbago, intestinal pains and boils, and he was too weak now to care about compromise. In any case they knew who he was: he had become a household name throughout the western part of the peninsula. Everyone had heard of the mad Engleysy, the Nasrani who wandered with the desert tribes and wrote magic in books and practised medicine.

He walked into trouble at Teyma because of the writing as well. Initially he was unaware of it; he assumed that the suspicion with which he was regarded was simply another example of the 'town' Arab's dislike of outsiders. But, in fact, shortly after his previous departure from Teyma part of the wall of the great well-pit of el-Hadaj had fallen in, and when it became difficult to repair it the townspeople concluded that Doughty had caused its collapse by writing in his book. They talked – and decided. Now they were out to cut his throat in reprisal. Fortunately it occurred to a local official that if Doughty actually had caused the wall to fall, then Doughty could cause it to rise again. If he failed, his throat was still available for cutting. Faced with the problem and the consequences of failure, Doughty calmly produced a plan to rebuild the structure. They were satisfied. In fact, nothing ever was rebuilt, partly because of the cost involved, mostly because of laziness.

Teyma marked a turning point in Doughty's travels. His days with the desert Bedouin were nearly over. Now he spent most of his time in the towns. In some ways they were safer for him. The desert Bedouin travelled in constant fear of being attacked and robbed by other tribes. Life was less safe, less respected. Nevertheless, the fanaticism that always caused him trouble showed up more in the towns, and as a result in most towns Doughty was maltreated. Teyma was the exception, after the initial difficulties were resolved. He found it an attractive place: clay-built, in good repair, surrounded by date palms and orchards of plum trees. 'Delightful now was the green sight of Teyma,' he wrote, 'the haven of our desert.' It was an oasis teeming with riches, after the barren desolation of the

Harra: poultry providing eggs and meat; crops of millet, grain, tobacco, pomegranate, figs, lemons and grapes. He was tempted to accept invitations to stay on, but after six weeks the pull of Kheybar became irresistible.

No one would take him directly to Kheybar. It was in an area of Arabia absolutely forbidden to non-Moslems. He decided to go to Hayil and ask the Emir Ibn Rashid to give him safe conduct. The journey was fiercely hard, taking Doughty over a wide sandstone mountain platform more than 5000 feet high, in temperatures of 80°F. It took him six days to reach the sand desert beyond, three more days to come to the town.

Hayil and Kheybar formed the fulcrum of his wanderings. His experiences there were a microcosm of his experiences in all the towns he visited – a mixture of tolerance and fanatic mistrust. Hayil was the capital of Northern Arabia, a town of 2000 inhabitants, and Doughty was the

Hayil, a wild fortress town, then the capital of Northern Arabia

first European to enter it since Gifford Palgrave had been there in disguise fourteen years earlier.

Mohammed Ibn Rashid, the leading Arab of his day, was courteous enough at first. Doughty was allowed to 'practise' medicine, and though it brought him little in the way of money it did bring him a friend or two who were to prove vital later. But by the ninth day gossip about his writings and drawing had spread. The inevitable incidents began. He was attacked and roughed up by one of the Emir's servants, and a few days later he was robbed. Finally, Ibn Rashid's patience gave out and Doughty was thrown into the street. Once more he decided to leave Arabia. He'd had enough. He sold his tent. With only a little over £7 in his purse Baghdad might well have been as far away as the moon.

But instead of Baghdad, he found an escort to take him to Kheybar and on 28 November he reached one of the four walled hamlets which made up the town. It depressed him at once. The air was dank, the water foul and the place swarming with flies. Even now he couldn't bring himself to pretend he was a Moslem, though that would probably have been enough to secure his safety. But for a day or two he resisted the cries of his conscience to tell everyone he was a Nasrani. Then, once again his behaviour gave him away. He had never been seen to pray, and when he blundered into a mosque with his shoes on there was no hiding the truth. His host tried to persuade him to leave at once. Kheybar was Hejaz – a place where no Christian was tolerated.

Doughty refused to go: 'The traveller must be himself, in men's eyes a man worthy to live under the bent of God's heaven, and were it without a religion; he is such who has a clean human heart and long-suffering.'

He stayed in Kheybar for three and a half months. The Pasha of Medina had heard of his presence and ordered the commandant of the garrison to treat him honourably. Even then, his property was seized and he became, in effect, a prisoner. But his sufferings this time were mostly from boredom. There was little of interest to see, and he wasn't allowed beyond the town limits without an escort in case he was attacked. His one pleasure was his association with the few friends he made in the place. It was

1. **Charles Montagu Doughty, played in the film by Paul Chapman.**

2. **Doughty spent the summer in the Fukara. The Bedouin moved constantly in search of fresh grazing and water. They had to. Water was always their most precious commodity. The Bedouin were shocked by Doughty's habit of using water to wash.**

3. **In Bedouin encampments it was the women who made and then always erected the tents; the men took no part in the labour of making camp.**

4. **'Kahil' was escorted from the town, driven on his way by a jeering, angry crowd. Again and again it was this stubbornness that was to cost him dear. He refused to compromise, remained at all times the Nasrani – the Christian infidel.**

5. **It seemed hopeless. He had been stripped, robbed, beaten. Without water he could not survive. He had lost most of his possessions, he was ill, and even his eyesight was failing.**

6. **It was Doughty's note-taking that was to cause trouble again and again. The Arabs took him for a Nasrani spy.**

7 and 8. **On the road to Mecca an Islamic pilgrim, driven beyond endurance by the presence of this 'infidel', attacks the Nasrani with a knife. He was saved only by intervention of the Emir's** *(continued p.49)*

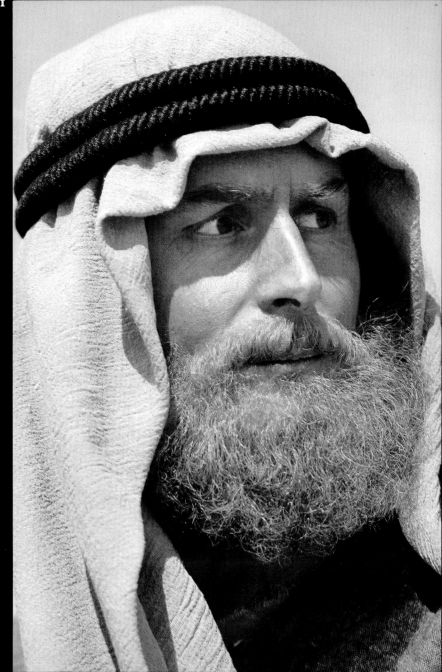

representative. But once
again, the man who would
not compromise had
jeopardised his own life by
refusing to recognise and
acknowledge the passion
of others.

The film was directed by
David McCallum, and shot in
the Bedouin Desert.

in Kheybar that he met the closest friend he was ever to make in Arabia, Mohammed en Nejumy (known as Amm Mohammed), who supported him bravely against all his detractors. 'Amm Mohammed went back to his own, we passed further,' says Doughty of their parting, 'and the world and death and the inhumanity of religions parted us for ever.'

He also wrote: 'Two chiefly are the perils in Arabia, famine and the dread-faced harpy of their religion. A third is the rash weapon of the every Ishmaelite robber. I decided my defence against the robber must be my poverty.'

It was 18 March 1878 before Doughty finally escaped from Kheybar. And on Sunday 1 April he was back in Hayil. His reception was what he might have expected. Ibn Rashid was absent. Aneybar, the black chamberlain, told Doughty to go – at once. While he waited at the palace gates for an escort, the fanatical crowd threatened him, demanded that he become a Moslem. It seemed to them little enough to ask. It was their town, their country, their religion. Most of his offensiveness, in their eyes, would disappear if he were one of them. All he had to do was say publicly: 'There is no god but Allah, and Mohammed is his messenger.' But for a man like Doughty it was impossible. 'It had cost me little or naught, to confess Konfuchu or Socrates to be apostles of Ullah,' he says, 'but I could not find it in my life to confess the barbaric prophet of Mecca and enter, under the yoke, into their solemn fools' paradise.'

'Once again my friends have asked me why must you say you are Nasrani. It is but a word to admit the prophet and you may live in peace. Should I not speak the truth, I have answered, here as in my own land? Do you not know the proverb, peace may walk through the world unarmed? This is foolishness, they told me. I replied, there is nothing more prudent than a wise folly.'

The refusal came near to costing him his life. A day later he was in the desert again with two escorting travelling companions who refused to let him ride their camels. 'An infirm traveller were best to ride always in the climate of Arabia; now by the cruelty of my companions, I went always on foot; and they themselves would ride.'

49

He knew they were going to desert him – they barely disguised their intentions – yet he had to keep them in sight. 'So it drew to the burning midst of the afternoon, when, what for the throes in my chest, I thought that the heart would burst. The hot blood at length spouted from my nostrils: I called to the rafiks who went riding together before me to halt, that I might lie down awhile, but they would not hear. Then I took up stones, to receive the dropping gore, lest I should come with a bloody shirt to the next Aarab: . . . in this haste there fell blood on my hands. When I overtook them, they seeing my bloody hands drew bridle in astonishment! . . . Whithersoever I rode I was likely to faint before I came to any human relief; . . . My eyes were dim with the suffered opthalmia, and not knowing where to look for them, how in the vastness of the desert landscape should I descry any Aarab? . . . Taking up stone I chafed my blood-stained hands, hoping to wash them when we should come to the Aarab; but this was the time of the spring pasture and oft-times the nomads have no water by them . . . "Watch, said he, and when any camel stales, run thou and rinse the hands: for seeing blood on thy hands, there will none of the Aarab eat with thee."'

For five days he survived. He buried his books in the sand – apart from the two German ones – to lighten his load. Finally his Arab escort deserted him, left him to the mercies of a Bedouin group. Fortunately he was well-treated, and two weeks later he was sufficiently recovered to make the nine-day journey eastwards to Boreyda. But once again his insensitivity to the politics of his situation landed him in trouble. He was surprised in the open by the muezzin's call to prayer, and rash enough to ignore it. He was questioned by officers of the Emir of Boreyda, then later attacked by six men who stole everything he had. They left him stripped to his drawers. The next day, half naked, half dead, totally humiliated, he left for Aneyza, and it was on that road that he reached the nadir of his Arabian experiences.

Here he was deserted, left without transport and shoeless in the scorching sands of the wady-er-Rumma. He was, also, as ill as he had been at any time in his wanderings.

He reached Aneyza, and was given water.

He recovered slowly. Days later he was allowed to practise medicine again. But as soon as it was realised who he was the zealots of the town drove him out once more. Preachers inveighed against him. Women and children were encouraged to harass him. His doorway was defiled, stones were thrown at his room. He was stoned in the street. Two friends he had made – Abdullah el-Kenneyny and Abdullah el-Bessam – could do little to help him. 'My now quiet and pleasant days . . . were troubled by the malignity of the fanatics.' He was escorted to Khubbera on a half-wild camel whose 'wild gait brought on an attack of diarrhoea' while the rough packsaddle chafed and cut his skin. 'I never suffered the like on the longest camel ride.'

He was three days in Khubbera before his friends from Aneyza came and brought him back. That was 28 May 1878. He stayed on the outskirts of the town for the whole of June. It was a monotonous experience. It at least gave him a chance to regain his strength. It gave him time, as well, to review his position. It was almost two years since he had joined the Haj south of Damascus. His strength was running out. His funds had almost gone, just £3 left. It was, all too obviously, time for him to leave Arabia at last. He spent his last evening in Aneyza in Abdullah el-Khenneyny's garden, where Abdullah el-Bessam and another friend, Hamed es-Saly, brought him a camel. On 5 July he left Aneyza and joined a caravan of 170 camels making for Mecca.

The journey from Aneyza to Ayn ez-Zeyma took seventeen days and covered 400 miles of sand, gravel, bare granite and black pumice. It was the hottest time of the year, and the closer they came to Mecca the more disagreeable his companions became. It was clear enough that he wasn't one of them. He was the only one not to strip and put on the symbolic loincloth of the pilgrim when they came within sight of Ayn ez-Zeyma. He was the only one not crying 'labbeyk'. Yet no one would agree to leave the caravan and escort him clear of Mecca to the coast at Jidda.

Jidda. Hostels for pilgrims on their way to Mecca.

Finally a nephew of Abdullah el-Bessam's agreed to go with Doughty. But it was too late. Doughty's presence had given such offence to one pilgrim, named Salem, that he rushed at him with a knife. It was, perhaps, the closest Doughty came to death during the whole of his travels. Only the intervention of Maabub, an old Negro officer of the Grand Sherif, saved him. Doughty and Salem were ordered back to Tayif to await the ruling of the authorities. On the way, in the dark, Doughty was robbed, beaten across the back of the head with a camel stick, his revolver stolen. Again Maabub managed to calm Doughty's attackers. Just before dawn the group reached Tayif.

For Doughty the tribulations were over. Husein, the Syrian officer of the Dowla in Tayif, was a liberal-minded man. He recovered the property that had been stolen from Doughty. Conversations that Doughty had with Husein convinced him that he was a man of intelligence and humanity – qualities he had so far found rare in Arab rulers.

Doughty left Tayif on 29 July 1878 with an escort of the Bishr bodyguard, and reached Jidda on 2 August. He had wandered the hinterland of Arabia, alone, for almost two years. Physically he was a wreck; months later he was still more dead than alive with bilharzia. There were psychological marks on him too that coloured the rest of his life.

At the end of November 1878, with his pressings and notebooks he arrived back in England. He was 35.

He made his way from Portsmouth to Martlesham. There he created quite a stir, though he

---

Sketches and notes from Doughty's notebook. He was thought a spy, because of his writing.

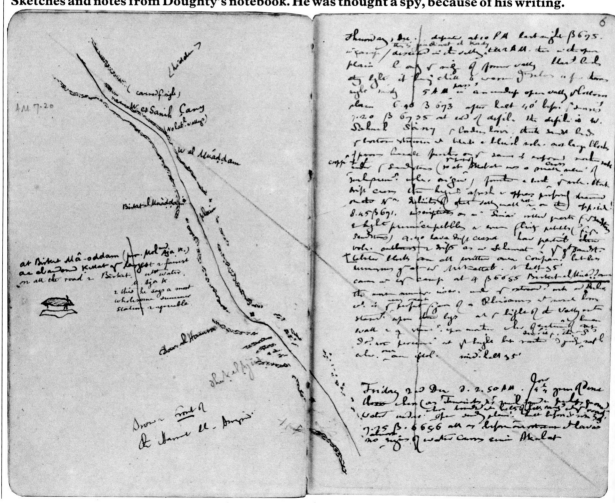

52

was almost certainly as unaware of the fact as he had single-mindedly been unaware of his impact as a Nasrani on the Arabs. 'He dressed', his friends recorded, 'in whitish cotton clothes of some eastern material and a green band often twisted about his waist; sockless feet thrust into heel-less sandals and using, when he went out, a large green umbrella. This, in December, struck us immensely! . . . he spoke seldom and then with some hesitation, as if his native language did not come quite easily to him. . . .'

With much difficulty Doughty managed to have archaeological reports published – first in Germany – and started a continuing series of sour arguments with the Royal Geographical Society and French and German museums over the sale of his pressings. He bitterly believed he was being treated most shabbily.

Pressings from the tombs at Medain Salih

In June 1879, six months after his return, he started writing *Travels in Arabia Deserta*. Five years later, in April 1884, he submitted it to publishers. The publishers replied that they found 'the style of the book so peculiar as to be at times hardly intelligible. . . . Most readers and all reviewers would say that parts of it are not English at all.' The publishers would only consent to publish if 'the book is put into shape by some competent man who can amend the style in accordance with the English idiom'.

He turned angrily, and in despair, to other publishers. After a year without success, it was eventually published under the sponsorship of Professor William Wright, an Arabic scholar, by the Pitt Press at Cambridge. The reviews were generally good, but sales were poor. The publishers made a loss of £383.

Doughty's wife, Caroline

In October 1886 Doughty married Caroline Amelia McMurdo at St John's Church, Fulham. His two daughters were born in 1892 and 1894.

When he set out on his travels, his declared aim was to prepare himself for his life's work – writing a major patriotic work of literature. Doughty went on writing.

53

In 1906 he published the first two volumes of his poem 'The Dawn in Britain', a monumental exercise of twenty-four cantos and more than 30,000 unrhymed decasyllabic lines. By 1908 an abbreviated edition of *Arabia Deserta* was enthusiastically reviewed.

More followed: books, poems 'The Cliffs' and 'The Clouds' were prophetic calls to arms in 1909 and 1912, just before World War I. This literary crystal gazing, almost more than any-

Doughty in later life

thing else, won him a degree of popularity and public acclaim. And in 1921 the literary world's 'glamour boy' of the desert, Lawrence, wrote an introduction to *Arabia Deserta* when it was re-issued.

He had – by then – been honoured, rewarded, applauded. He had remained throughout stubborn, inflexible, clumsy, convinced of his own rightness. Some thought him a great poet – yet few people outside university departments of English read 'The Cliffs' or 'The Clouds' today.

He died at the age of eighty-two in 1926, after a bad attack of laryngitis. He had been unwell since 1918. After his death, it was not his literary achievement that caught the imagination and remained in memory but that remarkable journey he had made fifty years before.

Among explorers, Doughty is in a category by himself. One might wonder even if he was an explorer at all. He discovered no unknown continents, like Columbus and Cook. He was by no means the first European to penetrate the Arabian peninsula. Gifford had been to Hayil before him, and Burton had even entered Mecca. But they had gone in disguise, pretending to be Moslems.

Doughty went as himself – an English Christian gentleman.

He complained of the fanaticism so often directed against him, yet he was no less fanatical himself. Time and again, a friendly Bedouin begged him to bend a little, to make some slight gesture of compromise that would have made life so much more endurable for him. On every occasion he refused. He was dogged, inflexible and largely without humour, yet we are in his debt for a marvellously rich picture of desert life, before any of the innovations of the twentieth century, or the glamorous fantasies of other explorers, impinged on it.

For Doughty was engaged in another exploration – of himself. He was driven, perhaps, by his early experiences – the loss of his parents in childhood, his own physical clumsiness, his communication difficulties, and perhaps, too, the logical outcome of his scientific tendencies.

Whatever the cause or motives, the fact remains that he placed himself in the crucible of the Arabian desert and then defied nature and mankind to do their damndest. His achievement was that he survived without compromise.

Stanley 1841–1904

In 1841 a six-year-old Welsh boy was left in a brutal workhouse, dumped by relatives who didn't want him, after his mother had rejected him. He ran away at fifteen to seek his fortune.

He became the explorer the world knows as Henry Morton Stanley.

He never forgot that early betrayal by his relatives and the rejection by his own family. He took the name of the American who adopted him after he'd run away to sea. He fought for the Confederates in the American Civil War, was captured, and enlisted on the other side. He was in the American Navy and roamed the world, seeking adventure and finally earning a living from journalism.

As a journalist, he was the man who found David Livingstone, who had 'disappeared' in Africa. It changed his life. He determined to finish Livingstone's work. And that determination led him to become the greatest explorer of his day, and the man who filled in the 'blank spaces' on the map of Africa, opening it up for the rest of the world.

All attempts to trade had come to nothing. The canoes were full of wounded. Out of the hundred men in the river party, no more than thirty were fit. For days they had been harassed from the banks by poisoned arrows. Even the land party had lost touch with them. They couldn't run any more. They had to make a stand.

The place was Vinya-Njara on the Congo; the time, a few days before Christmas 1876. Stanley turned the *Lady Alice* towards the bank that rose steeply out of the water. She had been built for him in England, in a Teddington boat yard, and then carried, in sections, from Zanzibar. He had named her *Lady Alice* after his fiancée, Alice Pike, of New York. He hoped to marry her on his return. At that moment it seemed unlikely he would ever see her again.

He took the Winchester from Maruki, one of the boys he had hired in Zanzibar, and leapt ashore. He called to Frank Pocock and climbed the bank towards the village while Uledi marshalled the men.

Pocock was the last of the three white men that Stanley had brought with him. His brother Edward Pocock had died of typhoid in the early days of the expedition. The other white man, Fred Barker, had died the year before. Pocock was left with 166 Africans under his command. '. . . a severe blow to me,' he noted. 'I may say I am alone in a wild country.'

Now he ran up the bank beside 'the Master' with the other Winchester in his hand.

The village was set back from the river on level ground with the thick forest behind it. It was a single street about three hundred yards long, with huts on either side of it. When they reached it it was empty. Uledi, a Zanzibari – 'lithe and active as a leopard, brave as a lion' – went through it with the men who were armed with Snider rifles and old percussion muzzle-loaders. There wasn't a soul left in the place. Everyone had run into the bush, although they hadn't gone far; their drums and war horns could still be heard, and the strange war cries. They were uttered, wrote Stanley, 'in tones so singular as

A battle on the river. Stanley's progress was constantly being challenged: 'The word was given to fire. It was every man for himself.'

to impress even my African comrades with a sense of its eccentricity'. A rhythmic 'Bo-bo, bo-bo, bo-bo-o-o-oh!'

The place had to be made defensible. Stanley pushed scouts out towards the forest in two arcs, one at either end of the village. Behind them the main force cut down anything between the village and the bush that would have given cover to an attacker – scrub, grass, weeds. Trees were cut and dragged across the two open ends of the street to form a stockade. Finally, two towers fifteen feet high were built, one at each end of the street, for marksmen. They were made of logs, cut to size behind the protective walls of the stockade, fastened together with bark rope and cane fibre. Each was large enough for ten riflemen, and gave a clear field of fire as far as the forest's edge.

It was the last thing Stanley wanted, a full-scale battle. He had seventy-two sick men with him – more than twice the number who were left fit to fight. But the alternative was to be killed. He still couldn't understand why he should have had to fight almost every inch of the way along the Lualaba, when all he was concerned with was finding out where it went.

The sick and wounded were brought from the river and put in the empty huts. Three had died during the night. Most were suffering from smallpox, their faces covered in pustules. They needed rest and absolute quiet if they were to have any hope at all of recovery. But the 'aboriginals' in the forest outside gave them no rest. They seemed determined to wipe out the entire expedition.

The arrows fell continuously, lobbed into the street from the edge of the forest. They were short, no more than a foot in length, fired from short, stiff bows covered in monkey hide. They relied for their effect less on their penetration than on the poison they carried. The odd sound they made in flight was more frightening to European ears than the whine of bullets.

The main attack, when it came, was preceded by the building sound of the war cries and the drums. A hail of arrows fell into the street, rattling on the roofs, sticking into the beaten earth. One of the tower marksmen cried out, then fell. Figures appeared at the forest edge,

small men armed with bows and throwing spears, difficult to hit because of their unpredictable movements. The scouts pulled back, running across the open ground towards the stockade. The attackers advanced, breaking into a fast run, drawing back their spear arms, beginning to bunch together as they came nearer. The cannonade of fire from the Snider rifles and the muskets caught them in the middle of the clearing and they fell. The survivors broke, paused for a moment in disbelief, then turned and ran back into the cover of the forest.

The lull was only temporary. War horns and drums sounded from the river. From the top of one of the towers, Pocock could see a great flotilla of war canoes coming at them across the water. At the same time, the attack from the forest was renewed. 'These bowmen climbed tall trees, and any person showing himself in the broad street of the great town became a target at once,' wrote Stanley. 'We were unable to bury our dead or attend to our seriously wounded.'

The combined attack was held. Just. The war canoes came within bow-shot and put down a hail of arrows, but the attackers' losses were terrible. The Sniders had a calibre of .577, the bullets were large enough to knock a man overboard. The river was littered with floating black bodies. 'The shrieks, cries, shouts of encouragement, the rattling volleys of musketry, the booming war horns, the yells and defiance of the combatants, the groans and screams of the women and children in the hospital camp, made together such a medley of hideous noise as can never be effaced from my memory,' said Stanley.

The heart of Africa had never heard such noise.

Then, when it seemed there could really be no hope, the besieged party heard firing in the distance upstream. The arrows stopped falling into the stockade. The natives broke from the forest and ran into the river and began to swim for the other side. The canoes turned in confusion and began to paddle away. Tippu Tib, the Arab leader of the land party, had arrived like a *deus ex machina* in the very nick of time.

It wasn't in Stanley's nature to leave things there. The thing had to be brought to a firm conclusion. The attackers had a camp on the far side of an island. That night it was windy and raining. Under cover of darkness, Stanley took the *Lady Alice* to the upstream end of the island whilst Frank Pocock went to the downstream end with twenty men in four canoes. The entire fleet of enemy canoes – thirty-six of them – lay there tied to trees. Stanley, Uledi and some of the men untied them and pushed them into the stream. They were picked up by Pocock in the channel below, and towed back to Vinya-Njara.

'The enemy had lost its battle fleet,' said Stanley. 'Thirty-six canoes. And with them, the means to make war.' They would have to negotiate a peace. On 22 December agreement was reached between the two sides. Fifteen canoes were returned to the natives, twenty-one retained by Stanley. The spoils of war. The expedition had lost four men killed, with another thirteen wounded, at the battle of Vinya-Njara. But the expedition had survived and won.

The dark centre of Africa would never be the same again.

Henry Morton Stanley became an explorer by accident. He had become a journalist in much the same way. When he left the United States Navy in 1865 at the end of the Civil War, he crossed to the west, visiting such places as Salt Lake City and Denver, and paying his way by writing about them. He was highly successful. He had, he discovered, an ability to write vivid, descriptive pieces that were in considerable demand. It was journalism and the search for copy that took him through Asia Minor and Tiflis to Tibet, rather than the thirst for adventure.

Back home in the United States, he joined the expedition against the Red Indians mounted by General Hancock in 1866, as correspondent for such papers as the *Missouri Democrat*. Inevitably, his reports reached the notice of the New York papers, and the *New York Herald* sent him as its correspondent with the British expedition against the Emperor Theodore of Abyssinia. It was Stanley who sent the first news of the fall of Magdala.

So effective was he as a reporter, so readable was his material, that the proprietor of the *Herald*, James Gordon Bennett, gave him a roving commission. In effect he had *carte blanche*. Then in 1869, Gordon Bennett Jr recalled him to New York and commissioned him to go in search of the Scottish explorer David Livingstone, whose long absence in Africa was arousing wide attention.

He left Zanzibar on 21 March 1871, and marched into the interior. He was still a journalist looking for a good story. But when he found Livingstone at Ujiji on 10 November, and uttered those classically understated words which made him famous, 'Dr Livingstone, I presume', something changed in him. Perhaps it was the African magic that caught him. Perhaps it was Livingstone's own magic. More likely it was a combination of both. But when he left Africa six months later, it was with more than just a good story. He had a purpose.

A few months later, he published an account of the journey, *How I Found Livingstone*. In London the story could hardly be believed. It was inconceivable that this 'loud, brash Yankee' who wasn't even an explorer should have gone into the unknown jungles and done what nobody else had been able to do. Yet he had Livingstone's journals with him to prove it. Gradually his account was accepted. He found himself famous. He gave a series of public lectures that added to his reputation, and in the end Queen Victoria asked to meet him. She gave him a gold snuff-box set with brilliants, and thanked him for finding Dr Livingstone.

He had achieved stardom as Henry Morton Stanley, the great American explorer.

It was what he wanted – acceptance in high places. Yet it was all a myth. He wasn't an explorer in the real sense. He couldn't begin to compare himself with Livingstone. He might never have gone to Africa if Bennett hadn't commissioned him to go. *How I Found Livingstone* had been highly successful, but it hardly pushed back the frontiers of human knowledge. He wasn't even an American, at least not by birth. The accent he used wasn't native to him. Even the name he used wasn't his own.

He was born in Denbigh, Wales, on 29 June 1841, and christened John Rowlands. He was probably illegitimate. His mother was poor and didn't want him, and he was first brought up by his maternal grandfather. Then his grandfather died. The boy was six. He was boarded out among various relatives and neighbours, but within a year the grownups in his life told John Rowlands one day that he was going on a visit to his Aunt Mary. That day he never saw his Aunt Mary. Instead, he was left in the workhouse at St Asaph, a particularly brutal establishment.

He was there until he was fifteen, when, big enough to do so, and tortured enough to want to, he thrashed the workhouse master – and ran away. He reached Liverpool eventually and went to sea as a cabin-boy.

He was eighteen when he left the sea, having found his way to New Orleans. An American, Henry Morton Stanley, befriended him, gave him a job, and finally adopted him. It was from him that he took his name. And he never forgot that early rejection by his own mother and betrayal by his family.

He joined the Confederate Army when the Civil War broke out, and in April 1862 he was captured at the Battle of Shiloh and spent two months in the prison at Camp Douglas, Chicago. He got his release by changing allegiance and enlisting in the Federal artillery, but a month later he was discharged as being unfit.

He was twenty-one and uncertain what to do. His benefactor was dead. His new country was at war, but he wasn't allowed to make a contribution. He retraced his steps. It was the first of several times. In November he landed in Liverpool. He was almost destitute; his clothes were shabby, his health poor. He went to Denbigh to see his mother, but she wouldn't let him in the house. It gave a massive reinforcement to the sense of rejection that was to dog him for the rest of his life. He went back to America and served in the American Navy until the end of the war. Then came journalism, and the historic pilgrimage to Livingstone.

What turned him into an explorer was the death of Livingstone. Stanley had found in Livingstone a wise and kind father figure – something he had sought all his life. He heard about Livingstone's death when he arrived back in England some time later, from Ashanti.

There and then he decided he must return to Africa to complete the exploration that Livingstone had left unfinished. Particularly, he wanted to solve the mystery of the River Lualaba in unexplored central Africa, which Livingstone had reached and believed to be the headwaters of the Nile.

Stanley announced his intention, saying: 'The purpose of the enterprise is to complete the work left unfinished by the lamented death of Doctor Livingstone and to solve if possible the remaining problems of the geography of Central Africa.'

It was a bold statement, from a man who could never himself be disregarded, and with this aim in view, a fund was raised with the backing of Lord Burnham, Gordon Bennett and other distinguished figures. The purpose was to finance an Anglo-American expedition under Stanley.

Despite his height – a little over five feet five inches – there was an extraordinary sense of power to him. He was broad-shouldered and strong, and when he left for Africa to continue Livingstone's work he weighed more than thirteen stone. He wore a dark, full beard. 'His appearance was certainly a remarkable one. I think I have never seen eyes set so straight across the face, or cheekbones so high and so outstanding,' one writer said.

There was also a clumsiness to him that was immediately striking. He had large feet and small hands, and whatever clothes he wore never seemed to fit. Queen Victoria said of him: 'I have this evening seen Mr Stanley, who discovered Livingstone, a determined, ugly little man – with a strong American twang.' Her assessment wasn't entirely accurate. When he was with friends and a little animated, his Welsh background was obvious enough in his speech.

He was indomitable, without question, otherwise he could never have survived a march from one side of Africa to the other. He conceived a single goal before he set off for Africa, and he never lost sight of it. If necessary, he was quite prepared to sacrifice himself or anyone else in order to reach it. He wasn't above beating one of his men or putting him in chains. He did it, he insisted, in the name of 'discipline' or 'justice', not capriciously.

HENRY M. STANLEY.

AT 19, John Rowlands, a poor Welsh boy, had emigrated to America, had been adopted by a merchant of the name of Stanley, and had assumed the latter name. At 22, his adopting father having died without a will, young Stanley was serving as a petty officer on board the war-ship *Minnesota*. At 26 he had become a journalist, and was about to represent the *New York Herald* with the British army in Abyssinia. On returning from this expedition he delivered lectures on his adventures, a handbill of which we reproduce on the page opposite, as a veritable curiosity. At 31 he had discovered Dr. Livingstone, and had returned

From a]   AGE 19.   [*Photograph.*

with glory. What Mr. Stanley has done recently is known to all the world.

*Always
Your loving Nephew
Henry Stanley
U.S.S. "Minnesota*

From a]   AGE 22.   [*Photograph.*

From a Photo. by]   AGE 26.   [*Rockwell & Co., New York.*

From a Photo. by]   AGE 31.   [*The Stereoscopic Co.*

From a Photo. by]   PRESENT DAY.   [*John Fergus, Cannes.*

Popular fame. *The Strand Magazine* **produces a potted biography of Henry Morton Stanley.**

His sense of responsibility was highly developed. The safety of the expedition was in his hands and he was well aware of it. He kept his enormous team together by constantly imposing his authority. 'I suddenly shot out my voice with the full power of my lungs, in sharp, quick accents of command to paddle ashore, and the effect was wonderful. It awoke them like soldiers to the call of duty. . . . I have often been struck at the power of a quick, decisive tone, it appears to have an electric effect, riding rough-shod over all fears, indecision, and tremor. . . . I had frequently, up river, when the people were inclined to get panic-stricken, or to despair, restored them to a sense of duty by affecting the sharp-cutting, steel-like, and imperious tone of voice, which seemed to be as much of a compelling power as powder to a bullet.'

He says of himself: 'While Frank [Pocock] was regarded more as a friend, I was looked at as a severe, exacting master in whose presence there could be no shirking.' It was a view that was not quite accurate. His great strength was his patience, which allowed him to listen to all manner of complaints without irritation. He was unsparing in his praise where he thought it was justified.

The 'master' praised Pocock for his coolness, and in a dispatch he wrote of Uledi, the coxswain of the *Lady Alice*: 'He is one of a hundred thousand. I doubt whether there is another in the Island of Zanzibar equal to him. There are few in this expedition who are not indebted to him for life or timely rescue or brave service. He was the first in war the most modest in peace. He was the best soldier, the best swimmer, the best carrier, the best sailor, the best workman in wood or iron and the most faithful of the black faithfuls.'

For such a concern for individual members of his party, he was regarded with affectionate respect. It says a great deal for his understanding and powers of leadership that he was able to persuade men to march seven thousand miles with him, for three years, through the uncharted forests of central Africa.

Africa, when Livingstone had first reached Cape Colony in 1849, was almost unknown. Apart from the lower course of the Nile, the middle of the Niger and the mouths of the Congo and the Zambezi, the map showed almost nothing. What Livingstone was principally concerned with was the hydrography of central Africa – the complex of water systems that the area gave rise to. With this in mind he traced the course of the Zambezi and discovered Lake Nyasa and the lakes to the west of it. He explored Lake Tanganyika, and it was on its shores that Stanley found him in 1871.

At the time of his death, Livingstone had followed the river Chambezi from Lake Bangweulu northwards into the Lualaba. For six hundred miles its course had been almost due north. It might be the Congo, but he hoped it would be the Nile. 'I have no fancy to be made into "black man's meat" for the sake of the Congo.' he said. He reached Nyangwe, and died without knowing the truth.

Stanley's army. The Anglo-American expedition for the exploration of Central Africa, 1878.

Stanley and three white companions arrived in Zanzibar in 1874 and began to assemble a large force of bearers for the journey into the interior. Two years later, after a march of six thousand miles, two of the white men were dead. Only Frank Pocock was still with Stanley as he approached the Lualaba at Nyangwe to take up the task left by Livingstone. 'If the River Lualaba flows north into the Nile it will lead us to Cairo,' he wrote. 'If on the other hand it flows west it must be the Congo – and that will lead us to the Atlantic.'

His expedition was huge; it moved like an army. The core of it consisted of 353 native porters recruited in Zanzibar, under the command of Manwa Sera, who took orders from no one but Stanley and Pocock. Manwa Sera was in his early thirties, bearded, finely built. Stanley found him always trustworthy and faithful. The indispensable Pocock himself was twenty-seven, a little taller than Stanley, with brown hair and eyes. He was from Kent where he had been a waterman on the Medway.

Under Manwa Sera came Wadi Safeni – 'sage Safeni', Stanley called him, and 'the councillor'. Others held high in Stanley's esteem as he approached the Lualaba were Uledi, coxswain of the *Lady Alice*, Hamadi the chief guide, Mar-

'He was tall,' said Stanley, 'blackbearded, negroid complexion, in the prime of life, straight, quick in his movements, a picture of energy and strength. A fine intelligent face with a nervous twitching of the eyes, gleaming white perfectly formed teeth.'

He had a considerable effect on Stanley at their first meeting. 'With the air of a well bred Arab, and almost courtier-like in his manner, he

Tippu Tib, the Arab slave trader

zouk the cook, Kacheche the senior guard, and such boys as Kalulu and Maruki. Zaidi, one of the younger chiefs, was also held in high regard for his 'tremendous courage and tenacity'.

Apart from the Swahili-speaking bearers under the command of Manwa Sera, there was an even larger party, commanded by an Arab.

His proper name was Hamed bin Mohammed bin Jumah bin Rajab el Murjebi – but he was called Tippu Tib. He said he was given the name because of the sound his muskets made when he was marauding in the interior. Others said he was named after a little bird of the region that had red-rimmed eyes and was always blinking.

welcomed me to Mwana Mamba's village, and his slaves being ready at hand with mat and bolster, he reclined vis a vis, while a buzz of admiration of his style was perceptible from the onlookers. After regarding him for a few minutes, I came to the conclusion that this Arab was a remarkable man – the most remarkable I had met among Arabs, Wa-Swahili, and half-castes in Africa. He was neat in his person, his clothes were of a spotless white, his fez cap brand new, his waist was encircled by a rich dowle, his dagger was splendid with silver filigree, and his tout ensemble was that of an Arab gentleman in very comfortable circumstances.'

Tippu Tib was, quite simply, the most notorious Arab slave trader west of Zanzibar.

He joined Stanley with his party of seven hundred – Arab warriors, women, children and slaves – as Stanley approached the Lualaba. He agreed to escort them through the dangerous country ahead. He did so in part because he took a liking to Stanley, and because Stanley was going to pay him, but also for another reason. Over a vast area of east Africa, stretching from the south-western corner of Lake Tanganyika some five hundred miles northwards towards the edge of the Upper Congo forest, the word of Tippu Tib was law. He took his caravans into the region freely, offering protection, extracting his tributes of slaves and ivory. By exploring with Stanley beyond the territories that he already controlled he saw every chance of extending them. The stories that came out of the unknown forest north of Nyangwe were of mountains of ivory.

This vast heterogeneous army of Arabs, Wa-Swahili, white men and slaves reached the Lualaba in October 1876. 'A secret rapture filled my soul as I gazed for the first time upon the majestic stream,' wrote Stanley. 'The mystery of the great River that for all these centuries nature has kept hidden from the world of science is waiting to be solved.'

Things had not gone too well just before that. 'Our expedition is no longer the tight compact force which was my pride. Desertion, illness and death have thinned our ranks.' He was ill himself. 'Another attack of malarious fever grips me. Treatment; 15 or 20 grains of quinine, taken with water from the river.' Even the quinine had its drawbacks. He had suffered from recurrent attacks of fever for years, ever since first contracting it in Arkansas in his youth. Earlier he had written, 'I am in such a state tonight that I can neither lie down or sit quietly in one position long. I am nervous and my head is very strange. I have the most fearful dreams every night and am afraid to shut my eyes lest I shall see the horrid things that haunt me. I will go walk, walk, walk in the forest to get rid of them. . . . I think it must be the quinine which I have taken in unusual doses that created this extraordinary state of nervousness of the head.'

1. Henry Morton Stanley, played in the film by Sean Lynch.

2. The *Lady Alice*, named after his fiancée Alice Pike of New York, was specially built by a boatyard on the River Thames, to be carried in sections through the jungle and then assembled for use on the Congo.

3. As they approached each village, Stanley would rise upright in the bow of the *Lady Alice*, holding beads and metal ware, giving the cry 'Ayemah, Ayemah', indicating his desire to trade. Almost invariably he was greeted with a shower of arrows.

4. This was the longest, hardest battle – the 45th. But Stanley and his small army won, drove off the attackers. The heart of Africa was never the same again.

5. Their arrows were short, their bows small. But the poison at their tips was invariably deadly. Eighteen months after starting on the three-year trek, Stanley's expedition was reduced from 750 to 312 men and women. And not all died from fever or disease.

6. At times the long, long trail of followers, guides, cooks, bearers and hunters stretched for more than two miles along the river bank. They marched with flags flying, bugles playing and drums beating. What native

(*continued p.65*)

villagers would not have been alarmed and defensive at the sight of this 'invading army'.

7. Despite orders from Stanley to the contrary, Frank Pocock, with five canoes of bearers, tried to shoot the most dangerous of the cataracts in an attempt to catch up with Stanley. Pocock was lost and drowned. Three others also drowned.

8. Stanley wrote: 'I have lost my dearly beloved Frank . . .' Stanley was now alone – the only white man left on the expedition.

The film was directed by Fred Burnley, and shot in the jungles and on the rivers of Equatorial Africa and Zaire (the Congo).

Stanley's plan, when he reached the river, was to take the entire party down it by boat. The *Lady Alice* was reassembled and put on the water, but the rest of the column had to march along the bank. 'Until we had enough canoes to float the entire expedition we had to assemble the *Lady Alice* and head down stream in advance of the main column to forage for food and search out camp sites.'

There were flaws in the plan. The natives refused to trade; food became scarce.

It is not difficult to see why. News of this enormous army must have reached the river tribesmen days before they even glimpsed its vanguard led by Hamadi in his red robe, carrying his ivory 'kudu' horn and copper bugle. The sight of a thousand people strung for half a mile or more in single file along the river bank, carrying guns and boxes, waving an enormous red and white striped flag with stars in one corner, marching in step to the beating of drums, must have filled them with more terror than they had ever experienced in the jungle. As Mary Kingsley observed twenty years later, it was no way to approach the African if you wanted his co-operation. As a trader one might hope to trade, but as an invading army it wasn't really sensible to expect anything but opposition.

There was another factor that added to Stanley's difficulties. Tippu Tib was accompanying him, and Tippu Tib's reputation must have been well known throughout the Upper Congo. To the African, it must have seemed that the whole of his country was being opened up to the slave trade. More than that, Tippu Tib regarded anything as fair game. Whatever he saw he took. 'I attacked the Shensis and took their boats and goats from them,' he relates. 'Every day I got 6 or 7 canoes and any number of goats.'

This lack of co-operation that the presence of so many of Tippu Tib's men produced in the African was perhaps affecting those in Stanley's own party, for on 14 November he sent three hundred of them back home. It still made little difference to the size of the army, which remained more than seven hundred strong.

Whatever the cause of the opposition from the tribesmen, they remained consistently hostile to Stanley. He would see a village on the bank, a market place in the middle of it. He would pick up some of his trading goods – bracelets of brass wire, strings of glass beads – and wave them in the air. 'Sennenneh! Sennenneh!' he called, standing in the bow of the *Lady Alice* and using the bleating cry that indicated he wanted to trade. The result was always the same. The villagers disappeared. A war cry would rise from the forest and arrows begin to fly. 'The natives are so wild here that they may not understand my pantomime for food,' he said. 'What a thin barrier separates ferocity from amiability. . . . I had hoped that if we came in peace we could make friends with these Aboriginal tribes. Now I regretted dividing the expedition.'

He decided to wait for Tippu Tib and Pocock. 'It was three days of waiting before the land columns caught up.' In the meantime he created a defensive position on the bank with the *Lady Alice* pulled clear of the water and forming some cover on the river side of his position. On the landward, he got his party, thirty-six in all, to make a palisade or 'boma' of brushwood that would give some protection against spears and arrows. Sentries were posted. He was particularly concerned aboat the safety of the *Lady Alice*. If she were lost they would have to abandon the river and the advantages that it gave them. 'We maintained a strict watch lest our boat should be stolen.'

The first indication of the arrival of the land party was the sound of musket fire from the bush. At first it seemed the start of an attack by the tribesmen and the men in the stockade on the river bank picked up their rifles and waited. Then Tippu Tib and Pocock appeared, with the first of the land party behind them. 'We were attacked,' said Pocock. 'A tribe who called themselves the Bakusu. Killed three of our party with arrows.'

The journey had taken a frightful toll. Tippu Tib's men were suffering from smallpox.

From a sketch by Stanley. At night they fenced themselves in, and drew the canoes ashore.

Frank Pocock, indispensable to Stanley

Stanley's men were free from that particular disease because he had them vaccinated against it a year earlier at Bagamoyo. But there were plenty of other diseases in Africa to affect them. Septic ulcers were particularly common, covering a whole face or limb with suppurating sores. 'I felt many times inclined to turn my face away at the sight of victims of diseases that would have provided enough for a dozen physicians,' wrote Stanley. 'Our medicines were limited and bore no guarantee of survival. In these areas it is advisable to acquire a knowledge of minor surgery. I decided we needed a floating hospital so we appropriated six canoes I had found along the river bank.'

Frank Pocock was indispensable to Stanley at such times. He had a simple humanity that communicated itself at once to the sick bearers. On the whole they accepted the medical treatment he gave them and were grateful. His humanity was particularly marked regarding Tippu Tib's slaves. Earlier at Ujiji he wrote, 'Ujiji is a disgrace to all other countries I have been in. In Africa the slaves of the Arabs rake about the market place like dogs, pick up pieces of sugar cane or anything that is like eatable, and seven out of ten are naked and nearly starved. Then as

the cruelty with which they are treated is enough to make one's flesh crawl in his bones to see and hear it . . . it's a pity that some means could not be made to put a stop to this human slaughter.' And later: 'When the drover of the slaves struck a fine young woman on the head with the paddle of a canoe and killed her, I had to walk away for my heart was full ready to burst and I could not help her.'

Pocock was put in charge of the floating hospital, which consisted of the six 'appropriated' canoes lashed together with cross-poles in pairs. The sick were paddled down-stream until they were well enough to rejoin the land party. 'For the accommodation of the raving and delirious sick we constructed a shed over the hospital canoe,' wrote Stanley.

If any of the sick failed to recover – and there were many deaths – they were wrapped in their own clothes with their arms tied to their sides and their feet fastened together. Weights were tied to them and they were dropped in the middle of the river. Tippu Tib said a prayer in Arabic if they had been with his party. 'River graves are a precaution against cannibals,' said Stanley.

The two parties were rejoined, and from that point forward Stanley insisted that they remain within signalling distance of each other. They used drums, with the drumbeats from the bank being returned by the *Lady Alice*. But the river was wide and the current strong, and inevitably the two parties began slowly to separate again.

A little later a village appeared in the middle of a clearing. Stanley took the *Lady Alice* cautiously towards the bank. Food was still the most pressing problem for both river and land parties, and Stanley, hopefully, went through the trade process again, holding up beads and copperware, bleating that strange cry, 'Sennenneh!', pointing to his mouth and stomach. Faces peered at him from the bush. Figures looked down from the trees, with bows in their hands. Once more the reception turned hostile as cries broke out in the black forest and arrows flew. Three of his men fell back, dead or mortally wounded by the poisoned darts. Once more he ordered the boat turned back towards the middle of the river out of reach of the missiles.

'We had sufficient cause to begin war,' he wrote. 'I was determined to occupy their village. We were desperate in our resolve not to die without fighting.'

That place was Vinya-Njara. The battle that followed was one of the most desperate experiences of the journey so far.

Christmas Day came only three days after the tribesmen conceded defeat. Tippu Tib had become tired of the expedition; he was anxious to return to Zanzibar with his caravan. He had collected a good deal of wealth on the journey so far, and he proposed to add to it on the way back. There is no doubt that Stanley would have preferred him to stay, but he didn't complain. He paid Tippu Tib the five thousand dollars he had promised him, and Christmas Day was spent in festivities. 'The great event was the race between Tippu Tib and Frank Pocock,' he wrote. 'The Arab had competed with unusual determination for the prize. The next day Tippu Tib and his private army bade farewell to my expedition. He had fulfilled the terms of our contract together.'

Tippu Tib's decision to leave the expedition nearly broke it. There was a good deal of dissension amongst Stanley's men. They had been away more than two years. They had just come through the battle of Vinya-Njara and many were sick. They wanted to return east with Tippu Tib.

'Stanley became very mournful,' said Tippu Tib. 'Even his food was no longer tasteful to him and he was on the point of weeping. In the evening he came to me and said: "My whole labour is lost if these men turn back. Then I too must turn back and my toil has been in vain. Help me now I implore you." I said to him: "God willing, I will help you under all circumstances!"

'I lay down to sleep, and next morning visited him and asked: "What have you decided?" He replied: "I have decided nothing, and I don't know what I am to do." Then I said to him: "Well now, follow my advice. Assemble all your people, then call me and speak to me with harsh words, and say: If you go back all my people will turn back. They cannot do otherwise. Now my work is for the State, and that is no other than Seyyid Burghash [Sultan of Zanzibar]. If my people turn back, I must turn back too. Then I shall tell the Sultan that it was Hamed bin Mohammed [Tippu Tib] who made my further journey impossible. Then the State will confiscate your goods. When you have said that, then I shall speak." Then I went away.

'In the afternoon he sent for me and called together his people, and spoke to me in presence of his men in harsh words, as I had prompted him. Thereupon I said to them: "You have heard Stanley's words; now get on your way and depart. Whoever follows me I will kill; for you would plunge me in ruin and my property would be confiscated by the Government. Then I should be as good as dead. My toil during many years would be in vain. Should I not certainly perish here? If you follow me, I will kill you." Thereupon I withdrew and they went on their way.

'Towards evening came Stanley's people, and their leader said to me: "Our time with this

Stanley kept meticulous expedition accounts

Henry. M. Stanley in acct with "Daily Telegraph" on behalf of "Daily Telegraph" & "New York Herald"

		£	s	d.
18 7/7	Brot ford.	1629	12	2.
To Tibu Tib for wcoct. 82 bcoo. which at Zanzibar rather is		484	1	,
Stores at Cape Town & Natal for Sick.		78	14	7.
Wages paid to Francis John & Edward. Pocock. —		200	,	,
Wages paid to Fred. Barker.	30	,	,	
Total amount of wages & rewards disbursed among 113 men. 22 women & 9 male relations in rupees. 17. 379. 57.		520	5	,
Expenses from Suez to Alexandria.	4	,	,	
Brindisi to England.	13	,	,	
Salary if agreable from Aug.st 1st /76 to Dec. 31st 1877.		416	13	4.
		£ 5276	6	1

* Credit See over.

...uropean is over; we positively must turn back.''... said to them: "Your words are idle – march ...n".'

Tippu Tib's departure wasn't without its ...ompensations. 'With 23 added canoes,' wrote ...tanley, 'the entire expedition can now be ...oated. And there will be no further arguments ...bout following the river!'

The river flowed easily, now majestic in its ...readth, carrying them steadily further north...vards. From Vinya-Njara they passed Mpika ...nd Kiamba and on towards Kirembuka, with ...tanley plotting every feature of the route, ...aking temperatures, checking heights above sea ...evel. Even during the fight at Vinya-Njara he ...till had had time to make anthropological obser...ations: 'The inhabitants of Vinya-Njara devote ...hemselves, among other occupations, to fishing, ...nd the manufacture of salt from the Pistia ...lants.'

'I have now', he said, '143 souls – men, women ...nd children. Out of these, only forty-eight have ...uns, and only thirty-two are effective. Add ...nyself and Frank Pocock and we are thirty-four ...ighting men. 109 are mere dummies which serve ...o frighten off savages deterred by a show of ...eads rather than arms.'

He had lost, by death or desertion, 210 of the ...earers he had recruited in Zanzibar.

...tanley's day, when he was free from native ...arassment, was well-ordered. The party broke ...amp early and took to the river between six and ...even in the morning. After an hour or two a halt ...vas made for breakfast. On 9 March 1877, Stan...ey wrote, 'Six miles below the confluence of the ...Nkutu river with the Livingstone we drew our ...essels close to a large thick grove, to cook break...ast. . . . Fires were kindled and the women were ...ttending to the porridge of cassava flour for ...heir husbands. Frank and I were hungrily ...waiting our cook's voice to announce our meal ...vas ready.'

On 28 April 1877, when supplies were low, he ...vrote, 'Our store of sugar had run out . . . our ...coffee was finished at Vinya-Njara and at Inkisi ...Falls our tea, alas! alas! came to an end.' They ...vere forced to take what they could find: 'Con...entment had to be found in boiled "duff " or cold cassava bread, ground nuts or peanuts, yams and green bananas.' But whereas the bearers made a simple dish from the ingredients, Stanley went to some trouble to produce something more appetising. 'First we rinsed in clear brook water from the ravines some choice cassava or manioc tops, and these were placed in the water to be bruised. Marzouk [the cook] understood that part very well, and soon pounded them to the consistency of a green porridge. To this I then added 50 shelled nuts of Arachis Hypogoea, three small specimens of the Dioscroea Alata boiled and sliced cold, a tablespoon of oil extracted from the Arachis Hypogoea, a tablespoonful of wine of the Elais Guineensis, a little salt, and sufficient powdered capsicum. This imposing and admirable mixture was pounded together, fried and brought into the tent along with toasted cassava pudding, hot and steaming, on the only Delft plate we possessed. . . . Frank and I rejoiced our souls and stomachs with the savoury mess.'

During the day, apart from the general business and administration of directing a large expedition, Stanley was concerned with various scientific observations. Solar readings were taken using a sextant and artificial horizon, and a chronometer carrying Greenwich Mean Time. With the help of a Nautical Almanac, the readings were converted into positions of latitude and longitude.

To determine his height above sea level, Stanley used a hypsometer, a device which works on the principle that the boiling point of water varies according to atmospheric pressure, and that such pressure varies according to the height above sea level. For the atmospheric pressure reading itself he relied on an aneroid barometer. All his instruments – some of which were duplicated so that a reading from one might be checked for accuracy against a reading from another – were later standardised at the Kew observatory, and corrections made to the on-the-spot readings where necessary.

He took a great deal of time making notes. His observations concern geographical features, rough calculations of distance and compass bearings. From time to time he noted 'a line of battle'. Named villages were marked. Unnamed features such as the great system of rapids he encountered in January 1877, were given names.

A halt was usually called about four in the afternoon. The expedition tied up the canoes and pulled the *Lady Alice* clear of the water on rollers. There was always a danger that if she was left in the water her thin skin might be damaged by some floating debris, or by some attacking tribesmen. The ground was cleared and a brushwood barrier built for defence on the landward side. The tents were put up for Stanley and Pocock and the more valuable provisions, the powder and ammunition in particular, were transferred to them from the boats.

When the cooking fires had been lit, Stanley would have tea made for himself and Pocock. 'I am like an old woman,' he wrote earlier, 'I love tea very much and can take a quart and a half without any inconvenience. That tea is all our refreshment. It is our beer, our champagne and our wine; and after the tea we lie down on the katanda [bed] take out our pipes and smoke. After a smoke we take out our notebooks and made a record of everything we have found out on the road. That would probably take an hour or half an hour, and it is hard work.'

Supper, the second and last meal of the day, was eaten at sunset, with the bearers sitting on the ground round the fires. When food was plentiful chicken, fish, cassava and bananas were enjoyed, but towards the end of the journey it became a very meagre meal; 'three fried bananas, twenty roasted nuts, a cup of muddy water' on 4 August 1877.

For a time after Vinya-Njara, the natives seemed less hostile. Then at Kirembuku came another attack. The inhabitants had stretched fishing nets acrosss the river in an attempt to trap the *Lady Alice* and the canoes. When the bearers hacked at the nets to get clear, the natives shot at them with arrows from the bank. Several were hit and wounded, one or two killed. Stanley had discovered that the poisonous effect of the arrows could be neutralised by the 'immediate and plentiful application of nitrate of silver', but such treatment was hardly possible under the circumstances. 'The Kirembuku seemed more interested in having us as game to be trapped, shot or bagged at sight!'

A day or two later, the first of a long series of cataracts came into view. The first of the canoes tried to shoot them but were lost. 'January 6th, 1877,' wrote Stanley. 'A mad confluence of tumbling rushing waters. To float the boats down the falls being impossible I set the men to cut a road through the jungle.' Their position was exactly 'South Latitude 0° – the equator'.

'The next day while the porters were still fairly fresh we made great efforts and by that afternoon had passed the falls and rapids of the first cataract.' The going was hard. No one was completely fit. A road had to be chopped through virgin forest, and then every single piece of equipment had to be manhandled along it. The *Lady Alice* had to be taken from the river and hauled up the bank, then carried with the canoes round the cataract to the smooth water beyond. Every case of supplies had to be unloaded. Every sick man had to be carried in a hammock.

Stanley was exhausted. The river still flowed northwards; the forest was unending. The bearers complained of lack of food and constantly threatened to desert. Many did so. Even Pocock had forgotten how to behave. 'I would discover him with naked feet,' said Stanley, 'and would reprove him for shamelessly exposing his white feet to the vulgar gaze of the aborigines! In Europe this would not be considered indelicate, but in barbarous Africa the feet should be covered as much as the body; for there is a small modicum of superiority shown even in clothing the feet. Not only on moral ground did I urge him to cover his feet, but also for his own comfort and health because of the danger from jigga and guinea-worm. I also discovered from the examples in my camp, that the least abrasion of the skin was likely, if not covered, to result in an ulcer.' His warning to Pocock, unfortunately, came too late.

The cataracts continued day after day, one great boiling tumble of water after another. At times it was possible to put the boats back in the water. At others they had to be carried along the bank. Then on the 11th, when at last the party had found a group of natives prepared to trade with it, Zaidi's canoe capsized in 'a furious stretch of water' with the loss of two men.

Stanley directing the rescue of Zaidi, and (*below*) hauling the canoes past Inkisi

When Stanley reached the scene, Zaidi was clinging to the remains of his canoe in the middle of the rapids with the water pouring over him. Uledi and Marzouk had gone to rescue him and they too were in the water. Then Zaidi, trying to grab one of the rescue ropes being thrown to him, lost his hold on the broken canoe. All three were swept further into the bubbling fury, bouncing and turning in the current. 'Below them was a mile of falls and rapids and great whirlpools.'

By pure good fortune, the current took them past a small islet and they were able to grasp the branches of overhanging vegetation and pull themselves ashore. 'But there were still 50 yards of wild waves between them and safety,' said Stanley. It was only at the twentieth attempt that a rope was thrown across to them from the shore, and they were hauled clear.

On 27 January Stanley wrote, 'We have now by-passed all the seven cataracts which I have named the Stanley Falls, thus closing a series of desperate labours which have occupied us for 23 days. But we still have to make our way up 200 yards of steep ground over which we have constructed a tram-way of wooden rollers.' Along this tramway everything was manhandled once more, and finally brought back to the river.

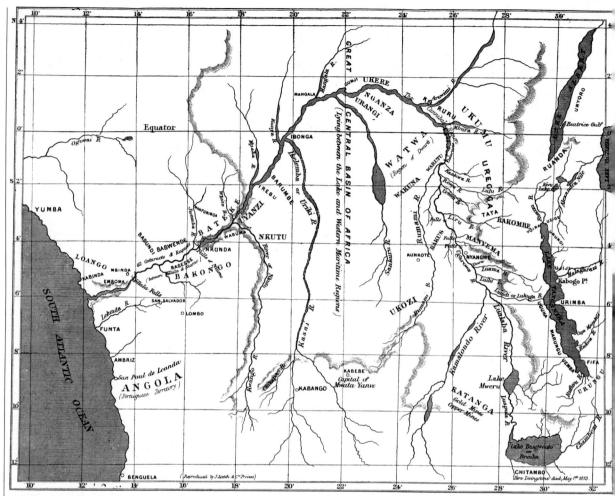

The river turned more to the west. It became obvious it was the Congo, not the Nile.

But something disturbing was happening to the river itself. It began gradually to turn more and more westwards. 'I had decided we should rest and barter for urgently needed food at a village they call Rubunga. For the first time for many weeks we enjoy a calmness of mind. A hearty geniality pervades the market where every mortal thing known in Africa is purchaseable. As well as trade we required information. I had sent my native captain to ascertain the local name for this river. The Lualaba is *not* the source of the Nile. Now I know that this terrible river will eventually lead us to the Atlantic.' The Lualaba had become the Congo.

Progress along the river now became comparatively fast and easy, and for 980 miles they were to find no cataracts or difficult obstacles in it. It was indeed a massive artery into the very heart of Africa. But the friendliness that Stanley experienced at Rubunga was not to be repeated. The natives began to trouble him again, and when they reached the territory of the Bangala they were ambushed. Sixty war canoes were waiting for them, each carrying five musketmen. 'Livingstone called floating down the Lualaba a foolhardy feat, and had turned back,' wrote Stanley. 'I pen these lines with half a feeling that they will never be read by any other white person. It may be said truly that we are now running the gauntlet.'

The Bangala approached with massed cries of 'Yaha-ha-ha, Ya Bangala!' At fifty yards' range they opened fire. Their flintlocks were loaded with pieces of broken iron and copper ore that thudded into the shield bulwarks that Stanley had put up to protect the men in his boats. Women and children lay down in the bottoms of the canoes. His forty-four riflemen opened fire, with spearmen beside them to protect them if the enemy came within striking distance. The attackers wore white headgear 'like English University caps . . . there was a great deal of glitter and flash of metal, shining brass, copper, and bright steel among them.'

The expedition was out-gunned, seven to one. It would have been a massacre if the Sniders and Winchesters had not been vastly superior to the native flintlocks. Stanley's rifles had an effective range of more than one thousand yards. By comparison, the penetrating power of the flintlocks at fifty yards was rarely sufficient to pierce the hide shields round the canoes. The elephant gun that Stanley carried was sufficiently powerful to penetrate a canoe below the waterline.

In the end, they broke the line of Bangala canoes and escaped. A number of Stanley's men were injured by the broken shot from the muskets, but few seriously. 'It had been the fight of fights – our thirty-first on this terrible river. The savages suffered more severely than ever I supposed they were capable of bearing. The hostility they have for us is most strange for as soon as they see us they fire away as if we were lawful game and they required us for meat.' His own lack of injuries surprised him. 'Had I been a black man I should long ago have been slain. But even in the midst of battle my very appearance gives rise to a curiosity that deflects the aim.'

The river seemed without end.

'In the last six months', Stanley wrote in April 1877, 'we have followed this terrible river for 1235 miles.' It was the river now that was the enemy, rather than the people who inhabited its banks. The rapids below Stanley Pool took a terrible toll. Thirteen men were drowned in them. Of the twenty-one canoes he had taken after the battle of Vinya-Njara, Stanley now had nine left.

They felled trees and hollowed out new canoes. But the intelligence was depressing: one cataract after another lay ahead of them, they were told. The river was quite impassable. Bearers began to desert again. Stanley had those that were caught whipped. And then Pocock began to give him cause for serious concern.

On 16 May 1877, Stanley wrote: 'Frank began to be troubled with a small pimple on each foot,

At cataracts they felled trees for a 'road'

and even then he neglected the advice I persisted in giving him to protect them from being tainted by the poisonous foetor which flies extracted from the exposed sores of the Wangwana.' Nine days later he noted: 'Frank Pocock being too lame from his ulcers . . . the conduct of the canoe party was given to Manwa Sera.'

By 3 June Pocock's feet were so bad that he was crawling about on his hands and knees, and Stanley set off alone in the *Lady Alice* to establish the next camp. He told Pocock that on no account was he to move. A litter would be sent back to carry him. It was too much for Pocock. For a long time he had felt the burden of being alone in the heart of a foreign continent. His brother was dead. Fred Barker was dead. Now the only other white man was leaving him. He pulled himself into a canoe and set off after Stanley.

'Pocock having countermanded my orders, the other canoes were compelled to follow,' wrote Stanley. 'Ahead of them lay the booming cataract of Zinga. With great difficulty most of the canoes fought their way out of the treacherous rapids before it was too late. Only one, with its cargo of three souls, failed to clear the angry whirlpools. My brave honest kindly Frank Pocock was drowned.'

The incident almost broke Stanley. On 4 June he wrote: 'Unnerved by the terrible accident. Utterly unable to decide what to do. I have a horror of the river now. As I look on Frank's empty tent and recall his many qualities, his patient temper, his industry, his cheerfulness and tender love of me, I cannot express my feelings – or describe the vastness of my loss.'

That night he sat on a boulder in the moonlight above the Zinga falls, 'deluding myself with the vain hope that by some chance he might have escaped out of the dreadful whirlpool, picturing the horrible scene which an intense morbid imagination called up with such reality'.

On 11 June Pocock's bloated body was found floating downstream by a 'horrified' fisherman.

News of a trading station at Embomma, six days' march away, reached Stanley some time after Pocock's death. By then, his condition was desperate, his party totally dejected. Discipline had broken. Many had deserted. They were near death. He wrote two copies of a letter from the village of Nsanda on 4 August.

'To any Gentleman who speaks English at Embomma. Dear Sir, I have arrived at this place

---

Pocock's last entry in his journal, and the moving appreciation of his dead friend, which Stanley added later to the pages

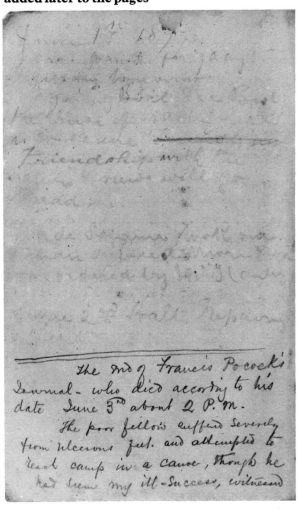

from Zanzibar with 115 souls, men, women and children. We are now in a state of imminent starvation. We can buy nothing from the natives, for they laugh at our kinds of cloth, beads and wire. There are no provisions in the country that may be purchased, except on market days, and a starving people cannot afford to wait for these markets. I, therefore, have made bold to despatch three of my young men, natives of Zanzibar, with this letter, craving relief from you. I do not know you; but I am told there is an Englishman at Embomma, and as you are a Christian and a gentleman, I beg you not to disregard my request. The boy Robert will be better able to describe our lean condition than I can tell you in this letter. We are in a state of the greatest distress; but if your supplies arrive in time, I may be able to reach Embomma within four days. I want three hundred cloths, each four yards long, of such quality as you trade with, which is very different from that we have; but better than all would be ten or fifteen man-loads of rice or grain to fill their pinched bellies immediately, as even with the cloths it would require time to purchase food, and starving people cannot wait. The supplies must arrive within two days, or I may have a fearful time of it among the dying. Of course I hold myself responsible for any expense you may incur in this business. What is wanted is immediate relief; and I pray you to use your utmost energies to forward it at once. For myself, if you have such little luxuries as tea, coffee, sugar and biscuits by you, such as one man can easily carry, I beg you on my own behalf that you will send a small supply, and add to the great debt of gratitude due to you upon the timely arrival of the supplies for my people. Until that time I beg you to believe me, Yours sincerely, Henry M. Stanley. Commanding Anglo-American Expedition for Exploration of Africa. P.S. You may not know me by name; therefore I add, I am the person that discovered Livingstone in 1871.'

He wrote additional versions of the letter in French and in Spanish – the only two other languages he knew – and told his four best men to carry it to Embomma. One had been mission-educated and spoke English.

The river had won.

He decided to abandon it and make for Embomma across country. The canoes were abandoned, the *Lady Alice* carried ceremoniously to her last resting place. 'At sunset we lifted the brave boat and carried her high above the Insangila cataract, out of the reach of marauding natives. After a journey of nearly seven thousand miles upon and down broad Africa, I abandoned her to the depredations of time and memory – to bleach and to rot.'

On the morning of 9 August 1877 – 999 days after leaving Zanzibar – Stanley was met by a relief column from Embomma. His letter had been read, and acted on.

Stanley wrote: 'We have attacked and destroyed 28 towns, three or four score villages. Fought 32 battles on land and water. Contended with 52 falls and rapids. Constructed 30 miles of tram-ways through forests. Hauled our canoes

Frank meanwhile resting in his canoe. The crew returned & said. the water was very bad, it would be impossible to pass. The crew say that Frank jeered them, and laughed them out of their fears, and after a while they roused up courage for the trial. saying to one another. our fate is in the hands of God – "Mambu Kwa Mungu"! and started. They could barely have counted 200 from the time they started from the litter cove, before the canoe was in the middle of the great rolling billows, with their flanks pitted with great whirlpools. into one of which the canoe was sucked bodily in, down to the bottom, and after a minute or so was shot up again with eight of the eleven that were in the canoe clinging to it. Three out of the eleven were drowned and one of the three, to my surprise and great grief was my faithful honest, gentle. Frank !!!

Henry M Stanley

75

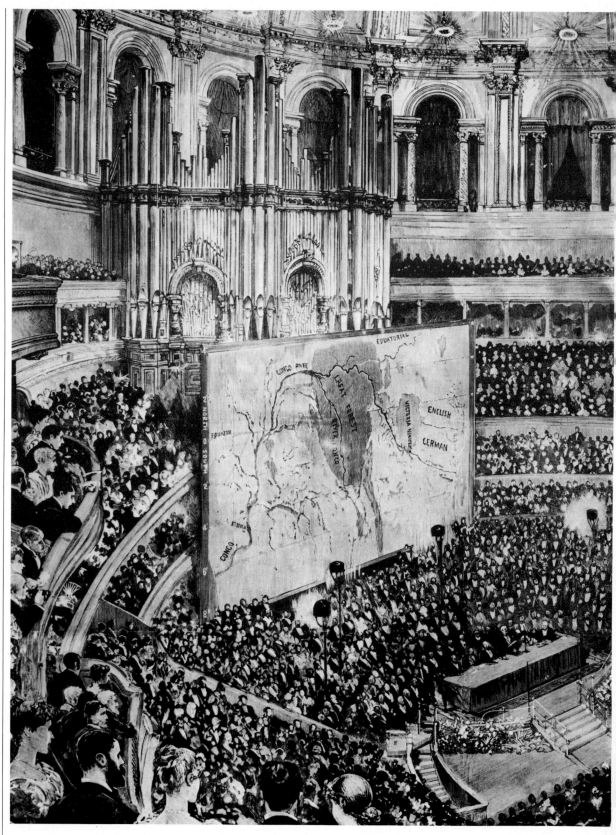

76 | **Stanley on his return, lecturing before the Royal Geographical Society at the Albert Hall**

and boat six miles up a mountain 1500 feet high. Lifted canoes by rough mechanical skill up gigantic boulders twenty feet high. All this since we came to the river. At times I did not believe there was any end to the great river. But God be praised, our wars and troubles are over. We have pierced the dark Continent from east to west – and traced its mightiest river to its ocean.'

In two days the expedition was in Boma and by the end of August it had been carried by Portuguese gunboat to Luanda, the capital of Angola. From there Stanley sent off some of the best dispatches of his journey, to the newspapers who had helped sponsor it. There, too, he was fêted as guest of honour by the Governor General, his bearers taken care of at Government expense.

The European and American reaction to Stanley's discoveries was not to reach him until he arrived in Capetown in October. By then, what he had done, the 'filling in of Africa's blank spaces', was being acclaimed as the single most important work of exploration of the age. Universities and learned societies vied with each other to honour Stanley. Newspapers and publishers queued to bid for his every word.

The price had been a high one. Of the 356 who had set out to explore Africa with him three years before, only 115 returned.

Stanley had left, rotting and bleached, on an African jungle mountain, the boat he named for the girl he returned to marry. And that would have been a moment to confirm his triumph; the final dispelling, perhaps, of the sense of rejection that drove him to such great achievement.

But Alice Pike, his American fiancée, had jilted him. She had married Albert Clifford Barney, heir to a railway fortune, even while Stanley struggled in Central Africa – as long ago as 11 January 1876. And by now they had a daughter.

Stanley never mentioned, in his diaries or journals, what the news must have meant to him; the savage disappointment and rejection he must have felt. He returned to England, his hair prematurely white and his weight down to seven stone, almost wasted away with his experience. Among the congratulatory telegrams and letters was a letter from Alice:

Alice Pike, Stanley's fiancée. He carried this picture with him throughout Africa.

'Poor Stanley! How much you have lost, but your gain has been great indeed. I shed tears when I read of the fate of Kalulu and the Lady Alice. I had hoped she would have proven a truer friend than the Alice she was named after, for you must know, by this time, I have done what millions of women have done before me, not been true to my promise. But you are so great, so honoured and so sought after, that you will scarcely miss your once true friend and always devoted admirer of your heroism. For indeed you are the hero of the day. That alone should console you for my loss.'

He never did say if it did console him. But he never forgot her.

Nor, it would seem, did she forget him. She had some talent as an artist, and twenty years after Stanley's death produced an extraordinary portrait of him in pastels: piercing-eyed, dark-browed, heroic – the way, perhaps, she had remembered him all those years.

Stanley wrote *Through the Dark Continent*, an account of his three-year journey, and published it in 1878, the year after his return to England. The book aroused considerable interest, confirmed his fame and achievement, but didn't produce the reaction he hoped in some quarters. He wanted his own country to see the significance of the great river he had conquered, that led, like a highway, into the heart of this rich new territory. He wanted to see *British* traders exploit its possibilities, and strengthen the empire by opening Africa commercially. He was to be disappointed.

It was Leopold II, King of the Belgians, who grasped the importance of the Congo. In 1878 Stanley went to Brussels to meet him. The result was a return to the Congo for Stanley, and his work there secured the Congo for King Leopold, leading, ultimately, to the setting up of the Congo Free State under Leopold's sovereignty.

In 1884 he returned to Europe and played a significant part in the Berlin Conference on African Affairs. He viewed the carving up of Africa among European nations with contempt and is quoted as saying it reminded him of the way 'my black followers used to rush with gleaming knives for slaughtered game during our travels'. But ironically it was Stanley, certainly more than any other explorer, who started what later became known as 'The Great Scramble'.

His third journey of exploration was made between 1887 and 1889. Ostensibly he was in the service of the Khedive of Egypt, and his primary task was to be the relief of Emin Pasha, Governor of the Equatorial Province of Egypt and the surviving lieutenant of Gordon of Khartoum, who was under pressure from the Mahdi. In fact, Stanley's real interest was the establishment of a British Protectorate in East Africa. His geographical discoveries were important, but the political significance of the expedition was the agreements Stanley made with various chiefs he contacted, in favour of Great Britain. These agreements were handed over to the East Africa Company for subsequent exploitation.

In later life Stanley became something of an English gentleman. He returned to British nationality and a country life. When he was nearly fifty, in 1890, he married Miss Dorothy Tennant, daughter of a British Member of Parliament, and herself a well-known artist. It was Dorothy who persuaded him to stand for Parliament, and in 1895 he was elected MP for Lambeth on the Liberal Unionist ticket. Four years later he was knighted.

Stanley had fulfilled his main ambition. He had completed the work that Livingstone started. And he had done much more. In terms of geographical knowledge gained, his achievement was greater than any other single explorer of his time.

Stanley's grave, not in Westminster Abbey, but in the village churchyard at Pirbright, Surrey

And it seemed now that at last even his own country had come to accept him. Yet before he died on 10 May 1904, he had expressed a wish to be buried beside Livingstone, in Westminster Abbey. In the event, the request was denied. It was the final rejection.

He was buried at Pirbright in Surrey. The monolith over his grave bears the inscription 'Henry Morton Stanley, 1841 – 1904', together with his African name, 'Bula Matari'. And the single word – 'Africa'.

Burke 1820–61 and Wills 1834–61

Robert O'Hara Burke and William Wills opened up the heartland of Australia, made the first journey from south to north. But as explorers they were disastrous; ill-organised, inefficient, unimaginative and, finally, failures.

Their achievement killed them both. Burke, an émigré Irishman and ex-policeman, took with him into the wilderness of Australia all the stubborn inflexibility, all the refusal to compromise, all the stiff-necked attitudes towards the Aborigines that, had those that appointed him but known it, were to seal his fate – and ensure his death.

His second-in-command, William Wills, became the supporting actor in an achievement crowned by tragedy.

In a sense they were both victims of the provincial committee in Melbourne that contracted and paid them to undertake the journey but, in fact, failed to appoint the right men for the job, failed to support them with enough money and supplies – and a clear enough brief to survive. The committee's purpose was achieved. But at a cost.

And yet between them Burke and Wills, with all their fumbling, their mistakes, their failures, managed to uncover the mystery of the centre of Australia; to open and pioneer the way for the vigorous Commonwealth country that thrives today.

They spent all day digging the grave. There were three of them: Burke, Wills and King. It was difficult to tell them apart. Their skin had been burned the colour of mahogany, their beards were long and matted. Their clothes hung in tatters from their emaciated bodies.

Each one took it in turn to chip, wearily, at the baked earth and rock with the short-handled post-hole spade they still had with them. They used their knives to break the ground. It was slow, painful. The sun climbed, scorching them and the ground they stood on. For days they had been surviving on the most meagre rations.

Now there was no strength in any of them.

By noon the hole was only ten or twelve inches deep. Wills handed out the ration of porridge, about a spoonful for each of them. They could hardly swallow the stuff but there was no hope at all for them without it. They sat on the ground with their feet in the hole. Above them black crows wheeled – and waited. Flies gathered thick on the uncovered parts of Charley Gray's dead body. No one bothered to wave them off any more. At last King, the youngest of them, took up the spade and began to chop at the earth once again.

Towards evening they had hacked out a hole some three feet deep. Even then they knew the dogs might get to him. It couldn't be helped. Time was also running out for the rest of them. They couldn't use any more of their last reserves of energy.

They lifted Charley Gray, put him gently in the hole and said a prayer over him.

He had cheated them all and they could blame some of their present predicament on him. But there was no point now in recrimination. Charley Gray had wasted away as the rest of them were now doing. He looked small and pathetic now, lying at their feet still wearing his short-sleeved shirt and flannel trousers. They pushed the heap of dried earth over him, hung his rifle on the tree above him.

'It took a full day to dig a grave, so weak was our condition,' wrote Wills in his journal. 'It was decided to use what little strength remained in us to make a last dash for the Depot and safety.'

The depot was at Cooper's Creek. William Brahe, the foreman, was waiting there with all the supplies: oatmeal and salt pork, rice, flour, preserved vegetables. More important, water. There were fresh horses and camels. When they had recovered their strength, they could ride all the way back to Melbourne in comfort. Whatever troubles and disasters there had been on the journey north, no one could say they hadn't done what they set out to do.

Cooper's Creek, according to Burke's estimation, was no more than four days away. Perhaps five, allowing for their condition. On the journey north he had been careful to identify each of his camps by number and to mark the numbers on trees or rocks. They were somewhere near Camp 68 now. The camp at Cooper's Creek was 65. Burke ordered everything that wasn't essential for this final journey to safety to be jettisoned. He considered killing one of the last two camels for meat. They were both in terrible condition. But they were necessary for carrying the remaining stores, and there was still a little left of the dried flesh of the pony, Billy, the last animal that they had killed. He loaded the animals with the few things he thought essential – two spades, a couple of guns, a few camel pads used for bedding – and set off south.

It was early evening on 21 April 1861 when the first of the eucalyptus trees came in sight, then the banks of dark green reeds that ran down into the water. Burke was riding the leading camel. It put up its head and flared its nostrils as it smelt the moist air. Wills and King were behind him, dragging the second animal by the lead rein. In ten minutes they would be safe, surrounded by friends, able to eat and drink as much as they could hold. There were changes of clothes at the depot: new boots to replace the worn out remains they had on at the moment, clean shirts and underwear instead of the stinking rags that covered them now.

Burke took out his revolver and fired into the air to let Brahe know they were coming.

There was no answering shot. Burke fired again. Still there was no response. He slipped off the animal and went ahead on foot, firing a third time. Something was wrong, he didn't know

With the return to Cooper's Creek, a sense of utter dejection settled on the three men

what. Was everyone asleep? He came through the eucalyptus grove and made for the great coolibah tree which had been the centre of the encampment.

The appalling truth began to dawn on him. Even then he refused to believe it.

He reached the stockade that Brahe had built, opened the big leather-covered door. The place was absolutely empty. The supplies that had been hung in the trees to keep them safe from the rats had gone. Here and there, bits of rope that had once held boxes of dried meat and flour dangled empty from the branches. The ground was covered in horse and camel dung and the remains of old packing cases. Brahe had gone and taken with him every single scrap of the supplies that had been brought with so much difficulty all the way from Melbourne.

It was beyond Burke's comprehension. The sole purpose of setting up the depot was so that it would be there when they got back. Now there was nothing. They might as well be back there with Charley Gray and the shallow grave. He turned to King and Wills. Wills was standing by the coolibah tree staring at a newly-carved inscription on the trunk. The message was brief and to the point:

DIG
3 FT. N.W.
APR. 21. 1861.

Wills took a stride in a north-westerly direction, then dropped to his knees. The ground was soft, where it had been recently disturbed. He began to scoop it out with his hands. King brought a spade and started to help. A bottle was unearthed, a note inside. King smashed it, handed the note to Burke. Burke read it aloud to them. His voice was cracked with tiredness and emotion, the accent still unmistakably Irish. The note read:

Coopers Creek
April 21st 1861

The Depot party of V.E.E. leaves the Camp today to return to the Darling. I intend to go South East from Camp 60, to get into our old track near Bulloo. Two of my companions and myself are quite well. The third – Patten – has been unable to walk for the last 18 days, as his leg has been severely hurt when thrown by one of the horses. No person has been up here from the Darling.

We have six camels and twelve horses in good working condition.

William Brahe

A sense of utter dejection settled on the three men. Wills wrote in his journal: 'After four months of the severest travelling and privation arrived at the Depot just in time to find it deserted. Brahe communicated the pleasing information that they have started today back to the Darling; their camels and horses all well and in good condition. Left some grub and some horse shoes and nails. Our own camels done in, our legs almost paralysed.'

They couldn't catch up. They were too weak, their camels nearly dead. They had missed contact by hours. It might as well have been weeks.

For Robert O'Hara Burke, the leader of the expedition, the discovery of Brahe's withdrawal from the depot was the last straw. From the very beginning everything had gone wrong. The men had given him trouble. The animals had proved unsatisfactory. Many of the stores had seemed to him unnecessary. It went back to the committee that had set up the expedition in the first place. Like most committees it had created something that looked impressive on paper but fell apart in the face of reality. The memory of the difficulties he had had from the start made his Irish temper boil with fury.

He was forty-one. But for the privations he had suffered, he would have been a finely built man, fit and well able to take care of himself. His life had always been an active one. . . .

He was born at St Cleram in County Galway, Ireland, and enlisted in the Austrian army as a young man. At twenty-eight he returned home and served for five years in the Royal Irish Constabulary. Ireland at the time was in a state of severe disruption. Famine – particularly the great famine of 1846 – was resulting in mass starvation. Those who could, emigrated. Burke left the country and went to Tasmania, later crossed to Melbourne and became an Inspector in the police force there.

In 1860 while he was a Superintendent in the gold-digging district of Castlemaine he saw an advertisement for an expedition leader at a salary of £500 per annum.

The advertisers were the Australian Exploration Fund Committee. The committee had been set up in September 1858 by the Philosophical Institute of Victoria, which a year later was to become the Royal Society of Victoria. Its duty was to 'enquire into and report upon' the exploration of the Australian interior. The committee had the backing of the legislature, which agreed to provide some of the funds necessary for an expedition.

Victoria had been made a colony in 1851 and given its own legislature instead of being governed from Sydney. This new-found identity seemed to require it to assert itself. One of the fields in which there was a significant contribution to be made, it was felt, was exploration.

The Australian hinterland was still very largely unknown. Captain Charles Sturt had gone west from New South Wales in 1845 and reached a little north of Cooper's Creek before the desert drove him back. A year earlier, Dr Leichhardt had made his way round the tropical north of the continent from Queensland. Between 1845 and 1858 Sir Thomas Mitchell, E. B. Kennedy and A. C. Gregory had all explored the Cooper's Creek area.

What remained almost a total mystery was the central heartland. Was it simply the wilderness that Sturt had encountered? Or was there, as many believed, an area of lakes beyond the desert, with a vast region of fertile pastures?

In March 1860 the legislature of South Australia offered a reward of £10,000 to the first man who could solve the problem once and for all by crossing the continent from south to north. John McDougall Stuart accepted the challenge, setting off from Adelaide on two separate occasions and reaching a latitude of 17°S.

The idea of a Victorian Exploring Expedition under the aegis of the Royal Society of Victoria caught the imagination. Ambrose Kyte, a local philanthropist, contributed £1000 towards the expedition's costs. Public subscription produced a further £2199 and the government contributed £6000. Chief Justice Sir William Stawell, Chairman of the Expedition, was delighted. The time had come to appoint a salaried leader. An advertisement was drafted and put in the press.

Apart from Burke, there were thirteen other applicants for the post. Burke had no knowledge of the bush and none of exploring. Yet neither had the committee. With one exception its members knew nothing about the problems of setting up an expedition for such an ambitious enterprise. Burke impressed them. Perhaps it was an Irish persuasiveness of manner, but if so, that talent rarely showed during the expedition itself. It was more likely that his police background inspired confidence in people who clearly saw the expedition in terms of a military enterprise.

Whatever the reason, Burke was appointed as leader.

The committee's enthusiasm grew. It decided that if the interior of the continent proved to be largely desert, then camels would be needed to cross it. It authorised the purchase of twenty-four of them from Afghanistan at a cost of £5497

– more than half the total sum available for the expedition.

Other expedition members were appointed. Two Germans, Dr Herman Beckler and Ludwig Becker, were appointed as doctor and naturalist respectively, at salaries of £300 per annum each. William Wills of the Melbourne Observatory was appointed as navigator and astronomer, also at £300 per annum. Charles D. Ferguson, an ex-American gold miner, was appointed foreman at £200 per annum. Perhaps the most puzzling appointment was that of George James Landells. He was to be second-in-command under Burke. Yet his salary was £600 per annum, £100 more than his leader's.

By the late summer of 1860, the committee had appointed a team of eighteen, including three sepoys (Indian soldiers) to look after the camels. Burke began to feel the weight of responsibility on his shoulders. He wanted to be off. The waiting made him irascible. Already it was obvious that the idea of mounting an expedition of this nature by committee had severe defects. These were to become increasingly apparent with the passage of time.

On 20 August the expedition left Melbourne to the sound of cheering crowds, bearing the

The expedition left Melbourne to cheering crowds. Ahead, 1500 miles of unknown territory.

good wishes of the whole colony. Before them lay 1500 miles of largely unknown territory until they reached the Gulf of Carpentaria on the north coast of the continent.

Burke led the way out of Royal Park into the open countryside. He wore a conical black hat, blue coat and red shirt. Behind him came the carts and the double line of camels and horses. There was already trouble with the animals. The horses, twenty-three of them, were frightened of the camels and the two lots had to be kept apart. Two of the sepoys walked beside the camels, whilst the third, Dost Mohammed, rode. Wills was on a camel, riding in the rear section of the great double saddle with his instruments in the front section. He had with him his journal, sextant, barometer, thermometer and compasses.

Beyond Melbourne, farmers rode over to watch the procession pass. They had never seen camels before. They seemed incredible beasts with their humps and great splayed nostrils, and metal-studded leather shoes on the feet. The riding camels had double saddles on their backs, with supplies in bags on either side. The pack animals carried 400 pounds of stores, arranged on flat wooden platforms built over saddle-frames. Below the platforms, barrels of water and other liquids were suspended.

In all, the procession carried twenty-one tons of provisions and equipment. There were arms and ammunition, rockets and fishing lines. There were tents, camp beds, boots and large-brimmed 'cabbage tree' hats. Dr Beckler had three cases of surgical instruments with him, and Becker the naturalist had brought packets of seeds in case the stories of a great central paradise proved true. Burke had brought copies of the works of Sturt, Gregory and Mitchell, together with volumes of light reading to while away the time. There were ten dozen mirrors and two pounds of beads to pacify the natives.

Edible stores consisted of flour, rice, oatmeal, sugar, dried meat, ginger and dried apples. In addition there was 'damper', small cakes of un-leavened bread that formed a convenient part of the daily ration. Apart from water there were eight demi-johns of lime juice and four gallons of brandy. For the camels – incredibly – there were sixty gallons of rum.

Once he reached the northern limits of Victoria, Burke began to assert himself. The expedition, as designed by the committee back in Melbourne, was an incoherent mess. He began to change it to bring it into line with his own concept. He wanted men of his own choice about him, rather than committee men. At Swan Hill, on 6 September, before he crossed the Murray River into New South Wales, he appointed, locally, two new members, Charley Gray and William Hodgkinson, bringing the party to twenty. At the same time he held a public auction of a quantity of the stores he was carrying.

It became apparent to everybody that what Burke was after was to impose his authority on the team. In itself, the intention was understandable. Jedediah Smith had felt the need to establish the authority of his leadership, as would Amundsen, later. Where Burke differed from them was only in the ways he chose to do it.

By the time the party reached Balranald on the Murrumbidgee river on 15 September, it was in disarray. Ferguson the foreman walked out. Burke dismissed five others: Creber, Cowen, Fletcher, Langan, and Drakeford the cook. He got rid of more stores that he considered un-necessary – two rifles, several revolvers, three tents and fifteen and a half hundredweight of sugar. In addition he dumped the entire stock of lime juice, the only safeguard he had against scurvy. Almost a hundred years earlier, Cook had shown how easily the disease could be avoided with the aid of lime juice in the diet.

The first day's march. The column became strung out. There was trouble with the animals.

Nothing demonstrated Burke's total lack of experience more clearly than this single action. It was to cost Patton, the blacksmith, his life.

As the month wore on, Burke tightened his grip. By 23 September they had reached the Darling River and established the first depot, covering an average of twenty miles a day. Landells, the second in command, was finding Burke increasingly difficult.

Then Burke, feeling the need to press forward more quickly, gave the order that no equipment weighing more than thirty pounds was to be taken any farther. Consequently the two scientists, Becker and Beckler, were forced to abandon their instruments. The effect was to turn them from specialists into little more than manual labourers.

It wasn't the end of Burke's reorganisation. On 8 October the party crossed the Darling on the way to Menindee, floating the camels over on giant inflatable bags or 'waterwings'. Two of the men were drunk on the rum meant for the camels. Burke accused Landells of being responsible. It was true to a point. Landells was responsible for the camels; the committee had stipulated that. Landells protested. Burke called him a liar, and with a sudden flare of temper ordered that in future there was to be no alcohol carried on the expedition. To demonstrate that he intended his instructions to be taken seriously, he grabbed a barrel of rum from one of the wagons and threw it to the ground. It

split open, the rum draining out. It was clear to Landells that there was no hope of their ever working together. He resigned.

The last resignation took place when they reached Menindee itself. Dr Beckler decided he'd had enough. His instruments had been left at the first depot; there was nothing medically useful he could do. He told Burke that he would stay until a replacement doctor arrived. The original fourteen white men that the Melbourne committee had appointed to accompany Burke had now been reduced to six.

At Menindee, also, there was disturbing news awaiting Burke. Wills noted: 'The Expedition under the command of Mr Burke, reached Menindie on the Darling River, 400 miles north of Melbourne, on the 16th October, 1860. The Committee sent news that another explorer might well be about to attempt the crossing of the Continent, in the same way.'

In Melbourne, the committee had seen the expedition as having at least an element of scientific respectability. By appointing Becker and Dr Beckler, who were intended to produce serious scientific observations, they hoped to enhance the status of the enterprise. Burke had almost completely put paid to this ambition by depriving the two scientists of the instruments necessary for their work. Now, with this threat that he might be beaten to the Gulf of Carpentaria, all pretence about the nature of the expedition was dropped.

85

Whatever his initial concept of the project had been, or had been seen to be, he saw it now – unashamedly – as a race.

So far as Burke was concerned, no one was going to get to the north before him.

Burke's intention had been to regroup at Menindee. The party had become extremely strung out because of the different speeds of its individual sections. In particular, the wagons were miles behind. But in view of the threat of competition, he changed his mind, decided not to wait for the tail to catch up. He began to make arrangements for an early advance. Wills wrote: 'After three days Mr Burke decided to leave the main party to rest up and get the tired animals conditioned while he moved on with an advance party to Cooper's Creek, a further 400 miles north, where the Committee requested we set up our base. Mr Landells, the second in command, had resigned over a difference of opinion concerning the camels. I was appointed in his place because, said Mr Burke, not only was I a surveyor, I also had a little medical training; an advantage since our medical officer has also resigned and was now awaiting his replacement from Melbourne.'

Burke recruited four other men, locals, before leaving for Cooper's Creek: Stone, Purcell, Smith and William Wright. Wright was to play a crucial part in succeeding events. His qualifications for his appointment to an important post were slim. Wills wrote of him: 'Mr Wright had been manager of a sheep station but had lost his job and asked to join the Expedition when we reached Menindie. He knew the country a good way round, and was coming part of the way with us. Because of the resignations, Mr Burke now decided to make him third in command – subject to the Committee's approval. It would be Mr Wright's task to see to it that the main party we had left behind in Menindie, joined us at Cooper's Creek as soon as possible.'

Burke left Menindee on 19 October. He had with him seven men: Wills, Brahe, King, Gray, McDonough, Patton and the sepoy Dost Mohammed. Fifteen camels and seventeen horses also went with him. For the first ten days, Wright and the other two sepoys accompanied the party. Wright was useful because he knew

the area. Then at Camp 45, called Torowotto Wright was sent back to Menindee to take charge of the preparations there.

They travelled for some time in a north-westerly direction, guided by three aborigines. At each camp, Burke left a record of its number. Camp 52 was made on 6 November, Camp 53 on the 7th, Camp 54 on the 8th. At the same time Wills took readings with the sextant to establish their position. Camp 52 was at 28°26′9″S, 143°E. Camp 54 was at 27°51′S, 142°40′E. On 11 November they struck Cooper's Creek at 27°49′S, 142°20′E, and began to follow it in a north-easterly direction.

For two weeks they followed the river, moving at times through areas of greenery and eucalyptus trees. Then on the 27th Burke made Camp 65 round the base of a great coolibah tree. This was to be the depot from which he was to

One of the larger water holes at Cooper's Creek. The water here is up to 90 feet deep.

make the last dash northwards. Its position was 27°37′8″S, 141°6′E. On the day of arrival, Wills took the temperature. It was 109°F in the shade.

The camp was well situated. Beyond the coolibah was the creek itself, a wide expanse of still water. On all sides there were trees that threw their welcome shade over horses and camels. The air was alive with the sound of birds.

But the place had its drawbacks. John King, the twenty-two-year-old whom Burke had put in charge of the camels after Landells had left, was pestered by the flies and mosquitoes. Even worse than the insects were the rats. A plague of them. McDonough became proficient in breaking their backs with a stick whenever he caught them at the supplies. The only way of saving food was to hang it on ropes from the trees.

They stayed at Cooper's Creek for five weeks. For Wills it was a pleasant time. He made surveys of the surrounding countryside, and according to him 'the feed was very good'. Burke found it less attractive. He was conscious that while he sat there under the trees some rival might be passing a mile or two away, gaining an advantage on the race north. Yet he had to stay. He was waiting for the party, under Wright, to reach him from Menindee. In Burke's view, the man was certainly taking his time. The galling fact was that Wright was Burke's own appointment. There was no blaming the committee this time. Nevertheless he found it difficult to control his temper.

The aborigines were another source of irritation to Burke. They stood amongst the trees, curious about the men who had suddenly come into their midst with strange beasts and mountains of supplies. They were naked and very thin. They carried long oval shields, spears, and various kinds of throwing sticks. Despite their apparent harmlessness, Burke wanted nothing

An Aborigine hunter with a spear and spear-thrower

to do with them. 'There is no danger from the natives if they are properly managed,' wrote Wills, echoing Burke's sentiments. 'Mr Burke wants them to be kept at a safe distance at all times and this we ensure by driving them off when they come too close.'

Burke's attitude is another indication of his inexperience. Jed Smith relied on the Indians he met whenever he could. Mary Kingsley would deliberately make friends with the natives. Both knew that without native cooperation survival would have been difficult, if not actually impossible. Perhaps more surprising, in an explorer, was Burke's total lack of curiosity about the aborigines. Even Pizarro, who was certainly no less single-minded than Burke, showed some genuine interest in the inhabitants of the countryside he was pillaging.

In the end, Burke's impatience was too much for him. He couldn't wait for Wright: 'On the 19th December, 1860, Mr Burke prepared to explore the country to the North. I estimate to the Gulf of Carpentaria; seven hundred miles,' wrote Wills, now the expedition's official recorder. 'The conduct of the men has been admirable. All of them wanted to go with us.'

Burke cut his team for the final leg to the bare minimum. He selected Wills, Gray and King to go with him. The party would take with it Burke's pony, Billy, and six of the camels, among them Golah Sing, Boocha, Rajah and Linda. 'Mr Brahe was made an officer and left in charge of Cooper's Creek Depot until our return in three months. Supplies for him and his men were due up from Menindie in a matter of days.' Brahe's new position was to be the last appointment that Burke made.

Burke left Cooper's Creek on 16 December at 6.40 in the morning, and made northwards, leading the way on Billy with Wills following on foot. Behind him came King in charge of the camels, with Charley Gray bringing up the rear.

North of Cooper's Creek, the greenery disappeared. The country was little more than scrub and saltbush. Wind whipped up the dust; visibility was poor and eyes became inflamed. The men wore goggles, and veils over their faces. Wills found it difficult to maintain direction because of the poor conditions. Grotesque rock shapes loomed out of the dust-haze – great eroded slabs of red and yellow.

Later the landscape turned to stone, a cruelly inhospitable sight. Wills wrote: 'Eleven hours on the road this day. Desert. All the creeks were dry. We pushed on, hoping to find them of an improved appearance. All of us kept vigilance on the sky for any flock of birds which might indicate the presence of water.' They decided to travel partly at night to avoid the terrible heat of the day.

When they did find water it was full of some milky deposit. That didn't deter them from drinking it. It was vital that their own stores of water should be kept as long as possible, in case of a real emergency.

The flat stone desert gave way to arid mountains, baking in the sun. The surface was broken by sharp ridges and outcrops of bare rock. 'Mr Burke determined to go straight at a line of ranges,' wrote Wills. 'The poor camels bleeding, groaning and sweating profusely from fear. Will give them a hot bath at first opportunity.' The result was inevitable. 'This morning, the camels refused to allow us to put their shoes back on.'

Burke had set himself a goal. First to the coast.

All pretence of serious scientific motivation was dropped. 'It was an expedition no longer – it was an endurance test, a race.'

Fortunately for Burke, Wills was less single minded. His scientific curiosity allowed him to take a slightly wider view. On the rare occasion when rain fell and the whole dead landscape erupted into ephemeral bloom, he discovered *portulaca*, 'a plant which serves as an excellent vegetable. This we boiled to supplement our rations.' No doubt it helped considerably in providing the essential fresh greens that Burke's diet lacked.

Dietary considerations, which had been planned so carefully by other explorers, never troubled Burke. King later told the Royal Commission set up to look into the expedition that on the way north they were constantly surrounded by wild game – kangaroos, emus, ducks and turkeys – but shot none of it because they believed they had enough food.

The stony Sturt. No place for man or camels.

The supplies were intended to last for three months; sufficient time, Burke calculated, to reach the north coast and return to the depot at Cooper's Creek. There were three hundred-weight of flour, fifty pounds of oatmeal, 100 pounds of dried horsemeat, 100 pounds of bacon and salt pork, forty pounds of biscuits, fifty pounds each of rice and sugar. In addition, they had twelve pounds of tea, five pounds of salt, some tins of preserved vegetables and butter. Guns and ammunition made up the rest of the supplies. They took no liquor, after the experience earlier when crossing the Darling, and no tents. The two pack camels, in addition to carrying the bulk of the stores, carried fifty pints of water each. Each of the four riding camels carried 130 pints. Each man carried five pints and Billy, Burke's pony, carried 150 pints. In all, they had about 100 gallons of water.

Burke allowed a daily ration per man of one pound of damper (unleavened breadcake), three-quarters of a pound of dried horsemeat, one-quarter pound of salt pork, four ounces of boiled rice, some sugar and tea. The diet shows none of that balance that Cook, on his voyages, had insisted on to ward off the scourge of scurvy; nor any of that variety that Amundsen, later, was to think so necessary.

Perhaps if Burke had known what was happening to the parties he had left behind him, he would have been more careful with his supplies. But he was still relying on the assumption that when he got back to the Cooper's Creek depot, Wright would have brought up the rest of the stores from Menindee.

At Cooper's Creek itself, Brahe had built a stockade of stakes cut from surrounding woods. It was a substantial achievement with walls more than eight feet high. It had a door covered with hide and enclosed an area twenty feet by eighteen. It was to protect the stores from attack. The stores Wright was bringing. But Wright never came.

And in Menindee, things had gone to pieces. Wright exercised no authority whatever. Perhaps it was lack of ability to do so that had caused his earlier dismissal as manager of a sheep station. The men refused to wash or see to the stores and spent their time drinking the camel rum and gambling. Tents had been torn, stores destroyed. None of the wagons he was supposed to be bringing up to the mark had been repaired.

Back with Burke's party, on the expedition that had become a race, the camel called Golah Sing had to be left behind. It was January 1861. Wills wrote: 'Now almost seven hundred miles north of Cooper's Creek heavy thunderstorms had broken over us with very little warning. The ground was now so boggy the camels could scarcely be got over it.'

The countryside had changed again. Deserts and bare mountain ranges had given way to lush tropical vegetation. The place was full of wild-life. There were snakes in the wet undergrowth and wild geese and pelicans on the water. Red-breasted cockatoos, pigeons and crows called from the dense foliage of the trees. It was certainly a contrast to the country they had already covered, though not necessarily any easier to cross. 'The dampness of the atmosphere prevented any evaporation, and the oppressive heat gave one a helpless feeling of lassitude I have never before experienced,' wrote Wills.

It was no less laborious for the animals and for the camels it was the worst possible country. Their feet had no purchase on the shifting mud of the creeks. At times they sank up to their bellies. In the end Burke made his final division of the expedition. 'Mr Burke decided that conditions would not allow the passage of the camels any farther. So we had left them on firm ground together with Charley Gray and John King. Our plan now was for just the two of us to make for the coast which could not be far off and then collect the others on the way back.'

The coast was, in fact, thirty miles away. They put three days of stores on the back of Burke's pony Billy, and set off on the last part of the journey on 3 February. But it was soon apparent to Burke that country that was impassable for camels was no less difficult for a horse. Billy slipped and fell again and again. Several times he almost drowned. At every creek he became bogged in the slimy mud and had to be dragged clear. In the end he could go no further. 'It was decided to leave the horse hobbled and push on. We called the place after him: 'Billy's Creek.'

Instead of the day and a half that Burke had

guessed it would take to reach the coast, it took a week. They cut through jungle, ploughed thigh-deep through mosquito-infested creeks, and finally reached the impenetrable coastal mangrove swamp on 11 February. They were caked in filth, hungry, thirsty and exhausted. The inadequate diet had taken its toll quite as much as the savage journey.

At first neither Burke nor Wills was certain that the goal had been reached. Before them stretched a forest of mangrove, the aerial roots thrusting down towards the water. There was no clear expanse of sea. It wasn't possible to go any further. Yet there were clear tidal marks on the tree roots, and the water had a marked saline taste. Then as they stood together looking to the north, uncertainty in their minds, a great screaming flock of seagulls flew overhead. They knew beyond doubt that they had been successful.

They had penetrated the mysterious heartland of Australia and crossed the great continent from south to north.

In the moment of triumph, Wills had misgivings: 'It had taken two months to reach here from Cooper's Creek, but only a month's supplies remained for our return. It was not a pleasant prospect that now lay ahead of us.'

They turned back – heading south.

They recovered Billy on the southward journey and picked up Gray and King a day or two later. Burke was no less worried than Wills about the stores. A survey showed they had left eighty-three pounds of flour, three pounds of pork, twenty-five pounds of dried meat, twelve pounds of biscuits and twelve pounds of rice. It was half the quantity of provisions they had needed on the outward journey. Burke decided on measures to meet the emergency. 'To lighten our load for the return we dumped the camp oven and other articles, including a considerable quantity of books we had carried for reading amusement. Mr Burke ordered that rations were to be cut by half because our supplies were running low.'

Then, for ten days it rained. Thunderstorm followed thunderstorm. The whole world seemed reduced to water. Men and animals were drenched to the skin. The high humidity pro-

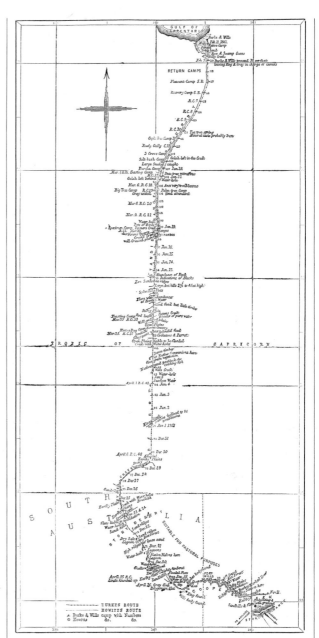

Their route across the heart of Australia

duced a general lassitude that made every movement an effort. Burke's temper wore thin. He could give orders. He could shout. But what the party lacked – what the whole expedition lacked – was leadership.

On the 19th, at a place they called 'Boocha's Camp', one of the camels had to be slaughtered for meat.

They moved at last out of the humid tropical belt into the dry uplands of the desert. Things were far from well. Their clothes were in a state of total disrepair. Their boots had been worn through by the combined effects of water and rock surfaces. Almost the only lightening of the gloom came when they found Golah Sing, the camel that had been left on their way north.

By mid-March, the food was unaccountably low. It seemed that there had been some miscalculation in the rations. Now it would require every possible extra economy to eke out what was left in order to reach Cooper's Creek alive.

Then on the 25th, Burke discovered the truth. He came across Charley Gray, hidden away from the rest of them, with a half-empty bag of flour beside him. His beard was coated with the stuff. It had fallen down his shirt front, on to the knees of his flannel trousers.

Burke lost control. It was beyond his belief that any man could behave like that, knowing he was risking the lives of his companions. He took Gray by the shoulders, pulled him to his feet, shook him, and slapped him several times in the face. If he had still the strength left to do so, he would have knocked him down. But he hadn't. When he could control himself, he looked at Gray as if he thought him the lowest thing on earth. Then he turned and walked away.

It accounted for the discrepancies. It had been going on for some time. 'There's no knowing how much Gray robbed us,' wrote Wills. 'Certainly, a lot of things had run unaccountably short. Gray had always been in charge of the stores until this time. Now Mr Burke relieved him of the responsibility because he was determined to see that we all got our fair shares of what was going.'

Occasionally another of the camels was killed. At Boocha's Rest (Camp 42 R) on the 30th the camel Boocha was slaughtered and cut up for food, a good deal of the body being roughly dried in the sun and stored for later use. What couldn't be used on the spot or 'jerked' by drying had to be dumped.

Then on 10 April at Camp 52R, it was the turn of Billy the pony. Wills wrote: 'We reckoned we were about a week out from the Depot at Cooper's Creek. A few days before one of the camels perished and not long after that it was clear that Billy, the horse, was so knocked up he had little chance of crossing the desert. To im-

prove our own chances we thought it best to reduce him to horse meat at once and did so. We found it healthy and tender without the slightest trace of fat.'

By the 15th of the month, all of them were sick, though some were worse than others. 'Charley Gray can no longer walk,' wrote Wills. 'All getting symptoms Charley complained of before, that is, aching limbs and headaches.' There were two camels left, and for a time they carried Gray slung in an improvised hammock under the pack of one of them. But it was clear his strength was going.

On the morning of 17 April, King lay in the open with a couple of camel pads over him. They were made of canvas stuffed with horsehair and they kept the chill night air off him. He had a premonition that something had happened, and when he lifted himself on an elbow he saw Burke bending over Charley Gray. When King went over to them he found Charley was dead, his face quite yellow. It wasn't unexpected, but it was nonetheless a shock.

He went to get the spade that lay with the rest of the stores. . . .

There is little doubt that when, on 21 April, Burke found Cooper's Creek empty, he went to pieces. True, he had told Brahe he would be back in three months and it had taken him four. But it seemed to him incredible that Brahe should have made no attempt to look for him, or waited longer before assuming the whole party were dead.

What affected him most was the horrible irony of the situation: Brahe had left just seven hours before Burke's arrival. If Charlie Gray had survived, or if they had not spent a day hacking out a grave for him, they could at this moment be feasting on rice and pork and dried horsemeat, instead of facing the real prospect of starvation.

As far as Burke was concerned, two choices faced him. He could set off in pursuit of Brahe in the direction of the depot at Menindee; or he could make across country for Mount Hopeless where there was a cattle station. Wills argued strongly for the former course. It was a route they had already covered. If anything slowed Brahe's progress there was a chance of catching

They set off to cross a further 200 miles of desert heading for Mount Hopeless

up with him. But in the end Burke overruled him. On 23 April they set off with the two camels to cross a further 200 miles of desert between there and Mount Hopeless.

Besides the note buried at the foot of the coolibah tree, Brahe had left some supplies, which Burke's party now found: fifty pounds of flour, twenty pounds of rice, sixty pounds of oatmeal, sixty pounds of sugar, eighteen pounds of dried meat and a supply of horseshoes and nails. If he had shown any ability to live off the land, Burke might still have come through safely. But he was a man of almost infinite inflexibility, brought up for most of his adult life within a rigid system of police work that was never noted for encouraging individual enterprise. Had he, for instance, been capable of a different attitude towards the aborigines – who had been aware of his every move since the moment he left civilisation – the outcome might have been different. They had lived for generations in the hinterland; the most cursory gestures of friendship towards them

might have guaranteed his survival. As it was, Burke continued to regard them with the greatest suspicion, and to keep them at arms' length. So, with so little resourcefulness of his own to fall back on, a successful link-up at the depot became crucial to the operation.

Why had it happened? Why had the depot at Cooper's Creek been abandoned? Brahe had not been without his own problems. Wright had never arrived. The rats had become a plague from which nothing was safe; some days the men killed as many as forty, cracking their backs with sticks. Then, gradually, scurvy began to appear, and in time everyone was affected. As time passed with neither Wright nor Burke showing up, Brahe became increasingly anxious. He noted: 'It is four months since Mr Burke and Mr Wills left. Patton is ill and cannot walk and we are all suffering from sore gums. We have eaten little: there are plenty of supplies. Mr Wright has not shown and no message from Menindie has been received.'

After leaving Cooper's Creek on 21 April, Brahe followed the trail south. Eight days later, in the early hours of the morning, he met Wright, who was finally bringing his party up from Menindee. Brahe's story was incredible.

Wright had been unable to get his party ready because he lacked money to re-equip it. Only when the committee in Melbourne had sent him £400 had he been able to make the final arrangements for departure. He had left Menindee on 26 January, having been there for fourteen weeks. Dr Beckler, who was still with the party since no replacement for him had arrived, was sent on ahead with the camels. The horses were difficult to control and eventually broke into two groups. The three parties, Beckler's and the two horse groups, found constant difficulty in keeping contact with one another. In the first day, the distance covered was only five miles.

Wright's entire enterprise was without direction. Beyond the vague intention of reaching Cooper's Creek, he had no coherent plan. The result was inevitable. Throughout February and March he moved in a general northerly direction, by way of Nuntherunge Creek and Yetawinge Creek. At Torowotto, what leadership he had possessed disappeared entirely. The party moved back and forth from Torowotto looking for food and water. They had little success. What records they kept of their activities were brief: 'No water found'.

By the end of April, the horses and camels were in a sorry state, suffering considerably from sores, half-dead from starvation. The men were little better. Dr Beckler, Stone, Purcell and Smith were seriously ill with scurvy. On 29 April Mr Becker died. That same day, Brahe met the survivors of the group on his way south from Cooper's Creek.

Increasingly Brahe had been wondering if he had been right to leave Cooper's Creek without some proof that Burke and his party were dead. But he felt he had a responsibility to his own party, too. Scurvy had broken out and Patton, the blacksmith, was in a bad way. He died in fact in the early hours of 6 May, justifying to some extent Brahe's decision to pull his party back to Menindee. Nevertheless Brahe worried. In the end he persuaded Wright to go back with him to Cooper's Creek to confirm that Burke was lost.

The two men rode into the deserted depot at Camp 65 – just a little after Burke had led his men towards Mount Hopeless.

To Brahe, Wright had become a terrible irritation. And in his preoccupation with the man, he missed all the signs that would so easily have told him that Burke had been back to Cooper's Creek since Brahe and his men had left it. A rake previously left on top of the stockade was now leaning against the tree with its demanding inscription. There were holes in the leather covering of the door, where Burke's party had cut new soles for their shoes. Brahe noticed nothing. The cache he had left for Burke looked undisturbed at the foot of the coolibah tree. It never occurred to him to open it. Had he done so, he would have found a note for him left by Wills.

Fifteen minutes after Brahe and Wright reached the place, they left it. Brahe was satisfied that Burke and his party were lost for ever. They turned south, picked up their own parties waiting at Koorliatto, and made for Melbourne.

Burke's wanderings after leaving the depot for Mount Hopeless were little better-directed than Wright's had been on his way to Cooper's Creek. Mount Hopeless had been well named: 'Cooper's Creek ran out into desert,' said Wills. 'To attempt travelling further into it without hope of water would be the greatest folly. We were forced to turn back, our condition weak, our only hope of survival now was on Cooper's Creek itself. Where we had left some of the food still buried – and a message for anyone who might come by.'

Burke began a series of moves centred on Cooper's Creek, directed by one thing only – the need to find enough food to stay alive. The last camel was killed and eaten. Burke managed occasionally to shoot a crow and they shared the thin meat between them. For the rest, they lived like the aborigines. 'We gathered Nardoo seed like the natives to make it into cakes. It takes a long time and much exertion to collect a small amount. Although it fills our gut, it supplies little nutrition and passes through us mostly undigested. Birds are very shy of us but we managed to get a crow.'

Wills's diary. A page written just one month before his death.

The note left by Wills in the cache at the depot. Tragedy by now seemed inevitable.

remained hostile, frequently firing off his pistol when they approached.

By the end of May, Wills began to think there was little chance of survival. It seemed to him essential that some record of the expedition should be left where it could be found. He left

Birds were not the only things that were shy of them. The aborigines, too, hovered uncertainly on the edge of their activities; the men were aware that they were being watched all the time. Wills argued that they really must ask for help from them, but Burke found it difficult to unbend. Yet it was obvious that the blacks were concerned about the suffering of the party. They occasionally brought fish to them that they had caught in the creek. Once or twice Wills and King gave them gifts in return: a little sugar, pieces of material from their clothes. But Burke

Burke and King to return alone with his journals to the depot. Without Burke to drive them off, the aborigines approached Wills. They fed him with some of their own meagre food and carried his spade for him. At night he shared a gunya with one of them, Poko Tinnamira. The gunya was a primitive hovel made of woven stick and grass, but it kept out the night cold.

Wills reached the depot on 30 May and opened up the cache. It was undisturbed. Before resealing it he left another message: 'Both camels are dead and our provisions are done. We are trying to live the best way we can, like the Blacks. Our clothes are going to pieces fast. Send provisions and clothes as soon as possible.'

Wills returned to the others with the greatest difficulty. Even with the aborigines helping him, he found it a struggle to move. His body was wasted by starvation; his strength had almost gone. Burke and King were little better off, totally occupied with the search for food. They collected nardoo seeds and occasionally they managed to pick up a fish by the Creek. Then on 6 June the abandoned gunya they were sheltering in caught fire and the last of their stores were destroyed.

Burke finally decided to accept help from the Blacks. It was too late. The group that had been living near the creek had gone. 'We set off in search of the Blacks,' wrote Wills. 'After an exhausting trek and with the greatest fatigue and difficulty we reached the Blacks' camp. It was abandoned, greatly to our disappointment. We took possession of the best of the gunya shelters and decided to rest there a while.'

Towards the end of June, Wills's condition had deteriorated to the point where he could no longer stand. He lay in the gunya under two camel pads, wearing his flannel trousers, two ragged shirts and a torn waistcoat to keep out the cold. He knew he only had a few days to live. On 28 June, when King and Burke had gone off to look for the Blacks again, Wills wrote in his diary: 'My pulse is at 48, my legs and arms are skin and bone. I am very weak. I can only look out, like Mr Micawber, for something to turn up.'

Burke, too, had finally reached the end of his endurance. At daybreak on 30 June he couldn't get up. King, reporting later to the Royal Commission, said, 'Mr Burke gave me his watch which he said belonged to the Committee. He then said to me, "I hope you will remain with me here till I am quite dead; it is a comfort to know that someone is by: but when I am dying it is my wish that you should place the pistol in my right hand, and that you leave me unburied as I lie."'

He died. King became aware that he was being watched. When he looked round he saw the aborigines were standing some yards away. Some of them were weeping. When he stood up,

1. Left to right, back row: Robert O'Hara Burke (played in the film by Martin Shaw), Charley Gray (played by Martin Harris); front row: John King (played by Chris Haywood), William John Wills (played by John Bell).

2. Cooper's Creek. It was here that Burke reduced the party to four for the final drive to the north; here he planned to return to his base party – and the rest of the supplies.

3. Even the camels, purchased specially for the exploration in Afghanistan, and shipped in, found the going to the north almost too fierce.

4. By now the camels had been abandoned because of sub-tropical swamps. Burke's horse, Billy, sank frequently to its belly in the mud. The horse was eventually hobbled and left while Burke and Wills finished the journey on foot.

5. He had been a thief. He had stolen their rations. He might yet be responsible for their failure and even death. But now Charley Gray was dead. A grave had to be dug. He must be buried in the iron-hard ground.

6. Cooper's Creek, abandoned by Brahe and his party only hours before Burke and Wills and King staggered in. But it might as well have been days for all their chances of catching up. Brahe left a message in a

(continued p.97)

8

9

bottle buried under the tree. It was the lethal beginning of a chapter of disasters and mistakes.

7. Near the end. Finally, after driving off the Aborigines who might well have saved them, they unbent enough to search, in the desert, for native help – and failed to find it.

8. Burke died within sight of the Aborigines, who could have saved him by teaching him how to survive. He never knew it. His last words to King were: 'Leave me unburied, with my pistol in my hand.'

9. The only survivor was King. He was cared for by the Aborigines of Cooper's Creek, and eventually discovered by the rescue parties. Even then he was nearly mistaken for an Aborigine.

The film was directed by Tony Snowdon, and shot in the Central Australian Deserts.

they picked up pieces of greenery from the trees and came forward and began to cover Burke's body with them.

Two days after Burke's death, King returned to the gunya in which he had left Wills. He was horrified to find dogs near it, the gunya itself pulled apart. The place was full of flies and stank of decaying flesh.

Inside, Wills's remains lay on the ground. Beside him were the ripped camel pads and his diary. King put the diary in his pocket and slowly, weakly, buried Wills in the sand. It was the end. He turned away to see if he could find the Blacks again. He walked, limping, into the desert, believing in his heart that death lay ahead.

Melbourne was in uproar when Brahe and Wright returned. The committee couldn't believe that the expedition they had backed and planned had simply disappeared. Search parties were mounted, with the support of government money, from Victoria and other Australian provinces. A. W. Howitt was chosen to follow Burke's route from Melbourne. Frederick Walker took a party from Queensland through Rockhampton to the Gulf of Carpentaria. William Landsborough sailed to the Gulf and moved inland from there. John McKinlay went from Adelaide towards Cooper's Creek by way of Lake Torrens.

Brahe went with Howitt, retracing his steps through Menindee back to Cooper's Creek. Again he made no attempt to open the cache. which would have told him that Burke's party had been there. As far as he could see only the Blacks had visited the place.

Two days later, on 15 September, Edwin Welch, another member of Howitt's party, found a party of aborigines camped by the creek. When he rode up to them they scattered. Only one man remained. He was thin and weak, his skin burned to the colour of chocolate. Shreds of clothing hung from his back. His hair was long, his beard matted and filthy.

It was John King.

What had saved King in the end was the aborigines. He didn't find them; they found him. They had shown him how to make a 'wurley', the windbreak they set up each night to protect them when on the move. 'For about a month until the

The survivor, John King, was discovered by search parties, living with the Aborigines

relief party arrived, they treated me with uniform kindness, and looked upon me as one of themselves,' he said. Without them he would most certainly have died.

The few remains of Burke and Wills were brought back to Melbourne amongst public mourning. On 21 January 1863 the two were given a lavish state funeral. Whatever disastrous shortcomings and mistakes may have occurred now seemed forgotten.

The Royal Commission set up to enquire into the expedition was less forgiving. It laid blame for the expedition's disastrous outcome on the committee, on Wright, on Brahe – and on fate. Official attitudes towards Burke changed. Burke had left a gambling debt of £18 with the Melbourne Club. A wrangle developed between the club and the committee over it. The club refused to write off the debt; the committee refused to pay it. The man who had left Melbourne with the cheers of thousands in his ears had become a public embarrassment after his death.

The Burke expedition was a disaster. It was inexperienced, inefficient, ill conceived, badly led. Yet it needs to be remembered that Burke did accomplish just what the committee had asked him to.

He crossed the Australian continent from south to north and exploded the myth of a richly-watered hinterland. Where Stuart had twice failed, Burke succeeded. But Burke failed to survive – and survival is a crucial aspect of exploration.

No one can doubt Burke's courage, or endurance, or determination. What must be in doubt is his experience and his competence. As a leader his vision was narrow and rigid. His temper slipped too easily out of control. He was too unsure of himself to listen to the advice of others.

Melbourne 1863. A public funeral for the remains of Burke and Wills brought from the desert.

His attempts to impose authority produced stubborn situations and the reverse effect. His temperament might be partly attributed to his Irish nationality and background; his rigidity, to his police experience. Yet whatever explanations are put forward, the simple fact remains that he was the wrong man for the job. The expedition was a catastrophe not because of Burke but because of the committee that appointed him.

In retrospect, it seems that everything Burke did was wrong. Yet the motivation behind some of his actions was so nearly right. When he tried to establish his leadership he was doing no more than Cook and Jed Smith and Amundsen had considered essential. When he made for Mount Hopeless instead of Menindee, it was because the distance was shorter; there were no maps to show him that nothing but desert lay between. When he threw away his supplies to lighten his party's load, he was doing exactly what Cook did when stuck on the Barrier Reef. The fact that he got rid of the lime juice demonstrates his ignorance and inexperience, not his crass idiocy.

Where his real shortcomings showed was in his relationships with the natives. They were the only ones who could have helped him, and almost to the end he kept them at bay. His attitude here can't be dismissed as inexperience. Wills, who was no more experienced, could see clearly enough how necessary it was to get help from the aborigines if they were to survive.

But there was in Burke a stiff inflexibility. It refused to let him unbend, in case his authority was diminished. It refused to let him be in any way beholden to another human being, particularly an uncivilised native. It was a trait for which he suffered.

In the end it killed him.

Mary Kingsley 1862–1900

It was one of the shortest journeys in the annals of discovery, the briefest of explorations. It lasted barely a week, in 1895, covered no more than seventy miles. Yet it was a journey which was to have lasting impact on European thinking about Africa.

Mary Kingsley, a Victorian spinster, walked through 'the white man's grave', inhabited by cannibals, a place of disease and danger. And, through her eyes, the blinkered world of nineteenth-century Britain was brought a view of African life that was as startling as it was new.

She believed, and subsequently preached, that black African savages might not need 'civilising' or even converting to Christianity. In those days what she said was revolutionary.

She was born only days after her parents' marriage and that knowledge burned into her consciousness, affected her life. She was brought up, in a sense, the victim of Victorian attitudes as well as the eccentricities of a wild and irresponsible father and a sickly mother. When they both died, leaving her – at thirty – unmarried and without purpose, she felt the only thing left to do was to die.

She searched for a way. Her life had become a burden and so she chose deliberately to risk it in a manner that was unique and memorable.

The hall was full. Men and women in evening dress filled the galleries, crowded the main floor. Everybody sat still, waiting for her to begin.

She turned, caught the eye of the man at the magic lantern. He nodded back to her. She was dead tired. She had influenza. She felt used-up, despairing that no one had need of her anymore. In fourteen days she had delivered ten lectures, covered thirteen hundred miles.

Now it was Birmingham.

She began: '. . . You will think I remind you of your great aunt long since deceased . . .'

They had expected something more serious from this famous lady explorer, who had eaten with cannibals in the jungles of West Africa. What they wanted to hear about was the seventy-mile journey she had made three years earlier. What she wanted to tell them was other things. She wanted to question the missionary system that imposed Christianity on the existing cultures; to ask why the British Colonial Office should want to interfere with an African way of life without taking the trouble to understand it first. But she was too accomplished a speaker not to lighten the seriousness of her purpose with humour.

And, in any case, what she had said was true. She did look like a 'great aunt long since deceased'. She was slim, rather tall, and wearing a black blouse and stiff, long, full, silk skirt. Her hair was fair, smooth, parted in the middle. She wore a huge cameo brooch at her throat. Everything about her seemed somehow just out of date.

And it was all calculated. She was well aware of the effect she was creating: the brave little Victorian spinster who had exposed herself to the terrors of the jungle and survived. She had a true sense of 'theatre'. Perhaps she had inherited it from her father or one of her eccentric uncles. Everything about her 'was a bit of stagecraft, designed to heighten her achievements', a friend said of her at this time. 'What began as a covering, ended as a disguise.'

But her voice betrayed her. There was nothing helpless or 'little woman' in the way she spoke. It was a vibrant voice, not low, but resonant and beautifully controlled. She spoke slowly and distinctly, aware of the indifferent acoustics of the hall. No one had the least difficulty in hearing her. Her intellectual command was obvious, revealing 'a brain masculine in its strength and in the breadth of its outlook'. She said:

'I have a profound personal esteem for several missionaries. Indeed, taken as a whole, missionaries must be regarded as superbly brave, noble-minded men who go and risk their own lives, and often those of their wives and children to do what, from their point of view, is their simple duty. But often they fail to recognise the difference between the African and themselves. A blackman is no more an undeveloped white man than a rabbit is an undeveloped hare.'

She was born in Highgate, London, on 13 October 1862, and christened Mary Henrietta. Her father, George Kingsley, had an obsession for travel that frequently kept him away from home for months, sometimes for years. He was an extraordinary man: tall, impressive in speech and appearance, the second of three extraordinary brothers. He qualified as a doctor and then financed his wanderings by hiring himself as medical adviser to rich noblemen. All three brothers were interested in travel and adventure, natural history and writing. Charles, the eldest and best known of them, was a clergyman, a Christian controversialist and the author of such bestsellers as *Westward Ho!*, *Hereward the Wake*, *The Water Babies*. Henry, the youngest, worked as a stock-rider and mounted policeman in the Australian outback before returning to Europe and becoming a war correspondent in the Franco-Prussian War. For generations the Kingsleys had been country gentlemen, soldiers or parsons. All the brothers were splendidly in the centre of a tradition of Victorian eccentrics from such backgrounds.

In 1862 George Kingsley married Mary Bailey. Temperamentally they were poles apart. She was described as 'a lady whose extraordinary benevolence endeared her to everyone who was fortunate enough to come within the circle of her friendship, and whose faculty for managing affairs of business enabled her to take from her husband's shoulders the burden of many of the petty cares of life'.

(*Left to right*) **Charles Kingsley; George Kingsley, Mary's father; and Henry Kingsley**

A comfortable arrangement it would seem, though it is doubtful whether either of them was happy with it. It left George free to continue his travels, but while on the face of it Mrs Kingsley seemed to have accepted the arrangement, as time went on her health deteriorated and she hardly ever left the house.

Her behaviour left a deep impression on her daughter. 'The only thing that ever tempted her [mother] to go about among her neighbours was to assist them when they were sick in mind, body or estate,' she wrote later. 'So strongly marked a characteristic was this of our early home life that to this day I always feel I have no right to associate with people unless there is something the matter with them.'

Life in the Kingsley household was monotonous. In 1864, a son was born, but the two children never played together. In fact no one played in the house. Mary had her share of the housework, and baby Charles had to be specially taken care of. He had a sickly constitution. During her father's long absences she was forced, from an early age, to become her mother's close companion.

In 1867 George Kingsley went to the South Seas with the Earl of Pembroke. Mary was five at the time. She was eight when he returned. He spent most of the following five years in America and Canada. He pursued his studies in anthropology and natural history, shot wild animals and engaged in adventurous exploits, accounts of which filled his long letters home. His style was racy, vivid, full of wit. There is no doubt that later Mary's own use of language was influenced by it.

Mary was deeply attached to him. She was more like him than she was like her mother, or her brother Charles. If she ever loved anyone, she loved him. His letters brought 'the bright eye of danger' into the tedium of the house in Highgate. They opened, for her, windows on to the vast world beyond her carefully circumscribed experience:

'There was in him enough of the natural man to give him the instinctive feeling that the duty of a father of a family was to go out hunting and fighting while his wife kept the home.'

Yet her feelings for him didn't blind her to his shortcomings. He irritated her by the way he justified his travels as major contributions to human knowledge, when they were little more than self-indulgences. She knew that the worry and anxiety he caused her mother over the years was shortening her life. She was becoming a permanent invalid now, the burden of running the household falling on her daughter's shoulders.

Her father's irresponsibility was breathtaking. He wrote to say he was joining an expedition with General Custer, and shortly after that the London papers were full of the news of the extermination of Custer's force at the Little

103

Bighorn. It was several weeks before they heard that bad weather had prevented his joining the expedition.

Even at home he wasn't easy. He was out of place in that quiet household, with his stories of grizzly bears and Indians. He had a vile temper that depressed his wife further, though amused Mary when she learnt how to cope with it. He detested 'Mr Gladstone in print or a Roman Catholic priest in the flesh,' reacting to the former by tearing the newspaper to shreds. He hated noise. When he was at home Mrs Barrett, the maid, lived in terror of him and tried hard 'to avoid her pet accident, namely falling downstairs with a dustpan, scrubbing brush, pail and a shriek'.

Mary was cramped, physically, emotionally, intellectually. Her brother went to school, but she had to educate herself. Education was not thought necessary for a Victorian girl in her position. What education she did have was from the books in her father's study. She read Darwin and Sterne and Pliny and counted amongst her favourite books Burton's *Anatomy of Melancholy*, Johnson's *History of Robberies and Murders of the Most Notorious Pirates* and Bayle's *Dictionary*. Chemistry was a particular passion, but she lacked the opportunity to experiment.

The only formal education of any kind that she received was in German, which her father saw as being useful to him because of the research that she would be able to do on his behalf. Whatever he thought of her as a person, he clearly regarded her as someone whose skill he might turn to his own advantage. It was, too, very much how she saw herself: a dutiful Victorian daughter. Of the real human world outside she knew nothing. 'The whole of my childhood and youth was spent at home, in the house and garden,' she says. 'The living outside world I saw little of, and cared less for, for I felt myself out of place at the few parties I ever had the chance of going to, and I deservedly was unpopular with my own generation, for I knew nothing of play and such things.'

When Mary was seventeen, the family moved to Bexley Heath in Kent. Inevitably, the spot they chose was 'secluded'. Four years later,

when her brother Charles went up to Cambridge, they moved there: to Number Seven Mortimer Street, overlooking Parker's Piece. Her father began to spend less time away. He built up a small circle of friends in the town and began work, writing his anthropological findings. For the next nine years Mary devoted herself to working for him, whenever it was possible to leave her mother. She had access now to first-class libraries. She continued her studies in mathematics and science with renewed energy. She met some of the scholarly friends of her father and almost for the first time was able to test her mind against others.

Yet the Kingsleys remained cut off from society. Those who met the young woman at that time found her attractive and intensely curious. But no one could really get to know her. She was almost constantly shut up at home. Only once did Mary leave the house to go for a short holiday in Wales, but the moment she arrived she was called back by telegram. She couldn't ignore the summons. 'I have always a feeling of responsibility,' she wrote later. 'All through the 15 years during which I nursed my mother and watched over my brother's delicate health I never felt "it was all for the best", but only that perhaps I could make things better for them, if only I knew how, or were more able: and I tried my best, and I know I failed, for my mother's sufferings were terrible, and my brother's health is now far from what I should wish. . . .'

The blow, when it fell, came from an unexpected quarter. On 5 February 1892 she sat up all night with her mother, which was not unusual. In the morning she took her father's letters upstairs to him. He was dead in his bed.

With marvellous charity, considering the way she had been used, she was able to say of him later that he had lived 'the very happy honourable life of a noble, perfect English gentleman. A man who all his life long, wild as the circumstances of it had been, never did a mean act or thought a mean thought, and never felt fear.' No doubt it was him she had in mind when she wrote elsewhere: 'I have always admired men for their strength, their courage, their enterprise, their unceasing struggle for the beyond.'

The family grave in Highgate Cemetery. Both parents and Mary's brother are buried here.

Her misery wasn't over. Within twelve weeks her mother died, and shortly afterwards her brother Charles left England for the east. It was a devastating break. She was twenty-nine. For the whole of her conscious life she had been devoted to her parents and brother. Now everything had gone. The *raison d'être* of her life had disappeared, and life itself scarcely seemed worth continuing.

Her share of the estate was £4000. She took a holiday in the Canary Islands. There she met the men who traded with the African coast: ships' captains, agents for European firms. The tales they told caught her imagination. She heard of Sierra Leone from men who had gone there; that

was more even than her father had done. She heard tales of mangrove swamps that were impassable, rivers teeming with strange fish. She heard of cannibals. Suddenly she knew that there was work for her again, a continuation of the work she had done for her father. At the same time she felt she would be working in her own right as a scientist.

'And then, when the fight was lost,' she said, after her parents' death, 'when there was no more odd jobs anyone wanted me to do at home, I out of my life in books, found something to do that my father had cared for, something for which I had been taught German so that I could do for him odd jobs in it. It was the study of early religion and law, and for it I had to go to West Africa.'

Characteristically, she could take a far from poignant view of the situation. A view that under the circumstances seems almost flippant: 'In 1893 for the first time in my life, I found myself in possession of 5 or 6 months which were not heavily forestalled, and, feeling like a boy with a new half-crown, I lay about in my mind, as Mr Bunyan would say, as to what to do with them. "Go and learn your tropics," said Science.' She puts it amusingly, with that style and wit that was so much a part of her. But it never quite hides the melancholy.

She made her first trip to the coast in 1893, with the intention of acclimatising herself and re-establishing contact with the traders. No one at home had been able to give her hard information. Friends tried to dissuade her. It was the 'White Man's Grave'. It was inhabited by head-hunters. A woman hadn't a chance of survival.

Her experience was quite the opposite. She found the traders uniformly kind and helpful. The port of Freetown took her straight back to the pages of Johnson's *History of Robberies and Murders of the Most Notorious Pirates*. It was still substantially as he had described it. She was captivated.

She had sailed from Liverpool in August 1893, in the *Lagos*, a small, overloaded cargo boat. The boat touched at a series of West African ports. Mary enjoyed the colourful scenes of embarkation and disembarkation from ferryboats tossing in the surf, and rambled with the

105

ship's purser through the markets of Freetown. She learned the rudiments of navigation from Captain Murray, and was even allowed to take the wheel on occasion. 'I have taken vessels of 2000 tons across that Bar and up the Forcados creeks as a pilot, three times,' she threw out in a letter to her publisher George Macmillan when he suggested rewording a passage on navigation in her *West African Travels*.

Mary landed eventually at Luanda in Angola. She pursued her anthropological researches up country, and farther north in what was then the Belgian Congo. References to her adventures survive in lectures, articles and letters; she never gave a consecutive account of them.

After that trip, she went home and began to plan. If West Africa was to be her life's work, she would do it properly. As a first step she consulted Dr Gunther, of the British Museum, who had written *A Study of Fishes*. He showed interest in a scheme she proposed to send him specimens of West African river fish for the Museum. He liked the idea and she decided that this would be the core of her work. It helped to identify the particular area she would have to visit, for it was the unknown fishes that Gunther was after, from the country north of the Congo. Her friends had been right in their warnings. It was cannibal country.

The Royal Geographical Society's publication, *Hints to Travellers*, was a mine of information. There was advice on photography and clothing; addresses from which arms and watches and compasses could be obtained; details of methods of collecting specimens. There was information on the best kinds of writing materials, and sections on medical care. Of great significance, no doubt, was the entry for dysentery: 'Of all the diseases to which the traveller in tropical climates is exposed, this is, probably, most to be feared. . . .' It might have been an entry such as this that decided Mary to take a course of medical training at the Kaiserworth Institute in Germany before departure.

The choice of clothes was important. She made few concessions. A white blouse; a long black skirt with capacious pockets – from which on one occasion she was able to produce three pocket handkerchiefs, a 'head' of tobacco and a

The Royal Geographical Society's *Hints to Travellers*: Victorian thoroughness exemplified

knife, and still presumably have room for her watch, compass and notebook. According to a friend, she always wore an old pair of her brother's trousers under her skirt when she was on expeditions. They would give some protection against the leeches that abounded in the rivers and swamps. She dismisses the idea herself, in her usual pithy way: 'One should not go about in Africa in something of which one would be ashamed at home. I hasten to assure you that I never ever wear a masculine collar and tie, and as for encasing the more earthward extremities of my anatomy in – you know what I mean – well, I would rather perish on the public scaffold!'

Boots should have 'broad and low heels, never

d, that to attempt "to rough it" unnecessarily is simply to invite
se, and too often death.
pressed by experience with these convictions, I have been careful to
a fairly roomy tent, 9 feet long, of good canvas. An iron bedstead,
cork bed, and two warm Austrian blankets. A folding chair, camp-
and a small portable table. The latter is an immense convenience
much writing has to be done.
short quick trips, in which I might be away from camp for a day
o, I have provided a palkee hammock, which forms a bed and tent
.
carrying any sick person an ordinary string hammock is taken.
squito curtain makes up the list of tent furniture.
tead of carrying an ordinary bucket canteen I have had a basket
up with all the necessary articles.
f course, take with me a small medicine-case, specially fitted with
to the treatment of fevers, diarrhœa, dysentery, liver disease, &c.,
esides, I have been careful to have some of the more useful medicines
arate bottles in case of accidents.
ong other useful articles, the following may be mentioned :—Water-
ground sheets; roll-up case of tools; one ·577 Express rifle, one
educed to ·450, a 12 bore gun, a revolver, with ammunition to
two axes; a hunting knife; two bill-hooks and two reaping-hooks,
used in camping and cutting a way through jungle and forest;
and necessary stationery; some books, especially such as can be
nd re-read.
se articles, with scientific instruments, photographic apparatus, &c.,
he chief part of my equipment.
ve not thought it necessary to lay in a supply of stores, such as
ffee, sugar, &c., as they can be got almost as cheaply in Zanzibar.
for bartering must also be got there, as I should otherwise run the
taking out what would, to a large extent, prove to be utterly
ess.
the country through which I have to pass is reported to be
ous, I shall arm as many of my men as possible with short Snider
and take revolvers for myself and the leaders.

mber 3, 1882.

---

exceeding one inch in height; broad tread, four inches wide for an ordinary foot; elevated toe-cap to make room for great toe'. Mary took good care of her boots, keeping them supple and waterproof with palm oil or animal fat, removing them and changing to slippers when not wearing them on the trail. 'It never does in this country to leave off boots altogether at any time and risk getting bitten by mosquitoes on the feet when you are on the march,' she says. 'The rub of your boot on the bite always produces a sore, and a sore when it comes in the gorilla country comes to stay.' On her second night in a cannibal village, however, she kept her boots on despite the fact that they were wet and her feet sore. She was afraid that otherwise she might not have been able to get them on in the morning.

Constance Larymore, travelling with her husband in Nigeria at this time, said that to leave off wearing corsets at any time 'for the sake of coolness is a huge mistake: there is nothing so fatiguing as to lose one's ordinary support . . . there is something about their absence almost as demoralising as hair in curling pins'. The advice of the Royal Geographical Society bears out Constance Larymore's contention, substituting a cummerbund for stays, or perhaps adding to it: 'the abdomen is supported and protected by a long wide silk scarf wound two or three times round the body'.

Regarding firearms, the recommendation was for a revolver at least. Mary had one with her in West Africa, though found it less useful than the Society suggested. Such things weren't as foreign to her as we might imagine. Her mother – if we can believe her daughter's remarks – was a renowned revolver shot. Where exactly in the Highgate house she found a place to practise remains a mystery. On the march, a revolver was useful, provided you had the sense to keep it loaded and in good working order. Mary never used her own weapon. It would have been suicidal. 'One white alone with no troops to back him means a clean finish.'

A knife was far more useful. A bowie 'with a shallow half moon cut out of the back at the point end, and this depression sharpened to a cutting edge'. Not a hinged-blade knife; in Africa everything goes rusty at the joints. In any case, 'hinge knives are liable to close on your own fingers'.

The real defence was neither knife nor revolver. It was the assurance of the traveller himself, the confidence he had in his own authority. In this, Mary Kingsley was remarkable. Where other explorers like Pizarro and Stanley thought in terms of arms when considering security, Mary thought in psychological terms. Safety lay not in finding suitable ground and disposing one's forces properly; it lay in understanding the ideas in the minds of opponents. 'These ideas, which I think I may say you will always find, give you safety.'

There was another defence. She had half realised it in the Canaries, when she had first met the men from the coast. It was trade. 'There is something reasonable about trade,' she says, 'especially if you show yourself an intelligent trader who knows the price of things. . . . It enables you to sit as an honoured guest at far-away inland village fires: it enables you to become the confidential friend of that ever-powerful factor in all human societies, the old ladies. It enables you to become an associate of the confraternity of Witch Doctors, things that being surrounded with an expedition of armed men must prevent your doing.'

Her whole expedition was based on this principle of trade. It was why it was so successful. Trade not only gave her an introduction to the unknown African societies that lay behind the coastal strip, it gave her independence as well. For £300 she could go to West Africa, collect specimens, conduct research into the religious practices of unknown cultures, and return safely, provided she could make up the rest of the money that was required by trading. Doughty had gone to Arabia with a similar idea. He would pay his way by practising medicine. It didn't work. It hadn't occurred to him that the Arabs might not wish to pay for medicine.

Mary Kingsley wasn't Doughty. Where he was vague she was precise. When she arrived at Talagouga on the River Ogowé in the summer of 1895, she had a box full of trade items – fish hooks, knives, coloured cloths – and she knew exactly what she wanted in exchange for each of them.

Mary explored the Ogowé on this second journey to Africa. Embarking in December 1894, she again made a leisurely progress along the West African coast, arriving at Calabar in January 1895. Here she spent five months studying wildlife in the swamps and estuaries of the so-called Oil Rivers, before moving on to what was then the French Congo. Up the Ogowé, she hoped to find rare fish specimens, and further inland, beyond the influence of the missionaries, what she called the 'good, rank fetish' of unexplored Africa.

She stayed with French Evangelist missionaries in Talagouga on the Ogowé, near Lambarene, which Albert Schweitzer was to make

A trading depot. Mary Kingsley admired the traders, based her expedition on trade.

famous. She formed the same impression of them that she had of other missionaries. They were brave and noble-minded, but they started from the wrong premise. They saw the African as a simpleton, a misguided savage – black with sin. From what she had observed of him so far, she thought him nothing of the sort. He was simply different. Polygamy was no more a sin than monogamy. It was simply a different way of looking at the married relationship.

She deplored this aspect of European influence. In comparison to the missionaries the traders seemed eminently honourable men. If anything, their presence had goaded the African into activities that ultimately would be beneficial to him, without destroying the complex cultures he had evolved. The missionaries – in particular the Protestant English ones – had done the opposite. Their effect was particularly obvious in the case of the coastal Igalwa tribe. They were a finely-built race. Their villages now were neat, full of European articles. Many of the tribesmen could read and write. But the whole fabric of their culture had been destroyed and they were dying out.

The missionaries' view of Mary was what might be expected. They gave her whatever help they could. She was brave, no question about it. She was ignorant, of course, because she hardly knew the place. She was idealising the African, when what he needed was educating. Her scientific investigations might be of some value to the British Museum, but they wouldn't advance the African one jot. As for her support for the traders, they were the people who had brought the worst aspects of European culture to the coast.

When she announced her intention of crossing the unknown territory between the river Ogowé and the river Rembwe, they thought she was mad. The French map of the area showed only one known feature, Lake Ayzingo. The rest was blank. The stories that came out of the area were enough to keep Europeans away. It was the

A Royal Geographical Society map of the area, about the time of Mary Kingsley's travels

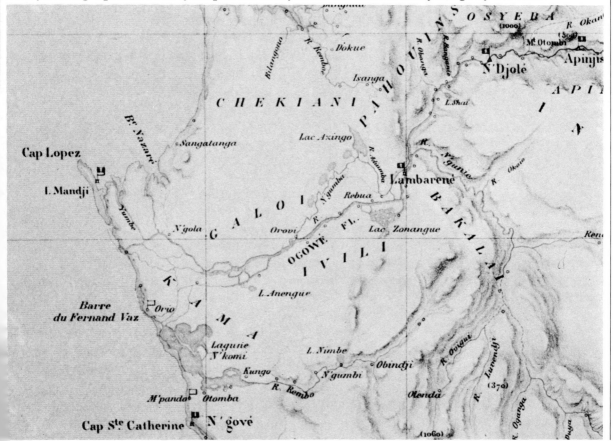

territory of the Fang tribe, the most notorious cannibals in the Congo's Gabon area.* Mary was well aware of the dangers. A missionary would have been killed and eaten on sight. But a trader – even a white woman trader – might survive.

On 22 July she left the river village of Kangwe in a canoe, with four Ajumba tribesmen and an interpreter of the Igalwa tribe. They were coastal men, familiar with Europeans and their ways. The river was broad, with long sand-banks breaking the water and islands covered in dark vegetation. The canoe was one of the fast Adooma type, narrow and flat-bottomed. The men paddled it standing up. They sang as they paddled, a rhythmic, melancholy sound that melted into the clamouring noise of the jungle on either side.

'Woe to the man in Africa who cannot stand perpetual uproar,' Mary wrote. 'Few things surprised me more than the rarity of silence and the intensity of it when you did get it.'

Her companions were an odd collection. From time to time they stopped the canoe and collected wild yams, then a mile downstream they threw them out on to a sand-bank to be collected by their friends on shore. Their names were impossible to remember, except for the interpreter's. He was called N'gouta. She remembered him because he was useless. He spoke hardly a word of English and contributed nothing to the paddling.

The others she called by their most obvious characteristic. *Grey Shirt* – he wore one of flannel – was a Christian, a man of, perhaps, a certain affluence whom she thought a gentleman and took a liking to.

Singlet was a Christian as well, and reminded her of a genial Irishman who for some reason had been born black. *Silent* was simply silent. He was a pagan, a thin elderly man who never said a word. *Pagan* was jet black, a big heavy man with massive muscular development. He was covered

in fetish charms designed to guard him from all the dangers of the river and the jungle.

All of them except Silent spoke some 'trade English' – 'pidgin' – that form of English that evolved through business dealings with non-English speaking groups in many parts of the world. Even if N'gouta had been a competent interpreter, his services would have been largely unnecessary.

They passed Lambarene Island and turned north-west out of the Ogowé into one of its tributaries, the O'Rembo Vongo. They were still in Ajumba territory. Passing canoes called to ask where they were going. 'Rembwe', called Grey Shirt. 'What!' called the others in disbelief.

In the early evening they reached Arevooma, Grey Shirt's village. She spent the night in Grey Shirt's house, an attractive place with walls of split bamboo and a palm-thatched roof, and set off next day for the country of the Fang.

The river was broad and slow-moving, the banks and jungle beyond alive with birds. The air was tremulous and deafening with their cries: hornbills, red and blue kingfishers, vultures sitting in trees or pulling at carrion on sand-banks, white cranes motionless at the water's edge, and great flocks of small black-and-white birds with bills like puffins.

The dense growth on either side was full of strange, shifting light, reminiscent of those Turner paintings she had seen as a young girl in Highgate. It all seemed, to her, like the African mind – strange, full of hidden richness. Unless you lived with it there was little hope of understanding it. And you couldn't live with it in any real sense unless you came to it alone, without preconceptions.

She was sitting against a pile of baggage in the middle of the canoe. Some of it, the powder bags and the flintlocks in their cases of leopard or gorilla skin, belonged to the men. The rest was hers. It was an extraordinary collection. There was the portmanteau full of trade tobacco, books and papers; the case of photographic materials; the collecting case with the bottles and spirit. A black bag full of personal belongings: blouses, skirts and underwear, stockings and sewing materials. A chest full of medicines that had been recommended by the Royal Geographical

---

* In her own account, Mary Kingsley incorrectly calls them 'Fan' tribesmen. The French colonists first called them Fang, their proper name. It was also a name not suited to Mary Kingsley's eventual purpose: to win sympathy and understanding for the African.

Lambarene on the River Ogowé. Later to be made famous by Albert Schweitzer.

Society and the Kaiserworth Institute. A mosquito bar, a net and framework for sleeping under. The trade box, the linchpin of her financial arrangements. And inevitably 'something to make tea in'. No wonder 'a gentleman danced and howled on the bank' when he caught sight of her.

From time to time, but only from time to time, trade was possible with villages en route. The canoe would make for the bank and Mary would barter. No coins were used. The nearest thing to currency were 'cheques' made out against the guarantee of a trading company. Mary had an arrangement with Hatton and Cookson, one of the principal traders on the coast, which allowed her to use this system. Such 'cheques' could be exchanged by the Africans for goods at one of the company's trading posts. More usual, though, was the simple exchange of goods. Ivory and rubber were amongst the principal commodities offered by the Africans. In exchange they wanted cloth and tools.

Each article used for trading had a definite exchange value. A tooth of ivory was equivalent to a European coat, for example. Similarly, six fish hooks had the same exchange value as one handkerchief, and could be used to buy a fixed quantity of rubber or ivory.

Towards midday, they began to run off the map. A tributary coming into the O'Rembo Vongo from the north suddenly emerged from the jungle. The map showed nothing. Grey Shirt said it was the Karkola and ran into Lake Ncovi to the north-west. They turned into it. She had heard of neither the river nor the lake. Nor had anyone else except the Ajumba and half a dozen other tribes. She became the first European to travel up the Karkola and record the existence of Lake Ncovi. She never accepted that she had 'discovered' them. It was her contention that those who lived there knew about them all the time. The attitude is consistent with her view that Africa should be seen in African, not European terms.

Lake Ncovi was a melancholy place, with uninhabited islands and a fringe of black-forested hills. Towards evening, M'fetta came into view. It stood on a small cliff covered in trees and creepers, with a rocky beach below. It was the first of the Fang villages.

The boatmen approached with caution. Grey Shirt and Pagan had once done business with two of the Fang from M'fetta, otherwise they wouldn't have gone at all. No love was lost between one tribe and another in this region. Everyone knew the Fang ate their enemies. They ran the canoe ashore and took up the flintlocks, removing the hide covers.

The Fang. From *Travels in West Africa*, 1897.

The Fang ran down from the village above. They carried guns and shovel-shaped knives, and they were obviously bent on a fight. Pagan and Grey Shirt stood on the beach facing them. They had slung their guns over their shoulders to indicate they didn't want trouble, and they were holding out their hands. Twenty yards from the two Ajumba, the Fang stopped and called to one another, deciding what to do. There was no sign of the two men with whom Pagan and Grey Shirt had done business.

Later, asked whether she knew what it was like to be frightened, Mary said, 'I have never felt that. I don't know what it is: I have an idea that if once I did feel so I should collapse entirely. But whenever I have been in real instant danger which simply needed every effort of every bit of me I had a strong salt taste in my mouth. Whenever I feel that I know I've got to take myself as seriously as I know how.'

It could well have been the end. The Fang's treatment of visitors was well known. Fortunately a man pushed forward on to the beach. He was typical of the Fang: a light bronze colour,

1. Mary Kingsley, played in the film by Penelope Lee.

2. It was a journey of no more than 70 miles, lasting barely a week, and yet it was to have a lasting impact on European ideas about Africa and Africans. She travelled alone with no army to protect her and only the concept of trade to help her.

3. A Fang tribesman. Mary Kingsley wrote: 'Why should we believe the African is a savage? A black man is no more an undeveloped white man than a rabbit is an undeveloped hare.' It was not a view popularly held in England. She insisted on its truth.

4. In the Fang villages she met and accepted a way of life rejected by European standards as cruel and heathen. She even took a 'protective' view when writing about them in her book, *Travels in West Africa*. Although she knew the correct spelling, she always described them as 'Fan' tribesmen. The word Fang would certainly not have helped understanding in Victorian England.

5. At night the forest was alive with noise, life and excitement. She may have come to Africa to die, but it was here – at night – she began again to live.

6. Fang women. Mary Kingsley stayed always in the villages, slept in the huts

(*continued p.113*)

provided for her by the tribespeople. The Fang were cannibals. Mary discovered that they kept, in a bag suspended from the roof of the guest hut, a collection of small human pieces – ears, a finger or toe – of those that they had eaten; but still respected.

The film was directed by Tony Snowdon, and shot in the Equatorial jungles of Gabon, with Fang tribesmen, in exactly the area where Mary Kingsley made her journey.

finely-built, about five foot eight in height. He wore a narrow band of worn leopard skin hanging from one shoulder. Apart from that he was naked. When he saw Pagan he rushed at him with a great cry, then stopped immediately in front of him, his arms held out in an embrace without actually touching him. It was Kiva, the business friend.

M'fetta was larger than most villages, with three or four streets of houses. The palava house, the centre of male Fang activities, stood in the innermost street. The curiosity of the Fang in the visitors was immense. Mary was surrounded by men, women and children, though never actually touched. 'Never lose your head' was one of her principal tenets. It was fortunate she had such control over herself. The only white person in Fang memory to have entered the village before was a French officer. He had paid Kiva six dollars to be his guide, and had never been seen again.

Mary required three guides to take them to Rembwe. The bargaining started. Everyone joined in, haggling, shouting, waving their arms. It was the African way. She'd seen it before. But it might take days before they came to an agreement, and the time simply wasn't available. It was no good, she said. If they couldn't reach agreement within the hour then she would have to call off the arrangement and go back to the Ogowé. Shortly afterwards, it was agreed that Kiva, Fika and Wiki would go with her.

Kiva's hut, where Mary was to spend the night, was fifteen feet square, with a sanded floor and a bamboo roof. It was furnished with a rough wooden bed and wooden pillow, and the skins of wild cat and leopard on the walls. Fetish charms hung from the ceiling, together with a brass rattle worn in the forest to scare away snakes.

The night was hot. She lay fully clothed, even to her boots. The lice and mosquitoes bit her, despite the mosquito bar. Beyond the silent village, the forest hummed with incessant life. She sat up and got clear of the net, went to the door and slid it open. Pagan was asleep across the doorway. She stepped over him. The night was intensely beautiful, a great canopy of brilliant stars over the forest.

She walked to the beach and took off her clothes and bathed in the lake, then dried herself on her cummerbund. She took one of the canoes and paddled into the middle of the lake. She was alone with Africa. Its power surrounded her. She gave herself up to it. 'Do not imagine', she wrote later of experiences like this, 'that it gives rise in what I am pleased to call my mind, to those complicated, poetical reflections natural beauty seems to bring out in other people's minds. It never works that way with me; I just lose all sense of human individuality, all memory of human life, with its grief and worry and doubt, and become part of the atmosphere. If I have a heaven, that will be mine.'

Next day, 24 July, they set off on foot for Efoua, the next village of the Fang. Another Fang had joined them, apparently out of curiosity. Mary called him the Duke: 'he was a gentleman with the manners of a duke and the habits of a dustbin'.

The pace of the march almost killed the Ajumba. They could paddle all day without flagging, but half an hour on foot turned them into panting weaklings. 'What saved us weaklings was their [the Fangs'] appetites,' said Mary. Every two hours the Fang would sit and eat, getting through a pound of meat each.

The forest, Mary found, was something you came to absorb and know slowly. At first you saw nothing 'but the vast column-like grey tree stems in their countless thousands'. Gradually you became acclimatised: 'Snakes, beetles, bats and beasts, people the region that at first seemed lifeless. It is the same with the better lit regions, where vegetation is many-formed and luxuriant. As you get used to it, what seemed at first to be an inextricable tangle ceases to be so. The separate sorts of plants stand out before your eyes with ever-increasing clearness.'

Whatever she said to minimise her response to it, it had caught her imagination for ever. Despite the humour and self-deprecation of so many of her remarks, she cannot hide the depth of her feeling: 'I do not recommend the African forest life to anyone. Unless you are interested in it and fall under its charm, it is the most awful life in death imaginable. It is like being shut up in a library whose books you cannot read, all the while tormented, terrified and bored. And if you do fall under its spell it takes all the colour out of other kinds of living. . . .'

Nonetheless, even for her it had its drawbacks. Kiva's snake rattle failed to drive all the reptiles from their path, and one morning N'gouta almost walked into a viper. It was hanging from a branch in front of him and only Duke's presence of mind saved him. He killed the snake and later cooked it. The Ajumba wouldn't touch it, nor would N'gouta – but Mary shared it with the Fang.

The incident was helpful. It strengthened her relationship with the cannibal tribesmen:

'A certain sort of friendship soon arose between the Fan and me. We each recognised that we belonged to that same section of the human race with whom it is better to drink than to fight. We knew we would each have killed the other if sufficient inducement were offered, and so we took a certain amount of care that the inducement should not arise.'

Later she fell into an elephant trap. Ivory was an important item of trade, perhaps the single most valuable commodity. Only the adult male natives could hunt elephant. The most usual method was the pitfall trap, dug across a track frequented by elephants and then covered with bamboo and leaves. Mary was bruised but unhurt, and Wiki pulled her out with one of the bush-ropes that hung in thousands from the trees. She was fortunate. The base of the pit, as was usual, was covered with spikes of sharpened ebony. The heavy folds of her skirt had prevented them from penetrating her flesh.

The Fang, she discovered, were skilled in the use of a wide range of hunting and fishing techniques. Pit traps were used for many kinds of game, and poisoned bait was successful against leopards and panthers. Wire nooses snared boar and antelope, and the children set snares of elephant hair for small animals. Bows, with bamboo arrows poisoned with 'strophantus' were used to hunt monkeys and the larger birds. Nets of the finest workmanship were used for fishing, and for trapping gazelles that had been driven into them by trained dogs.

They reached Efoua before nightfall on the 24th – essential if they were to have any hope of convincing the inhabitants of their peaceful intentions. They entered the village through a guardhouse, to find dancing taking place in the street beyond. A man was beating a large standing drum gripped between his knees. Another was playing a handja, a xylophone of gourds set in a frame. Bystanders tapped sticks together in unison. They fell back when the visitors appeared, the woman and children running into the huts then peering back through the doorways.

Kiva had been to the place before. When he was recognised, the tension eased. Their whole way of life was full of such moments for the Fang. Safety depended on the speed with which they could identify and react to the dangers that came to them from the forest. The shape of the village itself reflected their fears. It was a single street with a row of houses on either side. Both ends of the street were closed by guardhouses. At night, the place was a fortress. Even the goats were driven inside and occupied a special hut.

A Fang village was built to protect all its occupants against outside dangers

Again, it was trade that made Mary acceptable. No white person had ever been to Efoua before, yet she was able to stay the night in perfect safety because she could produce the accepted symbols of business: tobacco, pocket knives, coloured handkerchiefs. 'I told them I was on my way to the factory of Hatton and Cookson on the Rembwe, and they got it stuck in their heads that I was a sort of travelling salesman for the firm.'

Under a flag of trade it was possible to come in contact with people she might otherwise never have met. She traded tobacco for rubber with one of the Fang chiefs, then found his wife haggling with her for a red silk tie. Again, trade made it possible to be forthright. She could refuse the offer of an old rusty razor by way of trade. Under other circumstances her action might have been thought offensive.

The Fang were semi-nomadic. When an area of forest had been exhausted, they moved. Apart from hunting and fishing, they cultivated patches of clearing, planting vegetables and tobacco.

Their diet was reasonably varied, consisting of plantain, yams, maize, pumpkin, squash and pineapple. As well as the more usual flesh, snails and snakes were eaten, together with the fat maggot-like pupae of the rhinoceros beetle.

But the staple food was manioc. The big bulbous roots were poisonous and had to be soaked in water before they were safe. Then they were dried, grated or beaten into a dough. The sound of manioc being beaten in wooden mortars was one of the most characteristic sounds of West Africa. It was used to thicken broths or boiled by itself in long rolls. 'As you pass along you are perpetually meeting with a new named food, fou-fou on the Leeward, kank on the Windward, m'vada in Corisco, agooma in the Ogowé,' says Mary Kingsley. 'But acquaintance with it demonstrates that it is all the same – manioc. If I ever meet a tribe that refers to buttered muffins I shall know what to expect and so not get excited.'

Rubber was an important part of the Fang economy. It grew wild in the forest, and its collection was of particular importance to the

She managed to bring back, in excellent condition, 65 different species of fish and 18 different species of reptile

Green. del. et lith.

Mintern Bros. imp

Plate I.

A. CTENOPOMA KINGSLEYÆ. B. CT. NANUM. C. CT. GABONENSE.

young unmarried man. He used it to buy his first wife, if possible 'a good tough widow lady, deeply versed in the lore of trade'. With her help, he would in time add a further five or six to his household.

Wiki and Kiva explained how rubber was collected. It was a wasteful process. The entire vine was cut down and chopped into lengths a couple of feet long. The lengths were put in a metal dish, with six or eight inches projecting beyond the rim. These outer parts were heated by a ring of fire, and the liquid rubber bubbled out into the dish.

The house in which Mary stayed the night in Efoua belonged to a chief. It was made of bark on a wooden frame and divided into two small rooms. The furniture was sparse: a few skin decorations on the walls, a stool at the door, a plank bed. There was an odd smell about the place – something sickly, half-decayed. She traced it to a bag on the wall. 'It contained bits and pieces of humanity – eyes, ears, toes and the like.' The shock must have been appalling. However courteous they were being to her, the Fang were cannibals. She would do well to remember the fact. Yet even then the wry humour that gave her mind such balance couldn't be suppressed:

'I subsequently learnt,' she says, 'that although the Fan will eat their fellow friendly tribes-folk, yet they like to keep a little something belonging to them as a memento. This touching trait in their character I learnt from Wiki and though it's to their credit, under the circumstances, still it's an unpleasant practice when they hang the remains in the bedroom you occupy, particularly if the bereavement in your host's family has been recent.'

Her escorts were reluctant to go farther. Between Efoua and the Rembwe lay Egaja – 'the dreaded town'. They would have preferred to stay and hunt, but it wasn't hunting she had in mind.

They climbed a ridge of the Sierra del Cristal, then dropped into an area cut up by deep ravines. Beyond lay a swamp, one of the worst sort: deep and narrow with a deceptive crust on top that gave under the weight of a man and let him drop through into the ooze beneath. Pagan was up to his waist in a moment, and a second

later up to his neck. They used bush-ropes to pull him out, and bundles of brushwood to strengthen the surface.

By the afternoon of the first day they had come to a deep, rocky ravine with a fast-flowing river at the bottom. On the far side, built on top of a long bar of sand, stood Egaja. Duke stopped. The place had the most terrible reputation, the worst of any village in the region. Not one of them had been to the place, or had any business with it.

'The Duke who is of course a fine courageous fellow ready to engage in any undertaking, has suggested I should go ahead of the party when we enter the town because perhaps they would not shoot on sight if they happen to notice I am something queer.'

There was nothing for it but to go on. She would never have gone back in any case; it wasn't in her nature. With all the self-assurance she could summon – 'the mainspring of your power in West Africa' – she walked alone into the village. The whole street was empty and silent. The others joined her, gradually regaining their courage when they saw that nothing had happened to her. Yet still nothing moved.

Finally a chief appeared, came towards her and stood looking at her. She was the first white person he had ever seen. He was tall and powerful, with a fine, intelligent face – a man to be reckoned with. He wore a black frock coat, bright blue felt sombrero hat and an ample robe of cotton check. He was deciding what should be done with this strange creature who had walked in from the forest.

She had to make an impact. There was no point in throwing yourself on the mercy of a man like this, and certainly no point in offering him trinkets to gain his friendship. She said to Pagan, 'Tell the Chief I hear this town is a thief town.'

Pagan was horrified. He refused. She said, 'Tell him, or I'll tell him myself.' Pagan turned and told the chief. He was dumbfounded. He protested that she was mistaken. It was a fine town, full of honest people. She said she would reserve her judgement then, until she had seen it for herself. It established a first measure of respect between them that later that night was to prove invaluable.

The chief's mother had an arm covered in ulcers, one of the worst cases Mary had ever seen. She bathed it in some of the Condy's fluid from the medicine box, with little hope of curing it. The chief was grateful, the rest of the village curious. They began to come to her from every part of the street with their ailments. The men, their eye-teeth filed like daggers in the Fang fashion, showed her ulcers. One had a piece of broken spear lodged in his thigh, with an abscess formed round it. Others had parasitic diseases like filaria. Most had the open sores characteristic of central Africa.

She gave what treatment she could. It might have gone on all night if it hadn't been for a fight that started outside. The worst possible thing had happened. Kiva had been recognised by someone he owed a coat to. The creditor had him tied up and was proposing to eat him. A crowd had gathered and excitement was running high. Mary turned to the chief. There was nothing he could do, he said. He had no jurisdiction over the creditor and Kiva, since neither of them came from Egaja. It really seemed that Kiva was to be killed and eaten.

She had a high regard for the chief's intelligence and integrity. No doubt he knew it. She said that if it was his town, surely he had jurisdiction over what went on inside it. She offered to make out a voucher on Hatton and Cookson's so that the creditor could get himself a coat from one of their posts. She would, of course, deduct the cost from Kiva's pay. The chief was agreeable. But it didn't satisfy the creditor. He had quite decided to eat Kiva.

In the end, it was settled after a great deal of talk. The creditor agreed to accept a coat from Mary's trade box, and Kiva was cut loose. What had really worked was the combined authority of Mary Kingsley and the chief. It represented what she was to strive to promote in later years – a co-operation of European and African cultures, based on mutual regard.

29 July was the last day. The track through the forest led to a mangrove swamp of vast proportions. It was pointless to think of going round it when no one knew its extent. 'It stretched away in all directions, a great sheet of filthy water, out of which sprang gorgeous marsh plants, in islands, great banks of screw pine, and coppices of wine palm, with their lovely fronds reflected back by the still, mirror-like water.'

It took two and a quarter hours to cross it, wading neck-deep most of the time, with their belongings on their heads. At first the stink of foul water and decaying vegetation was nauseous. Later it became unnoticeable. In places the tangled aerial roots of the screw pine were almost impassable. Where the water was more open, great exotic blooms floated on the surface.

When they finally got clear of it, they had leeches round their necks 'like astrachan collars', and their hands were covered with them. They came off with salt, but the bleeding didn't stop at once and the flies settled on the wounds. Mary admitted later that she felt 'quite faint from loss of blood'.

That same day she reached Agonji on the Rembwe. The journey up the Karkola had taken six days. 'We have travelled across this small blank space on the map.' A distance of only seventy miles. But as she said herself, 'The armchair traveller should not be deceived by the length of the route on the map.'

'I went to West Africa to die,' she said, alluding to her feelings after the death of her parents. 'West Africa amused me and was kind to me, and was scientifically interesting, and did not want to kill me just then.' It was the most happy, the most independent, the most personally satisfying period Mary Kingsley was ever to have. When she left, she was never to see West Africa again.

She returned to England in the December of 1895, to find herself a celebrity. But her background claimed her again: the sense of responsibility that had weighed on her throughout the whole of her childhood and into womanhood. She wanted to travel more but she felt obliged to stay at home and keep house for her brother who had become – not surprisingly – a rather ineffective and selfish man. 'I must do it, it is duty: the religion I was brought up in.'

She published *Travels in West Africa*, an account of her journeys, in 1897. It was an immediate success, but it brought its own problems. It pulled her to the forefront of the

Abridged Popular Edition Now Ready. Extra Crown 8vo, 7 s. 6d.
***** A few copies of the original Library Edition still remain.
Price 21s. net.

TRAVELS
IN WEST AFRICA,

Congo Français, Corisco and Cameroons.

BY

MARY H. KINGSLEY.

WITH ILLUSTRATIONS.

CONTENTS.

INTRODUCTION—Liverpool to Sierra Leone and the Gold Coast—Fernando Po and the Bubis—Voyage down Coast—The Ogowé—The Rapids of the Ogowé—Lembarene—On the Way from Kangwe to Lake Ncovi—From Ncovi to Esoon—From Esoon to Agonjo—Bush Trade and Fan Customs—Down the Rembwé—Fetish—Ascent of the Great Peak of Cameroons—Trade and Labour in West Africa—Disease in West Africa—The Invention of the Cloth Loom.

PRESS OPINIONS.

ATHENÆUM.—"For all who know West Equatorial Africa Miss Kingsley's book will possess an absorbing interest, whilst those who have not yet visited that country will gain a vast amount of varied and useful information on many subjects. Long as this notice is, it is not so exhaustive as we could wish, but it is pleasant to find so much in this admirable book to praise and commend, and so little to disagree with."

ACADEMY.—"A very interesting and singularly instructive book."

WESTMINSTER GAZETTE.—"A notable book about a very remarkable tour."

ILLUSTRATED LONDON NEWS.—"The brightest and sprightliest narrative of travel that has appeared for many a day."

BLACK AND WHITE.—"By far the most important and most vivacious book of adventure published for many a day."

NATURE.—"The book stands alone as a vivid picture of West African life by a writer whose point of view is as nearly impartial as we can ever hope to see."

MACMILLAN AND CO., LTD., LONDON.

Press notices reproduced in the back of Mary Kingsley's book, *Travels in West Africa*

struggle between the traders and the Colonial Office. She came down on the side of the traders, maintaining that their effect on the African way of life was likely to be less harmful in the long run. And it was the African culture she was championing. She did so almost alone.

She lectured as widely as her strength would allow. Her heart – 'always a weak spot' – was troubling her. She wanted Europe, England in particular, to see that the African as she knew him had an existence in his own right, that he wasn't simply a second-class white man. She pressed the point in *West African Studies,* a brilliantly lucid and powerful political tract. It brought her praise that was like 'melted butter poured over her'. It brought her hatred too. She was called 'Liverpool's hired assassin', because of her defence of the traders.

The same year – 1898 – she was ill with influenza and later typhoid. They left her very weak.

In 1899 she met Matthew Nathan, the governor of Sierra Leone. For the first time in her life she became emotionally involved. It was hopeless. He was a confirmed bachelor. Perhaps that was how she wished it. She wrote to him, 'The fact is I am no more a human being than a gust of wind is. I have never had a human individual life. I have always been the doer of odd jobs – and lived in the joys, sorrows and worries of other people. It never occurs to me that I have any right to do anything more than now and then sit and warm myself at the fires of real human beings. I am grateful to them for letting me do this. I am fond of them, but I don't expect them to be fond of me, and it's just as well I don't. . . .'

She died on 3 June 1900, at the age of thirty-seven.

She had volunteered for service in the South African War, and was sent to nurse Boer prisoners in Simonstown, where she caught enteric fever. Nurse Rae, who was tending her, said, 'She rallied for a short time, but realised she was going. She asked to be left to die alone, saying she did not wish anyone to see her in her weakness. Animals, she said, went away to die alone, and she felt like them. It was hard for us to do this but we left the door ajar, and when we saw she was beyond knowledge went to her.'

She was carried from Simonstown on a warship and buried at sea as she had wished. 'It is the non-human world I belong to myself,' she had written to Nathan. 'My people are mangroves, swamps, rivers, and the sea and so on – we understand each other.'

The Fang villages would have been discovered without Mary Kingsley, though with far less understanding. Her journey was a remarkable achievement. Only her incredible courage – lack of awareness of fear, she would have called it – brought her through safely. But her real achievement was to bring a new view of African life to the colonising Europeans and the proselytising missionaries:

'These Negroes are a great world race – a race not passing off the stage of human affairs, but one that has an immense mound of history before it. The moulding of that history is in the hands of the Europeans, whose superior activity and superior power in arts and crafts give them mastery; but all that this mastery gives is the power to make the future of the Negro and the European prosperous, or to make it one of disaster and misery to both alike.'

Today, her views seem little less than prophetic: 'What we do in Africa today, a thousand years hence there will be Africans to thrive or suffer for it.' There will be Europeans too.

Part of a letter to John Holt, the Liverpool trader who became a close friend. She writes about Stanley and taxes imposed on the Africans.

Jedediah Smith
1799–1831

Jedediah Strong Smith, son of Methodist New England parents, became a Mountain Man – and a legend. Few today cannot have heard of Davy Crockett. Jedediah Smith was a forerunner of all the 'Davy Crocketts'.

With a band of paid trappers and hunters – including the first American Negro to explore through to California – Jedediah Smith set out in search of beaver and other furs.

He was, in fact, an explorer after trade; a traveller searching for profit. But he had a classical education, a stern sense of self-discipline, and a dedication to the ideas of discovery that seems to contradict his profit motive.

He pioneered and mapped the way for the opening of the American West. He won a route through from the frontier areas East beyond the Rockies, across the Sierras to what was then Spanish California.

But he did more than that. Until his incredible journeys no man had crossed the deserts and mountains that lay between the frontier towns east of Utah, and California. By doing so he ensured that, eventually, there would be a *United States*

Jed Smith: survivor. He'd been close to death, from starvation, a dozen times before. He'd survived scores of attacks by hostile Indians.

A few years earlier he'd even come through a near lethal mauling by a grizzly bear. His scalp had been ripped to the bone and one of his ears torn off. And even then he'd come out of the encounter with less damage than might have been expected, because he insisted on having the ear sewn back again with needle and thread.

But it seemed now that his luck had run out.

For two weeks he'd been crossing Southern California's Mojave Desert, with his party of Mountain Men and Indians. Days before, the last of the food and water had been finished. Fifteen of the horses he had bought in the Mojave Valley had already died from heat, exhaustion or starvation.

It looked, at last, as if Jedediah Smith, survivor, was going to 'go under'. It seemed as if he and his party were going to be beaten, by death, in this exploration, an exploration that was as much for profit and commerce as for discovery alone.

First and foremost he was a business man. Only secondly was he an explorer. He had an investment in reaching new beaver grounds with his party, and for days he had pushed them forward on one pretext or another. 'I urged and encouraged the men into this forbidding prospect with the promise that they would soon see a land of wealth and green as the Ammuchabas [the Mojave Indians] described to me,' he wrote.

He had nothing but instinct and Indian stories to back the promise. He was the first American, coming from the east, ever to enter that country.

Now he looked at the men with him, wondering who would be the first to crack.

It was the hottest time of the day. The desert ahead ran unbroken as far as the eye could see. The brilliant reflection of the light from sand

Harrison G. Rogers, clerk and second-in-command, was reading from the Bible to bring the others into a suitable state of mind. Perhaps for death, to meet their maker? His lips were cracked but there was still the strength of his Calvinist belief in his voice: 'If thou wilt diligently hearken to the voice of the Lord thy God, and wilt do that which is right in his sight, and wilt give ear to his commandments, and keep all his statutes, I will put none of these diseases upon thee, which I have brought upon the Egyptians; for I am the Lord that healeth thee.'

Only John Wilson, the carpenter, complained, but that was in character. He had been trouble from the very beginning, drinking whenever he could get his hands on a bottle, fighting with the others. Now he was the cause of more general grumbling amongst the party. Smith gave him an ultimatum: 'If you give me any more trouble I'll discharge you right here and you can make your way on your own.'

Smith had handed out chunks from the flesh of a cabbage pear, 'a plant that appears similar to the prickly pear that grows on the most parched ground. If chewed on it provides juice but is in no way palatable.' Wilson spat it out. Smith was inclined to thrash him, but neither of them was in any condition for a fight. Smith turned to the others with a sudden blast of fury, and cried, 'If you all used your eyes as much as your tongues, you'd have seen but a few minutes ago a dove fly West, and doves fly only a few miles from water.'

It was a lie. 'I framed a story to enliven their hopes then prepared once again to search for the water that would revive us.' It was typical of him that on such an occasion he should assume full responsibility for the survival of every man in his party. Like Amundsen later, Smith would stand no challenge to his authority. But – also like Amundsen – he never ceased to care for the well-being of his men.

Jed Smith was six feet tall, lean and wiry, with brown hair and blue eyes. He wore his hair long, in the characteristic way of Mountain Men. It covered most of the scar left by the grizzly that ran from his scalp down his forehead and through the eyebrow to his ear. He wore a fringed buckskin jacket over a red woollen vest and scarlet woollen trousers, moccasins on his feet and a woollen cap on his head. He carried a 'Green River' knife in his belt – a single-edged butcher's knife that received its name from the 'G.R.' initials of the early British specimens. He had pistols and a pouch for shot, and a 'possibles' pouch for miscellaneous contingencies. Over his left shoulder he carried a powder horn and a pouch full of bullets. His principal weapon was a rifled flintlock made by Jacob and Samuel Hawken of St Louis that had cost him $40. It took a charge of between sixty and 200 grains of powder, and was accurate, with a half ounce ball, up to 200 yards.

A Mountain Man. They pioneered the West.

Superficially he was indistinguishable from a hundred other Mountain Men, except for the fact that he was clean-shaven.

But his background set him apart. . . .

Jedediah Strong Smith was born in 1799 in the Susquehanna valley of New York State, the son of an old New England family. Throughout his life the accents of New

England persisted in his speech. He was tutored by a Dr Simons of Pennsylvania, and received a broad middle-class education. He was well-read in Greek mythology and had also read widely in the field of African and American exploration.

Throughout his life Smith remained a man devoted to his family and his church, once expressing, in one of his letters to his parents, deep concern for moral and religious principle: 'As it respects my spiritual welfare I hardly durst speak, I find myself one of the most ungrateful, unthankful Creatures imaginable. Oh when shall I be under the care of a Christian church?'

During his later life his companions amongst the rivers of the Rockies were at times more often than not drunken, gluttonous lechers, but Smith remained a practising Methodist who never smoked, never chewed tobacco, never swore and drank only on formal occasions.

At twenty-two Smith answered an advertisement in the St Louis *Gazette and Public*

For the Rocky Mountains.

THE subscribers wish to engage One Hundred MEN, to ascend the Missouri, to the

Rocky Mountains,

There to be employed as Hunters. As a compensation to each man fit for such business, **$200 Per Annum,** will be given for his services, as aforesaid.— For particulars, apply to J. V. Garnier, or W. Ashley, at St. Louis. The expedition will set out from this place, on or before the first day of March next.

Ashley & Henry.

jan 18.   40tf

The advertisement which Jed Smith answered

Advertiser. 'Enterprising Young Men', it read, '. . . to ascend the Missouri to its source, there to be employed for one, two or three years.' The advertiser was General William Henry Ashley, a partner in the fur-trading firm of Ashley and Henry of St Louis. Smith impressed General Ashley as 'a very intelligent and confidential young man', and after a term as a Captain in the Missouri Militia he became a partner in the firm.

For four years he led groups of trappers into the virgin forests of the lower Rockies, returning each year with vast quantities of beaver furs that Ashley sold to the European market at some seven or eight dollars each. Smith's own needs were meagre: fresh clothes from time to time, food, ammunition. The bulk of his earnings were sent back east to his parents.

But partnership with Ashley had its drawbacks. Smith felt restricted. He wanted to extend his activities beyond the routine of trapping beaver and hauling the pelts back to civilisation.

In 1826 he went into partnership with two other Mountain Men, David Jackson and Bill Sublette – known to the Indians as Cutface. His apparent intention was to increase the profitability of his business activities, though another motive was already beginning to take hold of him: 'I, of course, expected to find Beaver, which with us hunters is a primary object, but I was also led on by the love of novelty common to all which is much increased by the pursuit of its gratification.'

There were, however, problems that beset the Mountain Men in their hunt for beaver, and in particular those like Jed Smith who had developed a curiosity about the country itself. In the 1820s the west coast of North America was in a state of flux. No firm frontier line had been agreed between the Americans and the British in Canada. The British insisted that the border should lie along the Columbia river, giving them most of present-day Washington State. President John Quincy Adams, preoccupied with America's 'Manifest Destiny' to move west to the whole Pacific coast, wanted to continue the line of the 49th parallel of latitude westwards. He lacked the political power to do so. But what he did succeed in doing was in persuading Spain to accept that her authority should extend no further than the present northern boundary of California. Similarly he got the Russians to agree to make no claims south of the present southern tip of Alaska.

To the American trappers, the situation with the British was particularly irksome. A joint occupancy of the Oregon area had been signed in 1818, by which both parties were to exploit the region. But the British were free to move down the coast from the present British Columbia, whereas for the Americans the barrier of the Rocky Mountains blocked any approach from the east. The Hudson's Bay Company took full advantage of the situation for the British. From its base at fort Vancouver on the Columbia river, beaver was drained out of Oregon on a massive scale. The Smith, Jackson and Sublette partnership estimated that in the course of a few hunts the Hudson's Bay Company had taken 85,000 beaver pelts out of 'our Territory', worth $600,000. No love was lost between the two parties. While General William Clark, superintendent of Indian Affairs in St Louis, considered Jed Smith 'an intelligent enterprising citizen', Kittson of the Hudson's Bay Company called him a 'sly cunning Yankee'.

President Thomas Jefferson had to some extent anticipated the problem. In 1804 he had appointed Meriwether Lewis and General William Clark, two men with military experience, to investigate the new north-western territories that had been added to his country by the Louisiana Purchase from France. They went up the Missouri and Jefferson rivers into Idaho, then made the first crossing of the Rockies at a point north of Mexico, following the Columbia river to the Pacific. On their return into Montana they explored the regions drained by the Big Blackfoot and Yellowstone rivers. The reports of their discoveries stimulated the Missouri fur traders to extend their activities into the area. In 1807 a trading post was built on the Yellowstone at the mouth of the Big Horn river.

Jed Smith reinforced the work of Lewis and Clark, adding new discoveries of his own. In six years he covered more of the mountain region than any man before him. In 1824 he reached the Snake River from the Green River by way of the South Pass. By doing so he had opened up the Oregon Trail that later was to carry settlers in their thousands from St Louis and Independence to the Pacific Coast. He explored the Flathead Country of Montana, remapped the Yellowstone and Big Horn regions, and was one of the first white men to set eyes on the Great Salt Lake of northern Utah.

On 15 August 1826 Jed Smith was at Rendez-vous in Cache Valley on a tributary of the Bear River. His partners had already left for the north to trap the established beaver haunts along the Snake River. What Smith intended was to go south-west to look for new territory to hunt. He needed to, in view of the growing 'fur desert' being created by the Hudson's Bay Company. It was reasonable to suppose such territory existed; from Taos and Santa Fe in the south, hunters had already pushed northwards with considerable success. But apart from beaver hunting he had a second aim. He was going 'for the purpose of exploring the country S.W. [of Salt Lake] which was entirely unknown to me, and of which I could collect no satisfactory information from the Indians who inhabit this country on its N.E. borders.'

The scene at the aptly named temporary settlement of Rendezvous was much as it had been in previous years: Mountain Men collecting their mules and horses, checking their gear, some saying farewell to the squaws they had been living with – promising to see them in a year's time. Most were outfitted like Jed Smith, though there were variations. There were caps of beaver and fox and rabbit, as well as of wool. Some men wore coats of bright coloured blanket instead of the more usual fringed buffalo skin. Instead of woollen trousers, many sported breeches of leather. They wore leggings of smoked buffalo skin. Unsmoked leather shrank and tightened round the calf muscles. Many carried short-barrelled smooth-bore flintlocks with a range of fifty yards, instead of the more expensive Hawken that Smith possessed.

There was still a good deal of heavy eating and solid drinking going on, even as the Rendezvous broke up. A year was a long time. No one knew what hardships and privations had to be faced until next Rendezvous. Men leaned with their backs against pines, tearing meat off ham bones with their teeth, wiping their hands on their breeches or beards so that they stank of rancid fat. Others drank themselves into a stupor with 'mountain whisky', a concoction of raw alcohol and river water.

There was a good deal of shouting, some music, but little talk. Communication was mostly a matter of gesture and facial expression

Rendezvous, where the fur trappers met, rested and traded, before setting out each year

In the first place, they hadn't much to say to one another. In the second place, the habit of silence in the forest – because of the danger from Indians – couldn't be broken easily. What speech they used would have been largely incomprehensible to an outsider: 'Well hos! I'll dock off buffler, and then if thar's any meat that "runs" can take the shine outer dog, you can slide.' 'Hos' was a friend, 'buffler' meant myself, to 'run meat' was to chase game.

For Jed Smith, Rendezvous finished on 22 August when he left with his trapping party of fifteen men and fifty horses for the south-west. He would see Jackson and Sublette again at next year's Rendezvous, 3 July at Little Lake.

His companions were a seasoned lot: big, powerful men who had spent a lifetime on the trail of fox and beaver skins for the European market. Men like the half-French Abraham LaPlant, the blacksmith Silas Gobel, and Robert Evans, perhaps the toughest man amongst them. Arthur Black had been in the mountains longer than anyone. Peter Ranne was very unusual, a Negro, later to claim to be the first black American to reach California from the east.

It was hard going as they pushed higher into the Sierras through totally unknown territory. Smith rode well ahead of his men, checking the track, keeping a lookout for game – and Indians. He had some food with him, but whenever he could he preferred to live off the land. Behind him came the men and horses. They rode when the going was easier, but much of the time they had to walk, guiding their animals over the bare rock faces that rose among the sparse pine trees.

The animals laboured under a great range of equipment. The expedition had to be entirely self-supporting. There was dried buffalo meat to last for three weeks – charqui or jerky. It did nothing for the appetite but it kept starvation at bay. Pemmican was better. It was made by the Indians from dried ground meat, fat and herbs. Each animal also carried a sack of between six and ten beaver traps and a blanket with an extra pair of moccasins. There were also trade goods needed to obtain fresh mounts or supplies. There were hatchets, coffee pots, kettles, mugs, powder and shot. A mule carried between 200 and 300 pounds of supplies on an X-shaped wooden frame, a horse a little more.

From the start Smith had trouble with the men. They were used to hardship. It was nothing new to them to go without food, provided that every now and then they could gorge themselves on beaver tails or dog. What they couldn't understand was why he appeared to be leading them away from beaver country. They were trappers. Their whole livelihood depended on taking furs and making Rendezvous with them next year. Yet they had scarcely seen a sign of wildlife since they set out. Even Smith had to admit that things hardly looked encouraging:

'After three weeks of constant travel in a line South West, I struck a country of starvation which gave my party little encouragement. Our supply of dried buffalo meat was all but run out and there was no game except for an occasional black-tailed hare.'

Fortunately there were few Indians to trouble them. Those they saw were almost naked, 'and they kept as close to rock as Mountain sheep'.

Wilson caused the most difficulties. His stream of complaints grew increasingly irritating. 'This ain't takin' us to no Beaver country,' he kept saying. When the water ran out he shouted, 'If we don't find water soon, we's finished!' He took things out on his horse, kicking it continuously with his heels when the going was hard. Harrison Rogers found him difficult to discipline. Arthur Black, who had had more trail experience than anyone, cried out on one occasion, 'Shut up, I'm sick of listenin' to your whinin'!'

It came to a head on the approach to Beaver River. They were on almost barren ground, red sand with outcrops of red rock and occasional dwarf junipers and sagebrush. The horses by now were thin and tired, their heads hanging down. Some had died already, or had become too exhausted to stand; Smith shot them himself, putting his pistol a foot from the head before firing. Afterwards they stripped the edible meat from the carcase.

Suddenly a black-tailed hare broke cover and zigzagged through the dry sagebrush. Simultaneously Wilson and Robert Evans fired from the saddle and the creature rolled over. Together they dropped to the ground and raced towards it. Evans got there first, but as he picked it up, warm and oozing blood over his hand, Wilson pulled him down and tried to take it from him.

1. Jedediah Strong Smith, played in the film by Richard Clark.

2. They were trappers in search of beaver. They were the mountain men, the frontier explorers and traders who opened up a nation. They became a legend in their time, and part of the history of America. Peter Ranne (far left), a former Negro slave, was the first Negro ever to explore through to California.

3. Harrison Rogers. He, and the others, complained that there were not anything like enough beaver on the route that Jed Smith first led them. It was the search for beaver that drove them on. Hatters in London and New York needed the beaver fur; perfumers in Paris and Vienna wanted the casatoreum scent glands. And the beaver tails fed the hunters.

4. Rendezvous, where each year the trappers gathered in summer with their pack animals, their squaws, their liquor, and their weapons, before departing on their treks, through the wilds, in search of fur. It was from here that Jedediah Smith started out on the unknown journey to California.

5. Beyond the Sierras the Mojavi Desert. Even the Indians would not cross it. And so far no white man had survived it. Now they struggled on, not to find beaver, but survival.

(continued p.129)

128

. Jed Smith cut pieces of cactus for the men to chew and so gain some little moisture. They lay in holes they scooped out of the ground, covering themselves with sand to protect themselves from the heat.

. The mission at San Gabriel. Here the Indians had been taught, by Spanish monks, all the crafts and trades to make a self-supporting community. And, from here, they exported back to Spain the richest of all the produce.

. The friars at the mission lived well. Their hospitality to the explorers was generous. For Jedediah Smith and his men, this was a paradise, almost unbelievable after their harsh journey.

The film was directed by John Irvin, and shot in the Sierras, the deserts of the mid-West, and California where Jedediah Smith's journeys actually took place.

The others gathered round in the hope of seeing Wilson thrashed. The hare fell to the ground and was forgotten for the moment. Evans and Wilson stood, toe to toe, punching one another as hard as they could. Wilson's lip split wide open. Blood poured from Evans's nose, ran down into his greasy moustache and beard. Arthur Black was shouting for Evans to knock Wilson senseless. Another blow from Evans put Wilson on the ground.

As Evans dropped on top of him, punching him continuously in the face, Wilson managed to pull his Green River knife from its sheath. He would have put it into Evans without hesitation if Jed Smith hadn't kicked it out of his hand. Smith grabbed him by the collar of his buffalo skin jacket and hauled him to his feet, only to knock him down again with a blow to the face.

It was a common enough incident in the lives of the Mountain Men. Violence could erupt at any time. Smith wrote in his journal: 'The conditions of our journeying made the men troublesome and had it not been that close to noon Divine Providence graced us with both water and a hare, I believe I would have given two of them a flogging.' It says a great deal for Smith's confidence in himself that he should even have contemplated such a thing. The men compared favourably with Pizarro's conquistadors for physical toughness.

The water that Smith referred to was little better than thin mud. 'Although my trail had the configuration of a watercourse, I only managed to find water about every forty miles and named it Lost River.' It was in fact the dried-up course of the Beaver River. The water was full of live insects. That, and the tiny ration of meat that was left for each man, produced further complaints. Black wondered how long they were expected to last on it. Silas Gobel, one of the two blacksmiths in charge of the traps, was worried about the horses. Abraham LaPlant, addressing Smith as 'mon petit bourgeois', reminded him that he had signed for the expedition to hunt beaver, not to die of starvation in the wilderness. But nothing could deflect Smith from his goal. 'Murmurs from my men on their expectations of re-tracing our steps, I dispelled by indicating that there was no cause for concern,' he wrote. 'It was my intention to go on, in a southerly direction.'

In mid-September they reached the first substantial water supplies for a month. The place was Corn Creek – now the Santa Clara – a tributary of the Virgin River. Men and horses drank until they could hardly move. Smith took out a razor, bent over the water to remove his beard. 'My reckoning of the position', he said, 'was about 400 miles SSW of Salt Lake.' He couldn't be more precise. He had no instruments that would have let him calculate latitude and longitude.

Some of the men became aware of being watched. They turned to pick up their rifles, never far from their sides. When Smith lifted his head he saw an old Indian, bronzed and wrinkled, looking at him. The man vanished. A little downstream Smith came across a village. He went towards it, making the sign for peace that he had learned from the Plains Indians – hands clasped together at the level of the chest. 'Although at first alarmed, these poorest of Indians I have yet seen are of quiet and friendly disposition,' he wrote. 'It is a fortunate circumstance, for the horses are becoming weaker and more difficult to drive and my men complain of both hunger and fatigue.'

The Indians were Pai-Utes, poor relations of the proud Utes farther to the north who gave their name to present-day Utah. They were primitive in the extreme. They wore loincloths of rabbit skin and some of the old men had rabbit fur headbands; otherwise they were naked. They wore their hair almost to the shoulders and either fringed or parted in the middle. A few of the older men had beards. Very few wore any personal decoration apart from basic neck thongs of leather. All of them were filthy, as if it was no part of their way of life to wash.

Smith managed to get a little corn and some pumpkins from the Indians. There was little else to be had. They were 'diggers' rather than hunters; their diet was largely vegetarian. What meat they had came from the oddest sources. When the trappers were offered some they discovered it to be grasshoppers and grubs that had been dug out of the ground. 'With the country nearly destitute of game of any description except a few hares, the people ate any creature that nature allowed to live, although they did raise some little corn and pumpkin and had a works for making candy by boiling down cane grass.'

Some of the Pai-Utes lived in 'humpies', crude shelters made of long branches of willow and cottonwood with cornstalks and grass woven through them. Others lived in the open. 'Many of them live without any kind of lodge and rise from their bed of earth to rove about in search of

Pai-Ute Indians, 'the poorest I have yet seen'

roots or grubs,' Jed Smith wrote. Apart from the people themselves, the only things of interest to Smith were a green marble pipe, a flint knife and a chunk of rock salt. He traded for them and later sent them to General Clark in St Louis to be added to the collection of Indian artefacts the General was making.

There was little improvement in the land south of Corn Creek. They followed the course of the Virgin River – Smith had called it 'The Adams', in honour of the President – until it ran into Lake Mead. At the southern end of the lake another river came from the east and turned abruptly south. The water in it was the colour of rust. Something about it was familiar to Smith. 'By the formation of rocks and their direction, I believe I am now on the same river I first struck two years ago, about 500 or 600 miles north, after

The Colorado River. 600 miles farther south Jed Smith recognised that he'd crossed the Colorado.

I had found and crossed a Pass over the Rocky mountains.' It was a remarkable deduction. It was in fact the Colorado that he had encountered on both occasions.

If anything, conditions had grown worse. They had taken only forty beaver pelts on the journey so far. It averaged out at something like $15 a man for six weeks of strenuous activity. Robert Evans, frustrated almost beyond endurance, shouted, 'Why the hell we got to keep followin' a river with no beaver in it?' Wilson complained: 'This Booshway's (bourgeois) crazy, I'm tellin' you! There ain't no beaver here! I'm for turnin' back before it's too late!' LaPlant declared that when his contract ran out he was going back to Canada for sure.

Then Biscuit went down and couldn't get up again.

Biscuit was Peter Ranne's horse and the young Negro was attached to him. When Jedediah asked him if he couldn't get the horse back on its feet he replied, 'No, Captain, old Biscuit's give out for good.' Smith looked at the horse. It had simply dropped in its tracks from exhaustion and lack of food. The heavy pack-saddle had twisted in the fall and most of the stores were under the horse. Its eyes were already beginning to glaze.

Smith ordered the stores to be taken off and distributed amongst the other animals. It didn't make things easier for the survivors. Of the fifty animals that Smith had set out with, almost half were dead. Two of his party had deserted, taking their mounts with them. He took out his pistol and shot Biscuit, regretting there was nothing more he could do for the horse. 'It is always the most unpleasant of duties for a man to despatch an animal which has shown such willingness to follow him as its master.'

The men began to butcher the horse at once. Jed Smith turned to the red waters of the Colorado and wondered if things were any better on the far side. 'I decided to cross and make my way down from the opposite banks, but with the supplies again exhausted and my men further discouraged, I thought it most prudent to let them eat the horse and rest before urging them over.' But the far side was no better. There was the same rock and the same sparse vegetation for mile after mile.

Then towards the end of October 1826, the vegetation increased. Gradually a broad green valley came into sight, backed by hazy blue mountains. Willows were growing, and patches of mesquite producing edible beans. To the trappers it looked like an oasis filled with the riches of Paradise. They began to urge the animals forward, but the horses had no reserves left. They had lost a great deal of weight. They panted; their ears drooped. The gloss had gone out of their coats. Their hair was dry and standing on end. Some of them had ceased to urinate or defecate.

The men were in little better condition. Their cheeks were hollow and their eyes sunken. They were covered with dust, and every exertion was an effort. They were leading their horses. Most of them were carrying packs themselves to relieve the animals. Jed Smith walked in front as he always did. Behind him came his pack-horse carrying his belongings: bedroll, spare blankets, spare pack-saddle, traps and wooden chest. Despite his appearance, his spirits rose every step nearer he came to the valley ahead. 'I was now nearly destitute of horses and had learned what it was to do without food, eating like the Pai-Ulches [Pai-Utes] anything to which our Lord had given life, but the beginning of green vegetation gave fresh reason for hope.'

The hope was short-lived. Ahead of them stood two Indians with bows and arrows. They were six feet in height and powerfully built, tattooed and wearing breech-clouts. They were furious at the intrusion of Smith's party into their territory. 'It seemed that their inten-

tion was to fall upon us.' Someone shouted, 'Niggurs!' and the trappers formed up behind the 'Captain'. Despite their condition they were always ready to defend themselves. At the sight of the rifles pointing at them, the Indians disappeared.

The trappers' relief was momentary. A few yards farther and they could see one of the low log lodges of an Indian village. Ahead of Jedediah armed warriors began to appear. They carried bows and arrows already nocked into the strings. Some had long cylindrical clubs, brilliantly coloured. They were Mojaves, as different from the primitive Pai-Utes as could be imagined, and showing none of the latter's reticence. Nor were they half-starved. They stood across the path, barring it completely. Smith could also hear them in the bushes on either side of him. Traditionally Mojaves attacked en masse. It seemed to him they were only waiting for the first move from their leaders and then they would follow. If they attacked, there wasn't a hope for his party.

He gave his own commands. No one was to shoot. No one was to move or show any sign of fear. He put down his rifle and opened his 'possibles pouch'. It contained the odds and ends of his trade: flint and steel for making fire, a small box of castoreum for baiting beaver traps, spare gun flints, an awl, thread and a few keepsakes. It also contained some ribbons for trading. He took them out and slowly held up two pieces over his head.

The Indians waited. After a moment it was clear to Smith that curiosity was overcoming aggression. He might succeed in placating them if he moved very carefully. He took a step towards the lodge, then another. An Indian ran up to him with an arrow pointing directly at his throat, inches away. He had to stop or he would have walked into the man. Smith called to Rogers, 'If anything happens to me, get the men into a square immediately and prepare to defend your lives.' Then he looked at the tall Indian standing in his path. 'I offered gifts and prayed to God that they be accepted in the meaning they were given, for my party was not in condition to fight off an attack for long and the only way of escape led but to one of starvation.'

A young Indian came forward slowly and examined Smith for some time. At last he took the gifts from his hands and the tension between the two parties began to dissolve. Slowly Smith brought up the others. The Indians looked at them apprehensively, then gradually lowered their weapons. It was now safe to enter the village.

'The Nation I found in this fertile valley called themselves Ammuchabas,' wrote Smith in his journal. 'The men, much tattooed, were tall and of fine build and their only clothing was a short cloth to cover the extremes of their nakedness. Although of reddish brown skin, some of the women could have compared favourably in features with the fashionable ladies of St Louis.'

The Ammuchabas – Mojaves – were the most warlike of the Yuma tribes. They had lived on the Colorado for many hundreds of years. The men were all tall and dark, athletic and well proportioned; their average height was at least six feet. They were naked except for a breechclout. The women were plump and handsome, with bare breasts. They wore short petticoats of shredded willow bark around the waist that fell to the knees and which stuck out some eight

Mojave Indians, most warlike of the Yuma

inches behind, giving a 'bustle' effect that the white men found amusing.

Both sexes were barefoot. Their hair was long, often to the waist, and cut square across the forehead only a little above the eyebrows. When hunting, the men would tie it in loose braids behind. Occasionally it was caked with mud on top of the head to destroy the inevitable lice. Both sexes were tattooed with horizontal lines some six inches long, in blue, red and white. Sometimes the whole body was covered, sometimes only patches of it.

The trappers were very much taken by the attractive women, and Smith found much that was pleasant in the Mojave way of life by comparison with that of the Pai-Utes. The Indians lived in rectangular lodges with walls some two or three feet high. Interior height was given by excavation, and the thatched roof was supported by four central poles. 'The people cultivate the soil, and raise corn, beans, pumpkins, watermelons and muskmelons in abundance, and also a little wheat and cotton,' Jed Smith recorded. 'It was a happy providence that they accepted our gifts and friendship and I therefore remained fifteen days to allow my men to recuperate from their hunger and ordeals.' Of the general way of life of the Indians he was later to write: 'It would almost persuade a man to renounce the world, take the lodge, and live the careless, lazy life of an Indian.'

During the stay with the Mojaves, Smith's party was able to repair equipment that had been damaged on the journey south, and replace that which was beyond repair. Beans, corn and melons were traded. 'I was enabled to exchange my horses and purchase a few more off a few runaway Indians who stole some horses off the Spaniards. And I here also got information of the Spanish country, the Californias, the direction to which was indicated to me Westwards. But from what information I could gather the way was difficult and the Ammuchabas themselves no longer attempted its crossing.'

The men had no objection to Smith's plan to push on through the mountains to California. No white man had done it before, but it could hardly be worse than going back the way they had come. In any case, fifteen days of rest and 133 relaxation with the Mojaves had made them forget much of the hardship they had experienced, and – except for Wilson – the desire to be out on the trail was strong again in most of them.

By early November the party were ready to set out again with more than thirty new horses that Smith had managed to buy, and two Mojave guides. Almost immediately, they hit the terrible Mojave desert that the Indians had warned them about. It was worse even than the harshest descriptions of it – hot, without food, water or shelter, barren beyond belief.

They were in it for fifteen days, helplessly watching the horses die one after the other.

But finally they emerged into the beautiful and fertile valley of San Bernardino. They were the first whites (and one Negro) ever to cross the Rockies from the east into California.

What had brought them through without human casualties was Smith's superb gift of leadership. What sustained Smith was his unshakable belief in God, his determination to reach the goal he had set himself, and his frequent thoughts of home, 'of my parents, my brothers and sisters and friends, thoughts that sometimes gave pleasure for their memory, sometimes sadness for their distance'.

If the valley of the Mojave Indians had just seemed like paradise, the San Bernardino valley was surely Paradise. The air was cool and balmy, full of sweet perfumes. Fruit hung ripe on dark-leaved trees. The meadows were green, full of fat cattle. 'I got to admit there was times back there when I didn't think I'd see this,' said Arthur Black. Jedediah wrote, 'With the barren plain but a short distance behind us over the hills, it seemed to me that no man though he had travelled the whole majesty of the world could have set eyes on a more pleasant and fertile land.'

On 27 November the party reached the Mission of San Gabriel, a complex of long low buildings in the Spanish style with a central church. The Franciscans ran it under the supervision of Father José Sanchez. Smith 'was accorded a hospitality that might befit the King of Spain himself. I was shown their manufactories which were considerable in extent.'

The Mission was virtually a self-supporting society with 30,000 head of cattle and proportionate numbers of horses, sheep and hogs. It supported, according to Harrison Rogers' account, 'upwards of 1000 persons, employed men, women and children, Indians of different nations'. Father José explained the work of the Mission to Jed Smith. It grew tobacco and vines,

A model of Jedediah Smith and the party arriving at San Gabriel Mission, 1826

producing quantities of cigars and 'not only fine wines but brandies, whisky, gin and liqueurs'. Fruit was grown for sale outside the Mission. Beef and sheep were butchered and prepared for export. Mission Indians cured hides for transport to the coast where ships were waiting to take them to Europe. Tallow was made into candles and soap. 'I learned', wrote Smith, 'that they shipped to Europe each year many thousands of dollars worth of tallow and hides and many thousand dollars worth of soap.'

The hospitality that Smith received was also extended to his men. Rogers mentions 'boiled and roast meat and fowl, wine, brandy or ogadent, grapes brought as desert after dinner'. Understandably the Mountain Men took advantage of the quantities of drink available. Some drank themselves insensible. Others became unruly. Occasionally there was trouble between them and the local Mexican soldiers, dressed in their multicoloured uniforms decorated with pompoms and lace. Insubordination wasn't uncommon, caused largely by drink and boredom. On one occasion Smith found it necessary to flog James Reed, one of the blacksmiths, for his wild behaviour.

Father José Sanchez – 'old father Sanchez', Rogers called him – particularly impressed Jed Smith. He thought the priest 'the most Christian man I have yet met'. In many ways Father José represented the other side of Smith, the side that knew Greek mythology and was versed in the literature of exploration. There was something of the ideal father in him as well, which Smith may have responded to – kindly, protective, concerned for the great Mission family for which he was responsible.

Perhaps more important, this was one of Smith's closest encounters with the Roman Catholic religion. He had all the prejudices towards it of any strict puritan. He found in the event that they didn't stand up to rational investigation. And he was impressed by their tolerance. 'The people of the Missions expressed surprise at my journey,' he recorded, 'but that I was not Catholic made no difference to my treatment by those kind gentlemen and I was allowed full liberty of conscience on my Methodist beliefs.'

Smith wrote to the Spanish Governor of California to announce his arrival. He had previously displayed foresight by obtaining a passport from General Clark in St Louis in Clark's capacity as superintendent of Indian Affairs, and he enclosed this document. The Governor, His Excellency Don José Maria de Echeandia, called him to his office in San Diego.

There Smith was repeatedly interviewed to a point that amounted to interrogation. He wrote, 'In San Diego my arms were taken from me and I was looked upon with the greatest suspicion. I was not allowed to leave the country and for the third time was compelled to appear in the presence of the Governor to be questioned.'

The real nature of his position as far as the Mexicans were concerned began to dawn on him. He was a foreigner who had simply walked into their country from over the mountains. Perhaps they were right to be concerned about him. His thoughts turned to his beloved family in New England – father, mother, brothers and sisters. He had come a thousand miles from Rendezvous. From his base in St Louis he was almost 3000 miles. New England lay far beyond that. He wrote to his parents in his characteristic self-effacing way:

'Dear Father and Mother, Your unworthy son once more undertakes to address his much slighted parents.

'It is a long time since I left home and many times I have been ready to bring my business to a close and endeavour to come home; but have been hindered hitherto. The greatest pleasure I could enjoy would be the company of my family and friends, but whether I shall ever be allowed the priviledge, God only knows, I feel the need and watch and care of a Christian Church. I hope you will remember me before a Throne of grace.

'Perhaps you may think it strange that I do not give you some particulars with regard to what is passing . . .'

The fact was that Smith did not really know 'what was passing'. He had, actually, presented the Governor with one of the greatest dilemmas of his life.

The tall, thin Echeandia was already beset by worrying personal problems. He was ill. He was in the middle of an unhappy love affair that gave him no peace. Only recently he had moved his headquarters from Monterey to San Diego farther south to get clear of the coastal fogs that affected his health.

The Mexican state, whose government Echeandia represented, was very young. The revolution that had brought independence from Spain had taken place only four years earlier. California was the farthest-flung of its provinces, and it felt increasingly isolated and threatened from outside. Communications with Mexico City were intolerable. Every single order had to be taken across country, then carried by ship from San Blas to Monterey. Even the Governor's move to San Diego hardly improved matters. It still took weeks for him to get clarification of the instructions he received.

Politically, California's fear was of invasion from the sea. The British were in Oregon. The Russians were in Alaska. Both had the capacity – and most likely the will – to seize the country.

But traditionally it had always been accepted that the eastern boundary was secure. The Rockies and the deserts formed an impenetrable barrier in that direction. Now this comfortable myth was shattered. A tall blue-eyed American had walked clean through the wilderness with a party of trappers. By doing so he had presented Echeandia with a greater threat than any he had so far feared; the threat of invasion from the new America beyond the mountains.

Echeandia was in a quandary. Should he believe Smith's story that he was only a trapper looking for new beaver grounds? Or should he hold him until the government in Mexico City had considered the matter and given him instructions? 'The Governor', wrote Smith, 'is treating me as a spy.' Finally, Smith persuaded a number of Americans to vouch for him. They were the captains of ships lying along the coast waiting to load the hides and other produce for the east and Europe. Echeandia agreed that he could go, but only on condition that he go back the way he had come. And that was the last thing Smith intended.

He withdrew inland, apparently towards the desert, for 150 miles. Then he pushed north. By March he had covered 300 miles and found himself in the American River district. Wilson had

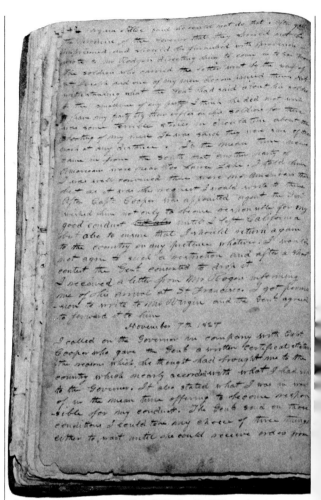

Jed Smith's journal, while in California

been giving trouble again. 'I discharged him and paid him off and he separated from us.' It wasn't the end of Wilson. He was picked up by the Californian Military Authority and put in prison. When he finally got back to America he sued Smith for underpayment, and won.

The American River district was rich in beaver. For almost the first time since they had left Rendezvous, the trappers were able to do what they had come to do. Day would dawn with a cry of 'Leve! Leve!' Some of the men were difficult to rouse, particularly if food and drink had been plentiful the night before. 'Darn breakfast, when a feller's fixed; I wouldn't git up for the fattest meat as runs on the peraera [prairie]; t'aint often this buffler is comfortable, an' when he is, he knows it.'

After breakfast, the party would move out in single file. The great danger was from Indians

A typical fur trappers' encampment, painted in 1837 by Alfred Jacob Miller

Scouts checked the track ahead. Guns were carried loaded across saddles. The Mountain Man was a skilled marksman. His way of life saw to that. He could reload and fire his gun three times a minute. At times he carried the ball in his mouth and spat it into the muzzle to save time. When pressed, he could dispense with the ramrod, compressing the charge by ramming the heel of the butt against the saddle.

At midday the party 'shaded out'. Horses were unsaddled, hobbled and allowed to graze. Men lay about smoking or dozing for an hour or so during the heat of the day, a process known as 'nooning'.

Mealtimes were irregular. Usually they were dependent on what was available to be killed. The evening meal, after camp had been made in some spot secure from attack, was usually roast or boiled meat. Buffalo was preferred, with dog a good second best, and the liver and intestines were eaten raw. Coffee was drunk in vast quantities – thick, sweet and black.

A 'hosguard' kept watch at night. The horses were hobbled. The men slept in their clothes with blankets of buffalo robes round them, loaded weapons at their side. In cold weather it was usual to sleep in pairs for additional warmth. Security was the prime consideration. The ideal campsite would have a river running along one flank and an open square in front, so that surprise attack would be more difficult.

Beaver trapping was a complex craft. A man had to stay in the water for long periods. Most Mountain Men suffered acutely from rheumatism as a result. The traps were set late in the evening near a beaver dam; they were jaw traps, activated by a plate and spring and secured to a stake by a length of chain. The trap was baited

Setting beaver traps. The men suffered rheumatism from working long hours in cold water.

with castoreum, a musky-smelling secretion taken from the beaver itself. It was rubbed on a twig suspended over the trap. The beaver, drawn to the smell, sprang the trap with a foot, by which it was then held fast until it died by drowning. A twelve-foot floatpole tied by a thong marked its position under the water.

The traps would be raised next morning, the beaver skinned on the spot, the trapper taking only the pelt, the castoreum gland, and the tail for eating. The pelt was roughly cured by scraping it free of meat, then stretching it to dry on a frame hoop of willow.

With the dismissal of Wilson and the discovery of beaver in such numbers, life now settled into a pleasant routine for Smith's party. 'My men were more content than they had been in the seven months since I left Salt Lake, happy to be trapping again,' wrote Smith. 'Even Arthur Black who had spent much

time in drunkenness at the Missions has become wearied of his own idleness. . . . The temperature remained warm and pleasant, and the waters have yielded pelts to a value of four thousand, five hundred dollars.'

But as the beaver pelts piled up before him, Smith had a new problem to occupy him. 'I must now make every endeavour to return to the Rendezvous at Salt Lake, to report to my partners and obtain fresh equipment.' The question was, which way should he go? Echeandia had ordered him back across the desert, but he had no intention of going. In the first place, the men wouldn't stand for it. In the second, curiosity made him wonder if there wasn't some other way through the mountains.

Towards the end of May 1827, Smith's party reached the Stanislaus Valley on the western slopes of the Sierra Nevada. Smith turned due east and pushed into the foothills. The result was

Trappers skinning beavers in the vicinity of the Oregon Trail. A contemporary drawing.

disastrous: 'I attempted to take my party across the mountain I named Mount Joseph in honour of the kind Father José Sanchez, to come on and join my partners at the Great Salt Lake, but I found the snow so deep that I could not cross my horses, five of which starved to death. I was compelled therefore to return to the valley which I had left.'

Another man would have gone round the Sierra, but not Smith. It was there; it had to be crossed. He turned back towards the forbidding peaks. 'This time I left the main party behind in charge of Mr Rogers, hoping I could return to them within about four months. . . . On the 20th May, 1827, I started with two men, Robert Evans and Silas Gobel, taking seven horses and two mules which I loaded with hay for horse feed.'

It took the three men eight days to cross the Sierra Nevada. It was a stupendous task. The pass that Smith had hoped was there didn't exist. The party had to cross the very summit of the mountains, at times half-buried in snow. The cold was intense. At night they huddled together round a small fire to stop themselves from freezing to death. 'It took all of my strength of will to prevent both myself and my men from giving up, but I forced a determination to go on.' The horses suffered even more than the men. There was nothing to protect them from the weather. They stood most of the time with the snow almost up to their bellies and the wind cutting into their hide. One fell into a ravine with a full pack on its back. It lay beyond their reach, buried in the snow hundreds of feet below. Another horse and a mule froze to death.

Beyond the mountains was the desert. The Great *Salt* Lake Desert. Cold was replaced by blazing heat; snow gave way to sand. It was a repetition of the earlier experience in the Mojave desert. The place was mercilessly arid, an unending expanse of waterless wilderness. Three of the remaining horses died and were cut up for meat.

Finally, it seemed that Smith had this time overreached himself.

'It now seemed possible, and even probable, that we might perish in the desert unheard of and unpitied.'

By 25 June the limits of endurance had been reached. 'As the sun of this day arose,' wrote Jed Smith, 'it seemed to us that we were the most unhappy beings on which it poured its floods of light.' The certainty of death that he now felt gave him a fresh insight into life: 'How trifling were all those things that hold such an absolute sway over the busy and prosperous world. My dreams were not of gold or ambitious honours, but of my distant, quiet home, of murmuring brooks, of cooling cascades.'

At ten in the morning the inevitable happened. 'Robert Evans laid down in the plain under a small tree, able to proceed no further.' Smith ordered him to his feet, but Evans couldn't move. Smith made the only decision possible: 'We could do no good by remaining to die with him and we were not able to help him along. . . . We left him with feelings only known to those who have been in the same situation.'

Within a mile or two, a hill appeared in the distance. A mirage, most likely. Even if it existed, it was too much to hope there would be water at the foot of it. Smith turned towards it. As he did so he caught sight of two Indians. He took cover with Gobel and watched them. They were making for the place where Evans lay. Some time after they had disappeared, two shots rang out from the desert. Gobel turned to Smith without speaking. It was clear enough to both of them what must have happened.

The hill was no mirage after all. Its form became clearer with every step. Smith pushed on towards it, pulling his half-dead horse behind him. He hardly dared believe it, but there was a patch of greenery ahead of him. He turned to Gobel and called to him, but his voice was cracked and almost inaudible. Gobel had seen the hill and was trying to run towards it, at times managing a few steps then dropping to his knees. The three remaining horses lifted their heads. They could smell the fresh grass. 'To our inexpressible joy, we found water,' wrote Smith. 'Gobel plunged into it at once and I could hardly wait to bath my burning forehead before I was pouring it down regardless of the consequences.'

The miracle wasn't over. As Smith turned back to look at the desert through which they had come, he caught sight of a thin column of smoke rising straight upwards in the distance. It dawned on him that despite the Indians and the shots, Evans might still be alive. He filled the big kettle with water and rode back into the desert. Evans was still under the tree. The rest, it seemed, had produced a partial recovery and he had fired the two shots and lit the fire as a signal for Smith. He hadn't seen the Indians at all.

He took the kettle in both hands and put it to his lips. 'He drank all the water, of which there was at least 4 or 5 quarts and then asked me why I had not brought more,' Smith recorded. The effect was almost instantaneous: 'I have observed that a man reduced by hunger is some days recovering his strength while a man equally reduced by the agony of thirst seems renovated almost immediately.'

Jed Smith reached Rendezvous at Little Lake at three in the afternoon on 3 July 1827. 'My arrival caused a considerable bustle in camp, for myself and party, having been away almost a year, had been given up for lost.' Of the nine animals with which he had left California only two had survived, 'and they were, like ourselves, mere skeletons'. He had covered the best part of 2000 miles and twice breached the great barrier of the Sierras.

The American west would never be the same again.

Jed Smith went back to California to collect the men and stores he had left there, returning by way of the Columbia River. He continued to map the area and spent some part of 1830–1 in St Louis preparing an elaborate map to accompany the publication of his journals. But his ambition no longer lay in the mountains: 'It has become my greatest desire to leave the wilderness and return to my family and friends: to live again in a civilised society and have the constant care of my

Indians and Mountain Men meet at Rendezvous on the frontier: a painting by Alfred Jacob Miller

A map of Jedediah Smith's travels. From *Jedediah Smith* by Dale L. Morgan.

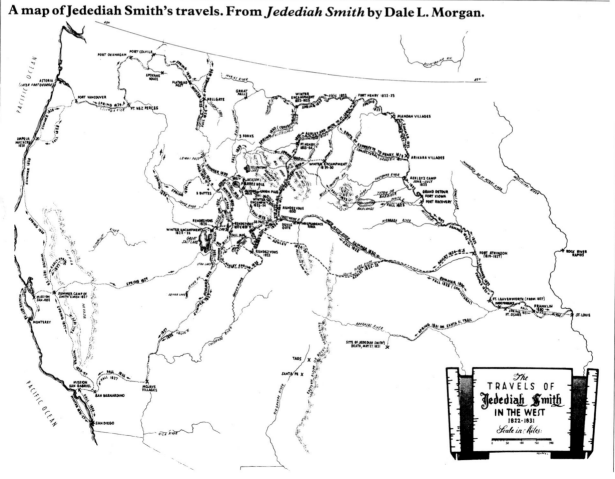

church. That I am presently prevented by circumstances only increases my longing, but it is now my determination.'

He never lived to see the wish fulfilled.

On 27 May 1831, he was alone on the Santa Fe Trail, riding as usual well ahead of the party of traders he was leading. He ran into a small band of Comanche Indians, 'the terror of the southern plains'. They were armed with trade muskets and eight-foot lances. The leader shot him without hesitation. Wounded, he still managed to make a fight of it.

But it was hopeless.

He was outnumbered by almost ten to one. They fell on him with lances, took his scalp and left him in a ravine for the dogs to tear.

The notes and maps he was carrying were scattered by the wind and never recovered.

When he died, Jedediah Smith was thirty-three.

An explorer almost inadvertently, his contribution to the development of the western United States is immeasurable. He did more than just cross over to California and back. He changed the known concept of North America, opened up the west and showed the way to one America. The mountains and deserts had been regarded up until then – even by the Indians – as impenetrable barriers that would for ever separate east from west. What Smith did was to demonstrate the essential unity of the two areas.

His personal ambitions had been very largely fulfilled. 'I started into the mountains with the determination of becoming a first rate hunter, of making myself thoroughly acquainted with the character and habits of the indians, of tracing out the sources of the Columbia river and following it to its mouth; and of making the whole profitable to me.' On almost every point he had been successful.

What sustained him throughout his journeys was his upbringing. He thought constantly of his family and his church. What sustained those he was with was his quality of leadership. It drew its strength essentially from his abiding concern for those he was responsible for: 'It is that I may be able to help those who stand in need that I face every danger,' he wrote. 'It is for this that I traverse the mountains covered with eternal snow . . . it is for this that I deprive myself of the privilege of society and the satisfaction of the converse of my friends.'

When his death was announced, the *Illinois Magazine* wrote, 'If there is any merit in untiring perseverance and terrible suffering in the prosecution of trade, in searching out new channels of commerce, in tracing out the courses of unknown rivers, in discovering the resources of unknown regions, in delineating the characters, situation, numbers and habits of unknown nations, Smith's name must be enrolled with those of Franklin and Parry, of Clapperton and Park.'

Friedrich Heinrich Alexander, Baron von Humboldt, was born into an upper-class (almost aristocratic) German family, and forced towards a commanding civil service position by a dominating mother. He broke away from the pattern of his background and parental ambition on his mother's death, to achieve in one, immensely long lifetime probably more than any other explorer in history.

In a life of ninety years, stretching from the age of Voltaire before the French Revolution until after the publication of Karl Marx's manifesto, he travelled, chronicled, recorded, investigated and discovered so much about this planet that, to this day, more than two thousand places – mountains, rivers, ocean currents, even a crater on the Moon – bear his name.

He loved passionately only once – another young man, early in his life. When that love died, the dominant driving force in him became his vision to produce a master work – a book in which he could put everything that was known about the Earth and the Universe, in which he could relate facts and discoveries in order to produce a unified view of nature. He wanted to prove the strongest connection between philosophy, and art, and geography, and history, and all the other sciences.

Many believe he did.

But since his death in 1859, the world of science and exploration has become a world of specialists. Humboldt was, therefore, perhaps the last universal man.

The Poison Master led the way. He was old and bent and almost naked. There was something of the wizard about him and Bonpland wondered if he could be trusted. Even Humboldt had lost a little of his assurance. He could still taste the bitter flavour of curare in his mouth. The old man had said it was harmless – as long as it didn't enter the bloodstream. If it was true, it seemed an extraordinary fact. If it wasn't, he could expect death, within a minute.

The village, itself, was primitive. The huts, made of sticks and leaves and twisted liana, were arranged round a central open space in which fires burned. The air was full of woodsmoke. And the smell of singed hair and cooking flesh was almost overpowering.

Some natives lay on the ground or sat with their backs propped against the huts. Some of them were incapable of moving, having been drinking heavily the fermented mash the women had prepared for them. Others were in a state of deep hallucination. They held little clay pots in their hands containing the drug niopo. From time to time they put the pots to their nostrils and inhaled.

But most of the tribe had gathered in the large central hut. A strange, thin, wailing music came from it as Humboldt and his friend, Aimé Bonpland, approached. Even now, Humboldt couldn't conceal a certain wry amusement at the incongruity of two well-dressed gentlemen wandering through this situation. He wondered what his aristocratic friends in Berlin and Paris would say if they could see him. Certainly, he would have some amusing stories to tell them – if he managed to live through the experience.

The scene inside the hut was extraordinary. At first the light was so dim it was difficult to make out more than the general movement of bodies, as they kept rough time to the music. Smoke from the fires filled the place, gradually filtering out through the loose thatch of the roof.

As his eyes became accustomed to the gloom, Humboldt made out some details. Food had been laid out and men were helping themselves to cassava cakes and leaves of cabbage. Women, some of them with children clinging to their backs, served drinks in stone vessels. Everyone except the Poison Master himself was drunk or drugged. To Humboldt, the scene was 'disagreeable to the eyes of civilised men'.

There were two musicians, squatting on the floor. They produced thin, plaintive sounds from a series of reeds that looked to Humboldt like the 'pipes of Pan'. In front of them, a circle of naked men held hands. The dancing – such as it was – was hypnotic. The dancers moved a little to left and then a little to right, in a series of repetitive and monotonous gestures that never developed and never seemed to come to an end. The scene of drunken stupidity was sickening to Humboldt. He turned to Father Zea, the Spanish missionary who now sat beside him on the floor. He wanted to ask him what exactly Christianity had done for these people during the three hundred years it had claimed to be responsible for them. But Father Zea was asleep.

Bonpland was appalled at what he saw beyond the musicians. Over the fire was a series of spits. He said in horrified disbelief, 'We're among cannibals!'

Through the smoke Humboldt could make out a number of bodies placed on the spits in a sitting position, roasting over the flames.

Then he saw that a row of cooked bodies, blackened by the fire, had been arranged along the walls of the hut. From time to time a woman went to one of them, tore off a limb and gave it to one of the men. Bonpland looked with revulsion at the bone he held in his hand. He said, 'We're eating their children!'

Humboldt got to his feet and went over to the spits. His scientific curiosity overcame his apprehension. He bent and examined the small creatures turning slowly over the fire. He had to agree with Bonpland – at first sight they did bear 'a hideous resemblance to a child'. But a closer investigation showed the truth to be less bizarre. 'Monsieur Bonpland was mistaken,' wrote Humboldt in his journal. 'We were not eating human beings but a species of monkey known as marimondes – or Ateles Belzebuth. Their taste was almost as disagreeable as their aspect.'

Even if Humboldt's worst fears had turned out to be justified, his insatiable curiosity would have led him on. As a child it had earned him the nickname 'little apothecary', because of his extensive collections of fossils and plants. Time had simply strengthened it, given it shape and direction. And led him deep into the Amazonian jungle. . . .

He was born on 14 September 1769, in Berlin, the second son of Major Alexander Georg von Humboldt. His father had been adjutant to the Duke of Brunswick during the wars under Frederick the Great, and the Duke was Humboldt's godfather. At the time of the boy's birth, his father was court chamberlain at Sans Souci, the King's country house near Potsdam. Schloss Tegel, the Humboldt family home where the boy spent most of his youth, was no more than a two-hour coach ride from Berlin. From birth, Humboldt was used to the company of courtiers, kings and scholars.

Schloss Tegel provided Humboldt with more than an aristocratic background of civilised human society. The house was set in open country, surrounded by forests, vineyards and mulberry plantations. The grounds contained exotic trees and plants, grown from cuttings taken from the Duke of Brunswick's own extensive collection. There could scarcely have been a better environment for a boy with a natural scientific curiosity.

Humboldt's father was a kind man. He was sociable and outgoing by nature, with a common-sense shrewdness produced by years in

Alexander Georg von Humboldt, his father

Schloss Tegel, the Humboldt family home

Frau Maria Elisabeth von Humboldt, his mother

145

the service of the state. He encouraged Humboldt and his elder brother Wilhelm to take an interest in the gardens of Schloss Tegel and in the countryside beyond.

His wife, Maria Elisabeth, could scarcely have been more different. Superficially, she had everything in her favour. She was good-looking, rich, well educated, stylish in her dress and manners. But there was about her a coldness that had a profound effect on Humboldt. She already had a son by an earlier marriage who had turned out to be troublesome, and her treatment of Humboldt and Wilhelm suggested a determination to keep the brothers in check from the start. In fact, it is doubtful whether she could have given them that warmth and open affection they needed even if she had wished. Human warmth and immediacy were not in her nature.

When he was six, Humboldt was given a personal tutor. His name was Campe. He was already well known for his translation into German of *Robinson Crusoe*, and although Humboldt never took to him, the idea of distant travel in strange romantic places might first have come to him from Campe. Campe was replaced in time by Kunth, a young man in his early twenties. Humboldt did take a liking to him. Kunth was a man very much under the influence of Rousseau's ideas, and his views on education and nature found a sympathetic response in the boy's developing mind. When Humboldt was ten his father died, and Kunth was probably the principal influence on the boy during his early teens.

Humboldt's relationship with his mother never improved. She took no interest in his collections of botanical and zoological specimens. She opposed his wish to be a soldier, insisting that he direct himself towards gaining a post in the civil service. When he was fifteen it seemed that matters might come to a head. Willdenow, the naturalist who had written *Flora of Berlin*, came to Tegel and encouraged Humboldt to continue his work in natural history. But his mother wouldn't hear of it. He was sent to the university in Frankfurt a.d. Oder, and later to Göttingen to read law.

But Humboldt's scientific drive was too strong to be crushed. He was prepared to do a

Karl Willdenow. He wrote *Flora of Berlin*

good deal to earn his mother's affection, but he couldn't suppress a natural talent. Göttingen was famous for its departments of philosophy and natural science, and Humboldt attended the lectures given in both of those as well as continuing his legal studies. More important, he met George Forster, who had travelled with Cook on the second journey to the South Seas. His imagination was fired. He knew he had to travel. The question was, when?

Like Amundsen who took up medical studies to please his mother, Humboldt continued to conform to *his* mother's wishes. She wanted as broad an education as possible for him. She believed in the eighteenth-century concept of the 'all-round man'. Goethe himself, the living epitome of the ideal, had visited Tegel. After she had moulded the boy to fit the concept, she wanted him to distinguish himself in the Civil Service. In 1791 he went to the Mining Academy at Freiberg. A year later, at the age of twenty-three, he was appointed to the post of Inspector of Mines for the whole Bayreuth and Fichtel Mountains area of Prussia.

For four years he fulfilled every ambition his mother had for him. He was, in fact, a brilliant Civil Servant. In a single year as a mining inspector, he doubled output. He drafted plans for a state pension scheme for miners, instituted social reform in the industry and even introduced evening classes for miners, which he paid for out of his own pocket. In 1793 he was appointed mining surveyor in Franconia and elected a member of the German Academy of Science.

A year later he was made Superintendent. He travelled to the Rhine and Brabant, and in December visited Goethe for a week in Jena. In 1790 Goethe had published his *Metamorphosis of Plants*, and there is no doubt that the acquaintance with Goethe kept alive Humboldt's scientific interest.

Humboldt's meteroric climb to distinction in the field his mother had chosen for him knew no limits. In 1795 he was promoted to the position of Supervisor-in-Chief, and his work took him to northern Italy and Switzerland.

Then, in 1797, his mother suddenly died. He was twenty-seven. He resigned at once from the civil service without apparent regret or second thoughts, and began to prepare himself for exploration. He studied astronomy and learnt how to take geographical bearings. He visited Goethe to discuss the projects he had in mind. They were vague and generalised. It was clearly necessary to make them more precise. He needed to decide exactly where he wished to explore, what he wanted to find out.

But, above all, he was free, at last, to do what he wanted. The sensation was intoxicating.

He went to Paris in 1798, with the vague intention of going on to Egypt to join a scientific expedition, following behind Napoleon's invading army. In Paris he met Aimé Bonpland. Bonpland was twenty-five. He was taller than Humboldt, dark, well built, good-looking, and in something of the same position as far as his own career went. His father and grandfather were surgeons and he had been trained in the family tradition. But his interest was in botany, which he was studying when Humboldt met him.

To Bonpland, a pooling of resources seemed an admirable idea. His own plans were even less

Aimé Bonpland, Humboldt's companion

precise than Humboldt's and the idea of joining Napoleon in Egypt seemed as good a way of starting his travels as any other. In October they left Paris for Marseilles, to take a ship from there for Algiers, and then overland to Egypt.

In Marseilles they hesitated. The ship they were due to take a passage on was wrecked, and while they waited, they began to wonder if Egypt was the right place after all. Humboldt wrote: 'From earliest youth I had dreamt longingly of travelling in faraway countries, rarely visited by Europeans. Even as a child, the sight of exotic trees, foreign maps and descriptions of tropic Zones, had been able to move me to tears. The yearning of my childhood was indeed a longing for a homeland for my soul.' It seemed suddenly that Egypt wasn't that homeland.

At the end of the year they turned to Spain. It wasn't to be their ultimate goal, but they both felt it would provide them with experience in geographical and botanical work until they decided where exactly to go.

By a quirk of fate similar to the one that much later was to give direction to Mary Kingsley – by 147 bringing her into contact with the traders from West Africa – Humboldt and Bonpland met d'Urquijo. D'Urquijo was Prime Minister of Spain, and the Queen of Spain's lover, a man of immense influence and able to obtain for them a unique entrée to the Spanish empire in South America. Hardly any foreigners were allowed in. But D'Urquijo liked the young men and took them under his patronage. The tales he told them of Spanish America seized their imagination. At last, the 'faraway countries' of Humboldt's dream had names and geographical locations. He set to work at once making preparations.

On 5 June 1799 Humboldt and Bonpland set sail from La Coruna. They sailed south for Tenerife, then south-west. The voyage was remarkable. Half the ship went down with typhoid and the destination had to be changed from Mexico to Venezuela. But as far as the two young men were concerned, every mile farther south increased their enthusiasm and excitement. On 16 July the coast of the New World came into view. Great palms rose from the shore; clouds of pink flamingos took off from the water. The extravagant sounds and colours were intoxicating. Bonpland pronounced the place to be quite simply 'paradise'.

'Our excitement on landing was enormous', wrote Humboldt. 'This was the moment I had dreamt of ever since my first tutor read me his translation of Robinson Crusoe! What a wealth of observation I shall collect here on the earth's construction. What happiness lies before me. I am dizzy with joy.'

His first action on landing was to take the temperature of the sand on the shore. It was, he discovered, 37.70°C.

Cumana, where they had landed, was a town of 18,000 inhabitants. The centre was full of churches and clergy, with well-spaced suburbs beyond. Humboldt wrote his first impressions to his brother Wilhelm:

'The town is still half-buried in rubble, for the same earthquake which, as is well known, caused such destruction in Quito in 1797 also destroyed part of Cumana. The town lies on a bay as beautiful as that of Toulon, behind an amphitheatre of 5 to 8 thousand feet high, wooded mountains. The houses are all built of white sina or atlas wood. By the side of the river, the Rio Cumana, there are seven monasteries and plantations which are like real English gardens.'

The two young men rented a house in the town and engaged two Negro women to look after them. At the same time they became acquainted with one of the canoe pilots on the river. He was a Guayaqui Indian by the name of Carlos de Pinero and he took them to meet his wife and children in the native quarter. Humboldt described the scene to Wilhelm:

'Outside the town one finds the dwellings of the copper indios: almost all the men of these tribes go naked. Their huts are made of bamboo and are covered with the leaves of the coconut palm. I went into one of them. The mother was sitting with her children, not on chairs, but on pieces of coral thrown up by the tide. They all had coconut shells before them instead of plates and were eating fish out of these. The doors of most of the houses are left open at night, the people are so good-natured.'

Everyone, in fact, was 'good-natured'. Everyone was curious to see these young men fresh from Europe, still wearing their white linen shirts and striped waistcoats and buckled shoes. The scientific instruments they had brought with them aroused particular curiosity. There were forty-two of them, each packed in its own heavy-duty wooden box lined with velvet. Everything was the very latest of its kind. The sextant was by Ramsden, the timekeeper by Berthoud, the demi-chronometer by Seyffert, the two telescopes by Dolland and Caroche. The two hygrometers for measuring humidity were made of hair and whalebone by Saussure and Deluc. Bennet and Saussure had supplied the two electrometers, made from gold leaf and elder pith. There was a snuffbox sextant by Troughton, for measuring at awkward angles, and an apparatus by Paul for determining height above sea-level by measuring the boiling point of water.

The compound microscope made by Hofmann aroused most interest amongst the elegantly dressed women of the town who called to see the young men. On one occasion Hum-

Humboldt and Bonpland at work in their South American 'laboratory' in Cumana

oldt took a louse from a servant's hair and put it under the instrument. The servant's mistress was horrified and threatened to dismiss the girl at once. Humboldt smiled, took a louse from the mistress's hair and put that under the microscope. The woman was speechles.'The poor lady was horrified to learn that the lice who lived in her servant's hair also inhabited her own.' It was the kind of situation Humboldt loved. He handled it with an easy charm that came to him almost too naturally, and at times lapsed into transparent flattery:

'I reassured her that there were thirty-seven different kinds of lice. And doubtless hers was an aristocrat among lice.'

At first the multitude of new sensations that crowded in on them at Cumana made rational and ordered scientific work impossible. Nevertheless, they were ecstatic at the opportunities. Humboldt wrote to his brother:

'Up to now we have been running around like mad things and in the first three days were unable to make any clear observations because we tended to drop one thing in order to grasp the next that offered itself. Bonpland says he will really go mad if there is not soon an end to the wonders. But more beautiful still than all the wonders individually is the impression conveyed by the whole of this vigorous, luxuriant and yet light, cheering and mild nature in its entirety. I can tell that I shall be very happy here.'

It was this 'nature' that Humboldt had come for. His wish was to build all its seemingly disparate parts into a unified, harmonious concept. 'Ceaselessly nature offers us new and fascinating objects for research. To analyse the atmosphere, measure its pressure, humidity and electrical charge, the strength of terrestrial magnetism, the temperature of the oceans, the geography of the skies and them to synthesise all these phenomena into a single philosophical viewpoint.'

The need to make sense of phenomena, to translate their condition, understand their meaning and position in the order of things, was central to Humboldt's view of the world. It wasn't sufficient just to discover or collect or classify. Science had to serve philosophy. 'Nature to me was no mere objective phenomenon, but a mirror image of the spirit of man.'

And it was in Cumana that Humboldt decided on a specific goal for the expedition. He and Bonpland would travel down the Orinoco, reach its source, and then confirm – or explode once and for all – the story of the Casiquaire, the unique natural canal that was supposed to join the Orinoco with the Amazon.

With a goal now clearly defined, Humboldt and Bonpland were anxious to set off. Humboldt had no fears about the conditions they were likely to encounter. Cumana had proved so much kinder than he had expected, he was led to observe that 'there seem to be no really hot places in the world'. He wrote to Wilhelm: 'I am not afraid of the hot zone. I have been in the tropics for almost four weeks now and have not suffered in any way at all. The thermometer always seems to show 20 to 22 degrees centigrade, but no more than that. But in the evening on the coast of Cayenne I found the cold uncomfortable at 15 degrees centigrade.'

The remaining time in Cumana was spent in acclimatisation and in building up a first collection of botanical specimens. Bonpland collected everything in triplicate, meticulously classifying and recording each item. Humboldt's excitement was unquenchable. After the staid world of the Prussian Civil Service, the country round Cumana seemed to tremble with the magic of nature. 'Like my revered friend Goethe, I worshipped nature,' he wrote.

It was at this time that Humboldt heard of the Mine of Fat. It seemed an extraordinary name for a cave. They were told it was the home of the Guacharo – the 'night bird'. The idea fascinated Humboldt. Guides led them to a great cave. They carried their torches high above their heads. Yellow light fell on the damp floor and threw great shadows up the walls. 'What strange

Mine of Fat cavern, home of the oilbird

vegetation sprouted in this forgotten darkness!' wrote Humboldt. 'Seed dropped by the so-called night birds, had germinated in the mould covering the rocks and the form and colour of the plants had been changed beyond all recognition. I was reminded of my research into photosynthesis in Freiberg. How Goethe would have loved to be confronted with this sight!'

Whatever Goethe's reaction might have been, that of the Indians was one of increasing terror. Pinero said that places that were never lit by sun or moon should be avoided by men. Humboldt dismissed such a view as humbug, reminding him that he was talking to a former Prussian assistant inspector of mines. 'Darkness is everywhere connected with death,' wrote Humboldt, remembering Pinero's fear. 'The Grotto of Caripe is the Tartarus of the Greeks. And the Guacharos which hover over the rivulet uttering plaintive cries, reminded one of the Stygian irds. The natives, restrained by their superstitions, refused to penetrate further into the cave. They still believed that the souls of their ancestors sojourn in the deep recesses of this cavern and that the plants were phantoms vanished from the face of the earth.'

Bonpland fired his gun into the darkness above them. One of the birds fell to the ground. Humboldt picked it up and opened its abdomen with a knife. 'We had found the Guacharo – or oilbird – up to this time a genus of bird thought to be merely legendary by students of zoology,' he wrote. 'Their peritoneum is loaded with fat which reaches from the abdomen to the anus, forming a kind of cushion between the legs.' The cave had proved to be exactly what the Indians called it – a mine of fat.

One thing marred Humboldt's stay in the 'paradise' of Cumana. His bungalow overlooked the market-place where, each morning, slaves were sold. Humboldt found the scene immensely distasteful. The idea of owning another human being, having the power of life and death over him and controlling all his movements, went against every principle in which he believed. He was a man of the French Revolution and believed in its political ideals. There was in him, concealed behind an exterior of slightly acid charm, a deep sense of compassion – and it was outraged by what he saw from his window. Yet there was nothing he could do about it, and – despite the revulsion he felt – the spectacle had a certain fascination.

The slaves were Negroes who had been brought by ship from West Africa. Humboldt calculated that of the 18,000 inhabitants of Cumana, 6000 were slaves – one third of the population. Each morning fifty or sixty were brought into the market in chains. Most of them were men, ranging from fifteen to twenty years old. Their naked bodies glistened with the coconut oil that they were forced to rub on their skin to give it an attractive black sheen. Many were slaves being put up for resale. They already bore the brands of their previous owners on their backs or arms. Prospective buyers examined them like animals, feeling muscles, checking skin condition, pushing open their mouths to examine teeth.

By November, Humboldt felt ready to tackle the Orinoco. On the sixteenth he sailed to Caracas with Bonpland and Pinero. For two months during the rainy season they catalogued the botanical and zoological specimens they had collected, and wrote detailed accounts of their discoveries.

Then on 7 February 1800 they left the coast and turned south.

Humboldt and Bonpland were on horseback. Pinero and a team of Indians followed on foot, leading two mules loaded with equipment and stores. At once the countryside and climate changed. The pleasant warmth of the coast turned into the fiercest kind of heat. Insects constantly plagued them. Humboldt realised how mistaken he had been in thinking there were 'no really hot places in the world'. At times the heat was so fierce they could only travel at night, resting during the day in hammocks slung between trees.

Further south conditions grew worse. 'In suffocating heat we crossed the great river plains, the Llanos, bigger than France, a hostile, sunbaked wilderness, inhabited by a strange variety of fauna,' wrote Humboldt. 'Everything here makes one think of the world in its primeval state. The fatigue of travelling beneath a burning sky, the eternal thirst one feels at a constant temperature of forty-one degrees Centigrade, the view of a horizon which seems forever in retreat – all these causes combine to make the Llanos melancholy and depressing.'

The great plain was covered in scrub and small atrophied trees. The cattle that roamed it in places were thin and sickly. At times there were monkeys and, occasionally, otters. Here and there snakes lay in the sun on bare rock faces. Water for men and animals became a serious problem. When they managed to beg some from the native farmers who were trying to scratch a living out of the dead earth, they had to filter it through linen to get rid of the filth it contained. Bonpland was doubtful whether, even then, it was safe. Humboldt said that if the natives drank it without coming to any harm, so could they. 'In spite of everything my health remains excellent,' he wrote.

South of the Llanos, conditions became less oppressive. 'Our physical circumstances improved as we approached the township of Calabozo, half-way between Caracas and the Orinoco. We were now collecting specimens of every kind,' wrote Humboldt.

And, as far as possible, they were also managing to live the life of civilised Europeans. Both men changed their clothes each day, washing the garments they had taken off in the nearest river or lake, shaving whenever they could with large open razors. They wore very much the costume they would have worn in Paris: soft-brimmed felt hats, white linen shirts, neckerchiefs of chequered linen, white cotton breeches. Over the shirts they wore striped waistcoats. The boots they wore came just below the knee.

In Calabozo they heard of *gymnotus electricus* – the South American electric eel. Humboldt once wrote a paper, when he was a student, on 'The Nervous and Muscular Irritation of Animal Fibres', and he had always had a keen interest in the electrical experiments of Galvani and Volta. He could hardly wait to investigate the powers of the electric eel. He made his headquarters in a farmhouse and set off to capture his first specimens. It proved more difficult than he imagined. Nothing would induce the Indians to go into the swamp water to pursue an eel. Humbolt wrote, 'Allegedly capable of killing man or beast by delivering shocks of six hundred volts, the *gymnotus* is a living, lethal, electrical apparatus.'

In the end, lured by the promise of money, local Indians hit on an idea. They would catch the eels for Humboldt after their electrical force had been discharged, and they would trigger that discharge with horses. 'The idea was that the horses would stampede the eels back towards the bank where we could catch them alive.'

It proved less simple than Humboldt thought. The horses raised no objection to going into the water. It was cool and they were thirsty. But when the terrible shocks began to hit them from invisible creatures in the water, they became hysterical. They turned and made for the bank, but the Indians beat them back with clubs and harpoons. When they were finally allowed to escape they sank to their knees on the bank, terrified and exhausted. 'The eels defended themselves against their attackers by discharg-

ing their electric batteries,' wrote Humboldt. 'The struggle between two such different species of animal offers a most rewarding and picturesque spectacle. Two horses drowned.' Bonpland was less objective. The whole thing had horrified him. He considered it nothing less than a massacre. 'But we have got the eels,' said Humboldt, pointing to the specimens that had been laid out on the ground. For him, it justified the suffering of the horses.

Some of the eels were put in a barrel of water. A frog and a turtle were dropped in beside them. The moment one of the eels touched them, they were electrocuted. Bonpland set up one of the electrometers to measure the electrical discharge, but there was no reading. Humboldt, impatient to discover where the electricity had disappeared to, put his hand into the barrel. A moment later he was screaming with pain. He wrote: 'I do not remember ever having received from the discharge of a large Leyden jar a more dreadful shock.'

For Humboldt, the eels raised a welter of questions: 'Why didn't the creature electrocute itself? Why wasn't it possible to observe the electrical discharge in the usual way? It did not register on the electrometer, there was no magnetic effect. . . .' On none of these points could he satisfy himself. 'After four successive hours of experimenting we felt a weakness in the muscles, a pain in the knees and a general sickness that lasted until the following day. But at least we could bring back to Europe the first scientific examination of this dreaded fish.'

Each night the men could hear the cries of jaguars in the jungle. Jaguars were the most dangerous and feared of the jungle predators. Bonpland and Humboldt were less bothered by them than the Indians. They took the view that they were safe enough in their hammocks, the instruments piled on the ground underneath them, as long as they kept a fire burning. But there were times when not a single piece of dry wood could be found and even Humboldt lay with his eyes open full of apprehension, listening to the roars of the beasts that surrounded them.

Occasionally they spent the night in some village and listened to the stories told by the Indians. At one place earlier in the journey they heard of a man who had suckled his son when his wife had died. Humboldt asked Bonpland to examine the man. His name was Francisco Lozano, and in Bonpland's professional opinion there was evidence that his small wrinkled breasts had been capable of producing milk.

Whenever they came across a mission, they found that the local missionary was always happy to welcome them for a night. Life in the jungle was tedious for many of these men. They were pleased – even overjoyed – to spend a few hours talking to interesting strangers from Europe. But Humboldt never took to them. He disliked their affluent way of life, with plenty of food and drink and all the work done for them by the Indians.

One he met had even forced the Indians to build twisting chimneys on his house – to remind him of the architecture of his native Aragon. Some were little more than fat boors. Others were sadists. As far as Humboldt was concerned, they only ever did him one positive service. They took his letters and saw that they were sent to his friends in Europe. Humboldt was a compulsive letter-writer. In the course of his lifetime he wrote and sent thousands and thousands of letters.

Humboldt's intention was to live off the land as much as possible. The expedition carried a little flour and sugar, but mostly they relied on the fish that Pinero caught with his harpoon and the game that was shot with bow and arrow. Pinero also did the cooking, using the campfire to grill meat or bake cassava cakes. The camp itself consisted of little more than the hammocks of the two explorers strung between trees, the fires to keep off the jaguars, and half a dozen cooking pots.

Each evening Humboldt and Bonpland made up their journals, writing sometimes for two hours by the light of the fires. From time to time they slapped at the mosquitoes, or put their heads into the smoke to get rid of the pests. Beyond the fires the jungle reverberated with noise. Monkeys howled, jaguars roared, parrots and other creatures screamed.

At San Fernando de Apure the expedition reached the northernmost tributary of the Orinoco. The harsh journey so far had done nothing to dampen Humboldt's enthusiasm. He wrote:

'As March ended we started to sail eastwards down the River Apure towards the Orinoco, towards the unknown. Accompanied by a convoy of gnats, jejenes and mosquitoes, we carried but few provisions. And we were armed with virtually nothing but our joie de vivre and our enthusiasm for scientific discovery.'

The expedition had acquired a large dugout canoe and Indians to paddle it. In the stern, a small shelter thatched with leaves had been built to keep off the sun. Humboldt had also been joined by another companion in San Fernando, the brother-in-law of the provincial governor. His name was Don Nicolas Sotto, and he had just arrived in Venezuela from Cadiz. Bonpland found him an irritating intrusion, but Humboldt found him amusing.

He was a splendid conversationalist, full of ready advice. When they pulled towards the shore and found the banks covered in gigantic crocodiles, Sotto announced, 'There is a simple way of escaping from the jaw of a crocodile. Just plunge your two fingers into his eyes.' Later, when the jaguars roared beyond the camp fires, he said to Humboldt, 'Should you meet a jaguar [in Spanish the word is tigre] in the jungle, just turn slowly and walk away. But slowly! Never look back, Señor Baron.'

The jungle never ceased to fascinate Humboldt. He could see in it that unity that so many scientists had seemed to miss. The jaguar was a part of it of course, but so was the ant. He marvelled, particularly, at the millions of tiny creatures that laboured ceaselessly around him. He was more afraid of them, he said, than ever he was of jaguars. 'They soldier on all day and half the night and they like to torture a tree to death. Nowhere else is death and growth so closely linked as in the tropical jungle.'

The nights fascinated him no less than the days. He wrote: 'Every night in the jungle a terrible cacophony begins . . . almost as bad as those cheap Spanish inns where one is kept awake all night by the twang of guitars being played in the next room.' It wasn't a complaint, merely an observation: 'I am in my element in this tropical paradise.'

The river broadened with every mile. They collected assiduously. Eventually their canoe was piled with botanical specimens. Cages swung from the stern canopy, full of monkeys and parrots. Pinero, in the end, became resigned to the fact that he was with a party of madmen.

Then ahead of them the river opened into what seemed to Humboldt to be almost a sea of deep brown water. He wrote:

'On April 5th we reached the junction of the Apur and the Orinoco, one of the most majestic rivers of the New World. We measured its width, at one point, as 3519 metres. It was to be our aim to explore and measure the Orinoco to create the first maps of this stream and to discover its link with the Amazon – the Casiquiare. A combination of stillness and vastness characterises its course. Indeed nature here seems to be greater than man himself.'

It was also on the banks of the Orinoco, a few days later, that Humboldt was to remember the piece of advice that Sotto had given him. The canoe had been beached and each member of the party was occupied with various scientific and camp-setting activities.

Humboldt walked into the jungle alone. It was alive with life. Monkeys watched him, peering down from the branches. A snake slipped quickly out of his path, its body as thick as an arm. Parrots in vivid blues, greens and reds screamed from the trees. It had on him the same effect that the West African jungle was to have on Mary Kingsley a century later. He found it the 'homeland for my soul'. It was what they both searched for.

Yet as he lost himself in its essence, Humboldt became aware that he was being watched.

The creature was on the ground, some distance ahead of him, half hidden by undergrowth and deep shade. He stopped and looked at it. It looked back, its eyes never moving from his face. His heart faltered. It was a jaguar, its head and flank a deep rufous brown broken by black spots. He could hear Sotto's voice: 'Just turn slowly and walk away'.

He turned, terribly painfully, slowly, trying not to move his arms at all. He wanted to run. He resisted the temptation. Very, very, slowly he began to walk. 'But slowly,' Sotto's voice seemed to be saying. He took ten paces, then another ten. The skin at the base of his skull and down his spine tingled. At any moment he expected to hear the creature, feel it knock him to the ground, smell its breath – meet death. The compulsion to turn round was almost irresistible. He could still hear Sotto's voice: 'Never look back, Señor Baron.' He didn't look back. He walked slowly back the way he had come, finally breaking into a run.

When at last he turned, sweat streaming down his face and into his neckerchief, the creature had gone. He had survived a face-to-face encounter with the greatest killer of the forest.

A day or two after Humboldt's escape, his friend Bonpland almost lost his life. The canoe was overloaded. In any case, its basic construction made it unstable. Now it was positively dangerous. Sotto, trying to ease his way past Humboldt to adjust the sail, knocked a book into the water. It was an important reference work and Humboldt made an instinctive grab for it. The canoe rocked and for a moment it seemed it would capsize.

Humboldt couldn't swim. There was no question of his going after the book. Before Sotto could stop him, Bonpland had pulled off his boots and jumped over the side. Sotto was horrified. The Indians stared at one another in disbelief. The river swarmed with piranha, the flesh-eating fish that hunted in packs and could easily strip a cow to its bare bones within a minute. When Bonpland surfaced, the book in his hand, Sotto shouted to him, almost hysterically. At any moment he expected to hear Bonpland scream, to see the first blood begin to stain the water.

Nothing happened. For some reason the piranha weren't there. Bonpland was hauled back on board unharmed. Humboldt was deeply impressed. He wrote: 'Never shall I forget Monsieur Bonpland's magnanimous devotion to me, a devotion of which he offered such ample proof on the Orinoco on April 6th, 1800.'

Three days later, the expedition reached Carichana, a mission village on the east bank of the river. The mission's three Franciscan friars had

---

Humboldt's camp on the banks of the Orinoco

shaven heads and long beards; their skin was yellow and wrinkled from the long-term malarial attacks from which they all suffered. Humboldt wrote: 'The poor missionaries received us in a spirit of friendliness and offered us all necessary information. They had all been suffering from tertian fever for several months.'

The missionaries were naturally curious to see two men walk out of the jungle, dressed in the height of European fashion. They could hardly believe Humboldt's explanation of his presence. 'The monks took us at first to be travelling hawkers,' wrote Humboldt. 'They simply could not believe that we had left our country to come to a foreign river to be eaten by mosquitoes.'

The missionaries lived in much the same way as their fellows further north, and to Humboldt their life seemed equally indolent. What work there was to be done was carried out by the Indians, in return for which they were given only red paint to daub on their naked bodies.

Humbolt could see little sign that Christianity had had any significant effect on the Indians: 'The colonised Indian is frequently no more a proper Christian than the independent heathen. Both are totally concerned with the needs of the moment – both are equally indifferent to Christian concepts.'

But it was still the cruelty and open slavery to which Humboldt objected most. One of the friars, Father Zea, offered to guide the expedition as far as the Rio Negro. When one Indian refused to go with him as crew, he thrashed him with a whip to a point where Bonpland cried out to him to stop. Father Zea talked of the need for 'discipline'. When Bonpland challenged him about the general status of the Indians, Zea said, 'The slave trade is necessary. . . . These savages are like children, only to be governed by force.'

Pizarro, three hundred years earlier, had expressed much the same sentiments.

Apart from the cruelty, Humboldt found the attitude out of which it arose philosophically unacceptable. 'The missionaries seemed to imagine that without acts of brutality the Indians would after a while stop serving us. A proposition I refuted absolutely. It was clearly the privilege of religion to console humanity for some of the evils committed in its name. Mon-

sieur Bonpland and I were shocked by the monks' tolerance of cruelty and slavery in their missions.' Nonetheless, Father Zea could be of inestimable value to the expedition. A compromise was necessary: 'Although he believed that all negroes were innately wicked and derived benefit from being slaves to Christians, I agreed that Father Bernardo Zea should act as our guide to the Rio Negro, an area he knew intimately.'

Whatever his views on Indians, Father Zea was a competent guide. He took them safely past the confluences of the Meta and the Tomo with the Orinoco, drawing Humboldt's attention from time to time to some natural feature he might otherwise have missed. Then as they approached Atures, it became obvious they would have to change into a different type of craft. 'We were approaching the Great Cataracts of the Orinoco. For several miles the broad river becomes obstructed by an archipelago of rocks and tiny islands, turning the water into foam.'

Their new boat was a smaller canoe, more manoeuvrable in the cataracts. It was crowded, and very uncomfortable. The stores and equipment had to be evenly distributed throughout its length, and when any one of them was required the boat had to be beached before it could be moved. But the boat had a great advantage over the previous bigger dugout canoe: it could be taken through the rapids whereas the dugout would have had to be carried round.

In any case, safety wasn't uppermost in the minds of those who travelled the Orinoco, as Humboldt wrote: 'It is neither the danger of navigating in small boats nor savage natives, nor the snakes or crocodiles that make Spaniards dread a voyage on the Orinoco. It is simply 'el sudar y las moscas – the sweat and the flies'.

According to Humboldt's calculations, 'the vertical height of the Orinoco's notorious rapids hardly measured more than twenty-eight feet'. Nonetheless the going was hard. There was no let-up in the oppressive, humid heat, or in the swarms of mosquitoes. Sometimes the Indians rowed for more than twelve hours at a stretch, with Humboldt feeding them with cassava cakes and plantains. At other times the men dropped into the water and dragged the canoe through the great beds of sharp rocks that lay in the river. Occasionally they beached to regain their strength, lighting smoky fires and burying themselves in sand to keep the mosquitoes at bay.

Beyond the rapids, they continued due south. There was no change in the jungle that lay on either side, nor in the appalling climate. From time to time they passed little mission houses, with their groups of aimless 'Christianised' Indians outside. There was a similarity between all of them, in Humboldt's view: a 'natural indolence' and a 'lack of any inclination to work'.

The Indians who had managed to stay clear of Spanish influence, for the most part were different. The Caribs who lived at the confluence of the Apure and Orinoco were splendid people, with finely developed bodies and thick dark hair, energetic and enterprising. Even the Guahiboes had an independence that Humboldt admired. The sight of them struck terror into his Indian guides. They were notoriously savage, hunting in packs on the upper Orinoco, their small rafts tied together in a great network. Animals and humans were all the same to them. They struck them down with their bows and poisoned arrows. But, for some reason they left Humboldt's party alone, and the real enemies remained 'el sudar y las moscas'.

On 1 May the expedition reached San Antonio de Yavita. A few miles south lay the Rio Negro, the great northern tributary of the Amazon. It took four days – and the combined efforts of twenty-three Indians – to carry the canoe and supplies from the Orinoco to the Negro. It seemed to Humboldt that a canal could usefully be built between the two rivers. Characteristically he immediately drafted a memorandum on the point to the King of Spain, and asked Father Ceresco of the San Antonio Mission to see that it was dispatched.

Humboldt's intention was to sail south down the Negro until he reached the Casiquiare. If the legend that puzzled the 'armchair geographers of Europe' was true, the Casiquiare would take him back to the Orinoco. From there he could retrace his steps northwards. But he reckoned without that ubiquitous bureaucracy that lies in wait for the traveller – even in the wildest of jungles. No sooner had he discovered the Casiquiare than he was arrested.

Humboldt and Bonpland were detained by three ragged soldiers armed with machetes. 'We had been told of a small border post called San Carlos, on the Brazilian frontier. But we had not anticipated an enforced visit,' Humboldt observed wryly. The post was no more than a few ramshackle huts in a clearing, with the Spanish flag flying from a pole in the middle. The commandant was in his thirties, arrogant and stupid. He was impervious to Humboldt's charm. 'The Commandant informed us that the authorities regarded us as spies. We were under arrest for concealing plans to spread dangerous new ideas and to be deported.'

If anything, Humboldt was amused. He was well used to bureaucracy. Bonpland, on the other hand, was furious. He was, he protested, a citizen of France. It meant nothing to the commandant. He had his orders. One foreigner was much the same as another. Humboldt wrote: 'The Commandant's suspicions had been aroused by our scientific instruments which in these regions had never before been in the hands of private individuals. Why indeed should two foreigners want to come so far to collect plants and measure rivers which did not even belong to them? Monsieur Bonpland reacted rather more violently than I had expected. He was not used to the ways of officialdom.'

Another man might have disappeared for ever in the maze of bureaucratic machinery that operated in the far-flung posts of the Spanish empire. But Humboldt had friends and he knew from long experience how to manipulate that machinery, how to use the system rather than confront it. Within days, he and Bonpland were free. He dismissed the affair as being hardly worth noticing: 'Border incidents like this may have served to amuse the local garrison. But the Commandant's superiors clearly thought otherwise. As he pointed out – one has friends.'

The insect swarms along the Casiquiare were frightful. The mosquitoes had proboscises long and rigid enough to pierce the thickest clothing. But Humboldt never complained and his enthusiasm never dimmed: 'The uninhabited, uncharted shores of this Casiquiare river had

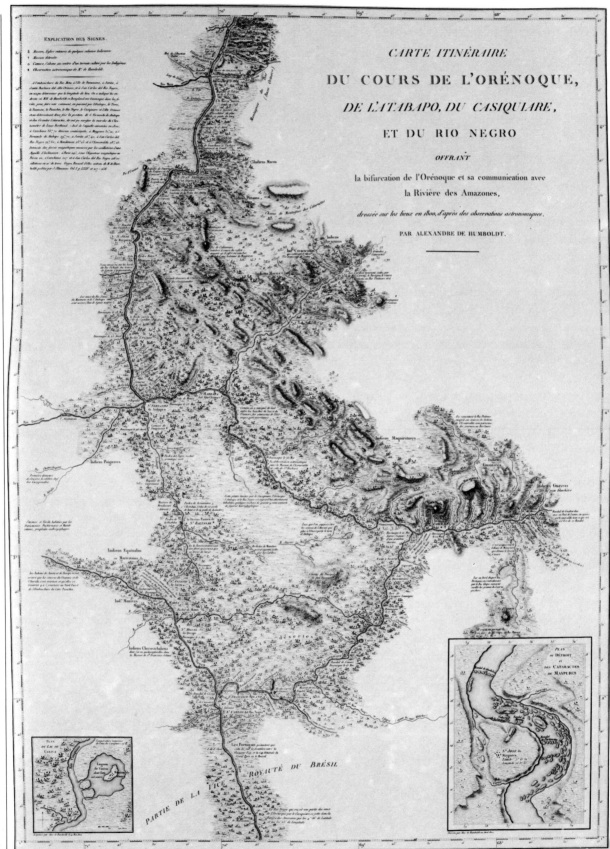

CARTE ITINÉRAIRE

DU COURS DE L'ORÉNOQUE,

DE L'ATABAPO, DU CASIQUIARE,

ET DU RIO NEGRO

OFFRANT

la bifurcation de l'Orénoque et sa communication avec
la Rivière des Amazones,

dressée sur les lieux en 1800, d'après des observations astronomiques.

PAR ALEXANDRE DE HUMBOLDT.

158

From *Atlas Geographique et Physique du Nouveau Continent*, by Humboldt and Bonpland

occupied my imagination like the legendary El Dorado. It is the only natural waterway in the world connecting two such gigantic river systems. What a prize of scientific knowledge with which to confront my friends in Berlin and Paris!'

However, Humboldt's excitement ceased to be infectious. Father Zea, Sotto and Bonpland suffered too much along the Casiquiare to be anything but depressed. They were covered in insect bites, their faces puffed and blistered. Food was scarce, the river water foul. Bonpland in particular was feeling unwell. 'Our spirits were beginning to suffer,' wrote Humboldt. 'We were in a desperate position, almost without food. We were reduced to eating ants and dry cacao, washed down with river water. This deadened our appetites for a few hours. And such was the humidity in this region that we could not even make a fire. For seven days – for the first time since leaving Cumana – I was unable to write my diary.'

For twelve days they moved north-east along the Casiquiare, 'through jungle overhanging so close to the river that we could see the jaguars – large jaguars I may add – up in the trees, because the dense undergrowth prevented them walking along on the ground'. Then, 'during the third week of May, we at last left the Casiquiare to rejoin the wide expanse of the Orinoco'.

The expedition had finally established the truth of what until then had only been rumours. There was, indeed, an extraordinary natural canal that joined the two vast and separate river systems of Orinoco and Amazon. Yet no one was in a condition to rejoice over the discovery. 'We approached a remote and terrible place called Esmeralda', wrote Humboldt. 'By now all of us had reached a stage of desperate hunger and total exhaustion. Here the insects are still more cruel and voracious than elsewhere on the Orinoco – Esmeralda gives the traveller the impression of having arrived at the end of the world.'

The party turned eastwards. Humboldt intended to reach the source of the Orinoco, then turn and retrace his steps, plotting its entire course as far as the mouth. They passed Mount Duida, a mountain which is not a volcano, but which still appears to be, 'belching fire and smoke', very close to where the river rises. But in the end they were driven back, though not by hunger or mosquitoes. 'The fierce and cannibal Guaica tribe prevented us from going further.' They returned to Esmeralda.

Humboldt had done what he set out to do. And he never stopped his compulsive collecting. The rigours of the journey had not tempered his insatiable craving for new knowledge and new experiences. Even the 'terrible place called Esmeralda' had facets that could excite him. He saw Indians shooting game with bows and arrows, animals dropping dead in their tracks. He wrote:

'Suddenly my spirits were unexpectedly revived. We had come to the source of a great legend of the New World – that of the poison curare. Up to this point no precise notion of its use and effects had reached Europe. Were Monsieur Bonpland and I to be the first white men to observe one of the Indians' most closely guarded scientific secrets?'

For killing, it seemed, curare was 'better than your black powder'. It was totally effective and absolutely silent. 'We found an old Indian chemist, known as the Poison Master, who proved to be only too willing to introduce curious strangers to the mysteries of his science,' wrote Humboldt. 'The Poison Master told us that the curare, the secret of whose manufacture is passed on from father to son, was far superior to anything made beyond the sea – like gunpowder. The chemical operation appeared to be extremely simple. A harmless liana – "bejuco de mavacure" – is converted into a black sticky tar. Its bark contains the poison. The herb juice kills silently when it enters the bloodstream. It is used for hunting and, strangely enough, as a remedy for stomach ache. The natives use it to kill birds and animals. But there is absolutely no danger in swallowing curare unless there is an abrasion on lips or gums.'

It was at the festival to celebrate the 'poison harvest' that Humboldt and Bonpland mistook roasting monkeys for human children. . . .

By the end of May, the expedition had renegotiated the Maipures rapids, on their way back down the Orinoco. The journey had taken its toll, yet there were still fascinating things to be seen. Humboldt wrote: 'Weakened by the ceaseless plague of insects and the insufficiency of edible food, we abandoned our plan to reach the source of the Orinoco and continued our journey downstream. Our poor canoe was by this time filled to an almost dangerous degree. But Father Zea and Don Nicolas Sotto would soon be leaving us to return to their missions. And with some additional effort we would be able to reach our next goal, the caverns of the extinct Atures tribe. . . . The prospect excited me.'

The cavern of Ataruipe lay at the foot of a steep mountain, beyond a cliff of wet rock. It was a vast cave, revealed, eventually, to them by the torches the Indian guides carried. Inside, arranged in rows, were large baskets. Each basket contained a human skeleton, placed in either a squatting or sitting position. The bones had been whitened by the sun, others were dyed red or formed into mummies and covered with a distinctive-smelling resin. In addition to the baskets, there were great painted jars almost six feet high, filled with the bones of entire families. In all, the place contained the remains of 600 people.

For the Indians who accompanied Humboldt and Bonpland, the cavern had a deep religious significance. They were in awe of it. It was said that a hundred years previously the entire Ature tribe had been driven into the cave by more powerful neighbours, and had died there. Humboldt, cutting through the superstition that he felt surrounded the place, took some of the bones. The natives were horrified. Humboldt wrote: 'Though I tried to tell our Indians that we were only collecting old crocodile bones, they were able to smell the resin. They clearly believed that their ancestors would be enraged by our scientific zeal. All these centuries of Christian teachings – and what has it achieved?'

By now, it was clear to Humboldt that the expedition was at an end. The party was exhausted and Bonpland had become seriously ill. They pushed towards the river's mouth – first north, then east – as quickly as possible. Bonpland had been suffering from a fever for almost six weeks, but sheer curiosity and determination had kept

1. Friedrich Heinrich Alexander, Baron von Humboldt, played in the film by Matthias Fuchs.

2. In the rain forests there was a myriad of botanical specimens to be collected. By the end of their exploration 3000 new plants and flowers, never before seen in Europe, had been catalogued and listed.

3. The electric eels fascinated Humboldt. He had the Indians drive horses into the water in order to observe the effect of the eels' stunning shocks on the frenzied animals.

4. The first cataracts. Humboldt and Bonpland changed to smaller dug-out canoes which could be portaged. During the whole exploration their canoes were invariably completely laden with specimens and animals they had collected.

5. There was no alternative. Faced with some of the thunderous cataracts, they had to carry their canoes, their possessions, their specimens, around the obstacles. All the time the heat and the mosquitoes took their toll.

6. Their canoe was dangerously overloaded with baskets, jars and boxes of collected specimens, animals and plants. Neither man was willing to sacrifice one item, one specimen.

(continued p.161)

7. Both of them made notes assiduously, despite mosquitoes, fever, and jungle predators. Humboldt's eventual account of his travels in the Americas amounted to more than a quarter of a million words.

8. Their collecting and cataloguing never stopped. There was no aspect of science or discovery that did not attract their attention and enthusiasm.

The film was directed by Fred Burnley, and shot in the Venezuelan jungles, on the Orinoco river, along the route taken by Humboldt and Aimé Bonpland.

him going. Now he lay on a stretcher on the floor of the boat, hardly able to move. It was typhus.

Humboldt nursed Bonpland with all the care of a devoted friend. Father Zea and Don Nicolas Sotto had, by then, left the expedition, and Bonpland was desperately ill. Even so, the boundless optimism and excitement that were so thoroughly a part of Humboldt's make-up were never far from the surface. He wrote:

'I felt a very deep sense of satisfaction. Soon we would be in Angostura, the capital of Guyana. And the first stage of our American expedition would be achieved. We had explored fifteen hundred miles of uncharted territory, we had scientifically measured more than fifty places and had taken important magnetic readings of the Casiquiare Canal, thus proving its existence. We had collected dozens of animals strange to European eyes and botanised diligently, gathering twelve thousand plant specimens, many of them new to science. I had written much and made a hundred different sketches. . . . '

Humboldt reached Angostura on 13 June. Bonpland was still desperately ill. 'Poor Monsieur Bonpland', wrote Humboldt. 'I could never hope to meet again such a shining example of loyalty, bravery and industry.' They were looked after and given rooms by the Governor of Guyana, Don Felipe de Ynciarte, who also gave Humboldt every possible help in nursing Bonpland. For prescriptions and treatment, Humboldt had to rely on Bonpland's own diagnosis of his condition. He was given angostura bitters – as they were in Angostura. Finally Bonpland began to respond to care and treatment. The fever broke and his temperature began to fall. It was a long time before he could travel again, but each day saw a gradual increase in his strength.

To the people of Angostura – as to nearly everyone they had encountered – it seemed extraordinary that two civilised Europeans should have journeyed into the uncharted jungle to find a river. But to Humboldt there was more to it than that. He tried to explain his motivation to Don Felipe de Ynciarte: 'The most important result of all thoughtful exploration, Excellency, is to recognise in the apparent confusion and opulence of nature a quintessential unity – to study each detail thoroughly yet never to be defeated by the contradictions of a mass of fact, to remember the elevated destiny of homo sapiens and thereby to grasp the spirit of nature, its essential meaning which lies concealed under a blanket of multifarious manifestations. . . .'

For four more years Humboldt and Bonpland travelled in the Americas. They explored jungles, visited volcanoes, and climbed mountains, reaching altitudes never before attained by any human being in history, nearly 20,000 feet, a quite fantastic achievement by the standards of the day. They explored Mexico for a year. But Humboldt's prolific letter-writing and diary-keeping appears to have dried up during his travels in Mexico. There is only a fragmentary record by him of his personal experiences.

In 1803, their fame having travelled ahead of them, they visited the United States. On his arrival in Philadelphia, Humboldt sent a letter to President Thomas Jefferson, presenting his compliments, expressing his admiration, and enclosing a parcel from the United States Consul in Havana, which Humboldt had just visited.

The American Philosophical Society made him a guest of honour. He was fêted, wined, dined – and finally invited to lunch with the President. America had just acquired Mexico. The President wanted a first-hand briefing from a distinguished recent visitor. He got it. It was to be the first of many significant endorsements for Humboldt's achievement.

In June 1804 he, Bonpland and another colleague sailed for Paris.

The private two-man expedition of Humboldt and Bonpland had cost Humboldt a third of his capital. They had travelled 6000 miles through remote rain forests and volcanic mountain ranges, and had returned to Europe with 60,000 plant specimens, a wealth of zoological, geological and ethnographical data; and notebooks, sketches and theories.

Humboldt and Bonpland, high in the Andes of Equador. A painting by F. G. Weitsch.

Humboldt as a personality was distinguished, witty, charming and educated, but, before his travels, not sufficiently interested in the company of women to marry. Indeed, as a young man he had developed a passionate homosexual relationship with an army lieutenant, Reinhard von Haeften. Haeften eventually married and Humboldt wrote a final letter, filled with pain and anguish, detaching himself from the relationship. The end of that affair probably also marked the end of Humboldt's active sexuality.

Bonpland, with whom he never exchanged a cross word, and in whose company he lived constantly for five years, was undoubtedly the 'truest' of friends. But only that.

Bonpland himself eventually returned to South America, after a disastrous marriage to a young French prostitute. There he was arrested by the mad dictator of Paraguay and virtually imprisoned for nine years. He never returned to Europe, and after his release lived as a primitive, settling down with a Brazilian girl for the rest of his days. By the end of his life he couldn't use a knife and fork. He died at the age of 85.

Bonpland also failed to contribute all that he should have to the great work which carried his name, *The Voyage of Humboldt and Bonpland*. When he first returned to Europe he was given the job of classifying all plant material gathered on the expedition and of publishing the results. There were about 60,000 specimens, representing 6000 species, more than 3000 of them new to science. But Bonpland procrastinated. The indefatigable fieldworker proved incompetent when it came to desk-work – temperamentally unsuited to it. And in the end he managed to edit only four of the seventeen volumes of *South American Botany* which were finally published.

He had been appointed Superintendent of the gardens at Empress Josephine's retreat at Malmaison, outside Paris, and there created one of the most beautiful flower gardens in the world.

Engravings of botanical specimens from Humboldt and Bonpland's *Plantes Equinoxiales*

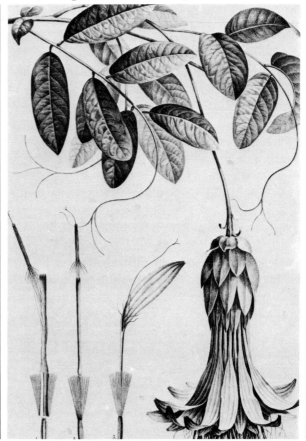

After Napoleon divorced Josephine, Bonpland became her confidant, and was with her when she died in 1814. It was shortly after then that he returned to South America and there finished his days.

Humboldt, who was thirty-five years old on his return to Europe, stayed in Paris until he was nearly sixty. He eventually took his place once more in Prussian society, and was finally summoned to join the court in Berlin. For thirty years he worked on a detailed account of his journey with Bonpland, finally publishing it in thirty-five volumes. But more than *The Voyage of Humboldt and Bonpland*, the public was attracted to his narrative account of his travels, *Personal Narrative of Travels to the Equinoctial Regions*, in three volumes, which was published in 1814.

His fame and reputation grew enormously. More than a thousand places, mountains and areas – even ocean currents and a crater on the moon – bore his name during his lifetime, and continue to do so. In his sixtieth year he returned to travelling, taking a scientific party through Russia and Siberia as far as the Chinese frontier.

His last thirty years were spent in a modest house in the grounds of Sans Souci and in his flat in Berlin. He wrote and lectured. From time to time he led diplomatic missions. Honours were showered on him from scientific and diplomatic quarters. At one time it was said that, apart from Napoleon Bonaparte, he was the most famous man in Europe. He was also, by then, pathetically poor. His publishing did not bring him riches. His travels cost him money. The distinguished orders and awards carried no pension or honorarium.

He continued to work until the end of his life on his 'master work', *Cosmos*, the book in which he wanted to put everything that was known about the earth and the universe. He received an average of 3000 letters a year and replied to at least 2000 in his own hand – and at his own expense. The third volume of *Cosmos*, his *Vision of the Nature of the World and the Forces of Earth*, came out in 1850. And in 1858, at the age of eighty-nine, Humboldt, by now the grand old man of European science, published the fourth volume. He prepared to write the fifth.

He toiled away at it, already having suffered a slight stroke in 1857, and a severely weakening attack of influenza in 1858. But he completed only eighty-five pages. He died on 6 May 1859, in his ninetieth year. He was buried in the family grave at Schloss Tegel.

For Humboldt, exploration was an act of complete dedication, of reverences. 'I worship nature,' he wrote. To him nature was 'a mirror image of the spirit of man'.

Compared with the men who discovered and opened up vast areas of the globe, unknown tracts of our planet – men such as Cook, Columbus and Pizarro – Humboldt was hardly an explorer at all.

Even his discovery of the natural canal, the Casiquiare, as a link between the Orinoco and the Amazon, was not original. The Spanish commandant at San Carlos, when he heard what Humboldt planned to do, shouted: 'You have come all the way from Germany to do this? No one here has doubted the communication for the past half a century!'

And yet, our whole view of the world was changed by the publication of Humboldt's account of his journey. If he did not discover new territories, then he discovered new ways of looking at the old ones. His achievement, his exploration, therefore, took place as much in the area of philosophy as in the field of geography. His fine mind did produce a unified view of nature. The achievement, though substantial, may not seem unique. Poets, mystics, visionaries had done as much before. But where Humboldt's view of nature *was* unique was in its being supported by scientifically acceptable fact.

He lived from the age of Voltaire before the French Revolution, and by the time he was dead Karl Marx had written the *Communist Manifesto*.

He was, perhaps, the last universal man. By the time he died the world had become a place of specialists. He was also probably the first truly scientific explorer, the founder, in fact, of the modern sciences of geography and geophysics.

James Cook 1728–79

James Cook, son of a Yorkshire farmer, learned his seamanship in the North Sea merchant coastal trade, went on to become the greatest maritime navigator and map-maker of his age – and probably of all time.

His unique skill, almost genius, in navigation made him first choice when the Navy (traditionally, at that time, a place for aristocratic preferment) needed to appoint a man who could lead a three-year-long expedition round the world and map and name all that he discovered in what was then unknown.

But James Cook was more than a merchant seaman turned naval officer; more than a working-class Yorkshire farmer's boy made good. He was one of the first truly enlightened naval commanders. He cared for his men and their well-being. He protected them – and they survived to describe their incredible journeys. And in Cook's days one in three of the men who set sail in His Majesty's ships was usually certain to die.

Cook was, too, a man who observed, understood, and believed he should not disturb, the native way of life that he found.

Sadly he was even able to forecast that the Polynesian and Pacific paradises he discovered for the rest of the world might well be changed for ever, even destroyed, by the 'civilised' invasion that would follow him.

James Cook was asleep when *Endeavour* struck. The impact flung the cot in which he lay against the side of the little cabin.

He jumped out, steadying the cot as it swung on the four ropes which suspended it from the deck beams. He paused only to light the lantern, then rushed on deck – still in his drawers.

He had known at once what it was.

Endeavour had struck the reef – and stuck fast. Even now he could hear the sharp spears of coral riving and tearing at the timbers.

Half the crew were already on deck ahead of him, the others piling up quickly from below. There was urgency, worry, but no panic. Orders were called out by the officers in firm, unemotional voices. The men leaped to respond, sails were furled, and three boats lowered to take soundings round the *Endeavour*. They were in waters where no man had sailed, and which no man had mapped before, 12,000 miles from England and home, off an alien shore. Was this the end for Cook and *Endeavour*?

Joseph Banks, one of the five remaining 'gentlemen' on board, said later: 'The officers . . . behaved with inimitable coolness void of all hurry and confusion.' But there was confusion among the poultry and animals kept on deck, some of which had escaped from their pens.

It was a clear, moonlit night, with only a light breeze from the south-east. Earlier, they had shortened sail and hauled off shore a mere six points from the wind. The intention was to stretch off all night, as Cook always did when surveying, 'hovering' in the same area rather than dropping anchor. At 6 pm the water was fourteen fathoms deepening to twenty-one – safe enough. Then, at nine, when all hands but the night watch were below in their hammocks, the water suddenly shallowed, the leadsman calling twelve, then ten, then eight fathoms. All hands were stood to stations ready to turn *Endeavour* into deeper water, even perhaps to anchor. It was a false alarm. The water deepened again, all hands were dismissed from watch. By ten they were back in twenty fathoms.

An hour later, however, they were back in seventeen fathoms. Then, before the leadsman could take another sounding, they were on to the reef and in danger.

***Endeavour* in rough seas**

Banks described it as 'a wall of coral rock rising almost perpendicularly out of the unfathomable ocean, always overflown at high water commonly seven or eight feet, and generally bare at low water. The large waves of the ocean meeting with so sudden a resistance make here a most terrible surf, breaking mountains high. . . .'

Two of the boats that had been lowered, a 16-foot yawl and a 12-foot pinnace, began taking soundings. The depth of water round the *Endeavour* varied from three feet to twelve fathoms. Cook ordered the third boat, a 20-foot long boat, to carry the starboard bow anchor well clear of the *Endeavour* and drop it. The long boat then took the second anchor, laid it out and tried to pull the ship clear of the reef, kedging off. It was hopeless. She was transfixed on the coral spikes.

It was also clear now that the situation was more serious than had at first appeared. The ship had struck at high tide. As the tide receded, she began to sink more securely into the coral. By midnight the outer wooden sheathing of the hull, together with the false keel, shattered under the weight of the ship herself. Pieces of planking floated to the surface and were tossed aside by the waves breaking over the reef. To the 'gentlemen' standing clear of the activity it seemed as though nothing could prevent the vessel breaking up. They might make it to the shore in this barren area, in one of the boats, but the chances of ever seeing England again, twelve thousand miles away, were slim. Yet still there was no panic. 'All this time the seamen worked with surprising cheerfulness and alacrity,' said Banks. 'No grumbling or growling was to be heard: not even an oath.'

Cook himself had absolute confidence in the ship. He had spent his youth, learned all his seamanship, in round-bottomed, shallow-draught vessels like this, carrying coal from Whitby in the north-east of England, down the coast or across the North Sea. In normal conditions she could stand up to almost anything the sea could do to her, though without a deep straight keel she wasn't the most comfortable thing to sail in. She was tough, designed that way. But she hadn't been built to withstand a hammering on a coral reef in the South Seas. She had to be lightened, if she was to be saved. And she had to be saved.

Apart from the hundred souls aboard, there were the priceless specimens that Banks and his party had been collecting, and six months of detailed chart-work round New Zealand and up the coast of eastern Australia.

It was 12 June 1770, still well before dawn.

The crew began to lighten her by throwing everything that was dispensable over the side. They began with the decayed stores, then the empty barrels and store cases. Then the oil jars and the stone ballast went. Finally they put the iron cannon balls over and six of the carriage guns weighing half a ton each, marking them with oval wooden 'nun' buoys in case there was a chance of recovering them later.

By 11 am nearly fifty tons of iron, guns, stores and ballast had been thrown over the side. It wasn't enough. High tide came, but it still needed another foot or two of water to refloat her. And, as the tide fell again, *Endeavour* began to make water. Two pumps were set up to take the water out of the hold. Everyone was turned to at the back-breaking work on the pump handles – officers and civilians, as well as the men. Each pump consisted of a wooden tube running from the main deck to the hold. The water was lifted by means of a lever-operated piston and system of valves. It was exhausting labour. Shifts of fifteen minutes each were all the men could manage before collapsing.

An hour later, the ship had slipped on the coral, heeling over several degrees to starboard. The situation looked critical. Throughout the afternoon the pumps worked without pause, but did no more than hold the position. By 5 pm the two remaining anchors had been taken out by the long boat and dropped, one on the starboard quarter and the other right astern. But as the tide began to rise again the ship made more water and a third pump had to be set up to keep pace with it.

By 9 pm the situation was hopeless. The ship had righted itself, but that only increased the leak. The three pumps couldn't control the crisis. An attempt was made to bring a fourth pump into use, but it was unsuccessful. Banks gave up all hope of seeing *Endeavour* saved and began to pack his chest, ready to abandon her.

Cook never faltered. His voice was calm, full of assurance. There was no question in anyone's mind about who was in command.

There seemed one last hope of getting her clear. When the tide began to rise again around 10 pm, everyone who wasn't on the pumps was called to the capstan. What Cook hoped was that *Endeavour* could be hauled off on her anchors. It was a calculated risk. As long as the ship remained stuck on the reef there was still a good chance of getting everyone off her, into the boats and on to the coast. But once she was dragged clear, across razor-sharp coral, she would fill very quickly. 'This threatened immediate destruction to us as soon as the ship was afloat,' wrote Cook. 'However I resolved to risk all and heave her off.'

She came clear at 10.20 pm, with a great tearing sound under the hull. As Cook had foreseen, the leak at once grew worse. The pumps worked

Endeavour, **careened for repairs after the Great Barrier Reef collision**

even more furiously, hauling up water and spewing it over the side. The hold filled to 3ft 9in. with sea water before the pumps showed any sign of holding the leak; then gradually the situation stabilised. 'No men ever behaved better than they have done on this occasion,' wrote Cook of those men who manned the pumps throughout the night.

But it was clear that something more was necessary if the ship was to be brought safely to the coast and repaired. At noon the following day there were still twelve miles of sea between *Endeavour* and land. The men couldn't pump for ever. They couldn't pump very much longer at all.

Cook decided to try 'fothering'. A sail, some twenty feet square, was laid out on deck and covered in oakum and wool. When the sailmaker had cross-stitched the material into the cloth, the whole thing was covered in dung from the animals' quarters to form a thick sticky coating, with another sail making a sandwich. This was dropped over the ship's bow and manoeuvred on warps from port and starboard against the hole in the planks. The pressure of the sea forced it inwards, effectively blocking the leak. Within half an hour the hold was pumped dry.

What Cooked had so abruptly discovered – and only just survived to report to the British Admiralty – was the Great Barrier Reef: twelve hundred miles of coral barrier guarding the northern half of the Australian east coast. And what had caused the near-disaster was, in fact, the very thing that had led the Admiralty to appoint him to the command of *Endeavour* in the first place. He had an ability, amounting to genius, for charting new territories. His brilliance as a navigator allowed him to take a ship closer to an unknown coastline than anyone else would have dared. It says a great deal in confirmation of his skill that on a voyage lasting three years his only miscalculation was this one, on the Barrier Reef.

The ostensible reason for the voyage that had brought him eventually to the Australian coast was a brief to accompany a party of scientists to the South Seas and return, as part of a circumnavigation of the world. The scientists' purpose was to record the transit of the planet Venus across the Sun, as Observed in Tahiti, in order to improve astronomical and navigational knowledge.

But a more significant reason, though one that was kept secret, was the instructions to Cook to discover the great continent thought at that time to lie south of Australia. If it was there then it was to be charted – and claimed – for Britain, before the French or the Dutch could get their hands on it.

Years before, Cook in his charting of Newfoundland and the St Lawrence had already demonstrated the capacity for such a task. Even so, it may still be thought surprising he was selected. The British Admiralty was notoriously inflexible and class-conscious in deciding which of its men were fit to be officers. Cook at the time was thirty-nine and, before his voyage, still non-commissioned. Despite his proved ability, his background was not promising in terms of promotion and preferment.

He was born on 28 October 1728, at Marton in north Yorkshire, the son of an agricultural labourer. At the age of twelve he was apprenticed to a haberdasher in the coastal village of Staithes. Six years later he went to Whitby, still on the north-east coast, and apprenticed himself to Walkers the shipowners. He did well and served with them for a number of years in the coal trade between Newcastle, Norway and the Baltic.

At twenty-seven, a tall, tough, good-looking and confident man, he was an established mate in the merchant service, with a reputation as a navigator and a sure future. But he joined the Royal Navy, 'having a mind', he said, 'to try my fortune that way'. He could only join as an able seaman, although it was a rank well below his considerable abilities. What secured his steady though modest advancement from then was his diligent study of mathematics and astronomy, the basis of all navigation. Such men were indispensable to the Navy. He was promoted in time to the senior non-commissioned rank of Master, and specialised in marine survey.

In 1759 – he was thirty-one at the time – he was given the command of the sloop *Grampus*, and subsequently of the *Garland* and then the *Solebay*. For the next eight years his meticulously precise surveys produced accurate charts of the coasts of Newfoundland and Labrador, and much of the eastern St Lawrence. Inevitably his work brought him increasingly to the notice of the more practical men inside the Admiralty. One commanding Admiral said of him: 'He is a person of great capacity, well qualified for greater undertakings.'

And those 'greater undertakings' were offered him in May 1768, when he was given instructions for the South Seas voyage. He was quickly commissioned as a lieutenant and given command of *Endeavour*. She had been built four years earlier in Whitby as a collier. The Navy Board had bought her for a little over £2000 and

spent another £5000 refitting her as a survey ship. The masts and yards were replaced, cabin and deck accommodation extended, and she was given a second skin of planking filled with large flat-headed copper nails to protect her from attack by *Teredo navalis*, the voracious tropical boring worm.

She was a workmanlike vessel, ugly and practical in appearance, measuring 106ft from stem to stern and 30ft across the bows. Her virtue as a survey vessel lay in her comparatively flat rounded bottom and her consequent shallow draught – only 14ft. 'A better ship for such a service I never would wish for,' said Cook when he saw her.

But one problem that *Endeavour* posed was accommodation. She had been built, as a coastal trader, for a crew of nineteen. Now she was expected to take almost a hundred naval seamen. Though the refit had done a great deal to overcome the problem, nevertheless the ship would be crowded – even for the Royal Navy. And now the problem was to be aggravated further. Cook received a totally unexpected communication from the Admiralty:

'The Council of the Royal Society have acquainted us that Joseph Banks, Esq, Fellow of the Society, a gentleman of large fortune, well versed in natural history, is very desirous of undertaking the same voyage. They have, therefore, earnestly requested that in regard to Mr Banks's great personal merit and for the advancement of useful knowledge, he, together with his Suite of eight persons with their baggage may be received on board. . . .'

Joseph Banks was an intensely enthusiastic amateur botanist, with that genuine, if dilettante, interest in natural history that was characteristic of a number of English eighteenth-century gentlemen. He was twenty-five, had come into a fortune four years earlier, and owned large estates in Lincolnshire which gave him an income of £6000 a year (in present-day terms something more than £50,000).

Two years earlier he had made his first scientific expedition, visiting eastern Canada to bring back a collection of insects and plants that had impressed the Royal Society. Equally impressive was his offer on behalf of Cook's expedition, to contribute to the expenses. It no doubt influenced the Admiralty's decision to recommend Banks to Cook. Banks admitted later that his contribution amounted to about £10,000.

Banks brought with him a friend, Dr Daniel Carl Solander, a pupil of Linnaeus and a distinguished botanist. Also in his party was Herman Spöring, a 38-year-old Finn who acted as Banks's scientific secretary. Alexander Buchan was a young topographical artist Banks had brought to do landscapes of the places visited. He was an epileptic, and his illness was to prove fatal before the voyage ended. And there was Sydney Parkinson, a draughtsman of twenty-three, a small thin man whose job was to make accurate drawings of the specimens Banks collected. Banks also brought along four servants, two of them Negroes, as well as two greyhounds to retrieve the specimens he shot. The Navy gulped and kept cool, and Cook managed to keep a straight face when they all boarded in Deptford.

Whatever Cook thought when the message concerning Banks reached him from the Admiralty, the two men took a liking to one another. It was fortunate. The voyage that Banks thought was simply going to take him to Tahiti and back was, in the end, going to last three years and take him round the world. The totally dissimilar backgrounds of the two men may actually have helped the relationship. There could be no question of competition between a member of the rich and landed upper class and a man who had been a haberdasher's apprentice at twelve.

On 19 August 1768, the *Endeavour* left Plymouth for the south. As far as was possible, she was a completely self-supporting community, almost an eighteenth-century village. She contained two carpenters, a cook, a surgeon and his mate, an armourer and a sailmaker. Between them there were few situations which could not be coped with. In addition, there were twelve marines whose duties were to act as guards. The average age on board ship was under twenty-

The Deptford dockyard where *Endeavour* was fitted out. She sailed from here on 21 July 1768.

five. The youngest, servant to Molyneux the Master, was twelve. The oldest, John Ravenhill the sailmaker, was forty-nine.

Cook had picked his supplies with care. There was coal which, until it was needed, acted as ballast. He had medical supplies for two years: drugs, saws, amputating knives, bone nippers and turnscrews, forceps and needles. There were tents, and even cork buoyancy jackets – since very few men could swim. There was gunpowder for the muskets, a forge and blacksmith's tools for the armourer, and a quite efficient distilling apparatus for purifying sea water.

There were the instruments to be used for navigation and surveying: compass, drawing materials, a chain, a theodolite, a mercury tray to form an artificial horizon. And there were also the more complicated instruments for sighting the transit of Venus that Cook and Charles Green, the Admiralty astronomer, would require: clocks, telescopes, quadrant, sextant, watch.

When it came to supplies, Cook was above all concerned for the well-being of his men. His care, in particular, to provide a balanced diet that would save them from the suffering and death that scurvy could cause, is similar to Amundsen's attitude more than a hundred years later.

Scurvy was still rife in the Navy in Cook's time. On long voyages it was commonly expected that perhaps fifty per cent of the crew would die of the disease. James Lind, Physician to the Royal Naval Hospital at Haslar, reported that on one ten-week voyage he had as many as 350 cases.

Scurvy was an abominable disease and it seems surprising that more official action wasn't taken against it. According to an account of 1736, scurvy 'appears with red spots on the arms and legs especially, which afterwards turn black and then blue; there is an extraordinary weakness, a redness, itching, and rottenness of gums and a looseness of teeth. . . . [The] mouth became stincking, [the] gummes so rotten that all the flesh did fall out.'

As early as 1593, Sir Richard Hawkins had discovered the effectiveness of orange and lemon juice in the diet as a way of preventing scurvy. Lind revived the idea. Yet it was not until 1795 that the Admiralty prescribed its use officially, after which scurvy disappeared. Before that date, freedom from scurvy depended entirely on the enlightenment of the particular captain. Fortunately for the crew of *Endeavour*, Cook was one of the most enlightened seamen of his day. He made himself acquainted with Lind's work, and although he did not adopt his precise anti-scurvy diet, he did utilise Lind's device for extracting salt from sea water and his method of fumigating living quarters with wood smoke; as well he used orange and lemon juice.

Cook's view was that scurvy was caused by lack of fresh food. Apart from the usual provisions of salt pork or beef or horse, biscuits, oatmeal and cheese, he provided pickled cabbage, portable soup (solid blocks of meat extract), onions and dried fruit. He kept six dozen hens alive in coops aft of the quarterdeck, to provide fresh eggs and meat. Throughout the voyage additional fresh meat was taken aboard whenever possible. On one occasion pigs were embarked; unfortunately they died of cold. On a more successful occasion sheep were penned on deck and appear to have survived satisfactorily.

Cook attached importance to onions as part of a diet designed to combat scurvy, issuing them to the crew every couple of days, though there was no fixed routine to this. Wort, the infusion of malt which ferments to form beer, was another scurvy preventative – and at times cure – that Cook had provided on *Endeavour*.

It was of course one thing to provide the right foods, another to get the men to eat them. They usually tasted terrible. In the first place, there was the problem of the ship herself, certainly as far as the inexperienced sailors who comprised Banks's party were concerned. *Endeavour* turned out to be a ponderous performer, with a top speed of no more than eight or nine knots. In heavy seas she rolled so badly that the very thought of food was nauseating. Banks himself was terribly sick during the early stages of the voyage.

Another problem was habit. Most men in the crew were used to eating salted horse flesh at sea. The chicken and other fresh meat that Cook provided seemed to them insipid by comparison. Some of them even refused it altogether:

'Punished Henry Stephens, Seaman, and Thomas Dunster, Marine, with twelve lashes each for refusing to take their allowance of fresh beef,' wrote Cook.

On another occasion Cook decided that the psychological approach might be more effective:

'Saturday, September 17th. Issued to the whole crew twenty pounds of onions per man. Served sauerkraut and portable soup to the ship's company. . . .The sauerkraut the men at first would not eat until I had it dressed every day for the officers' table and permitted all the officers without exception to make use of it. This practice was not continued above a week before I found it necessary to put everyone on board to an allowance, for such are the tempers and dispositions of seamen in general that the moment they see their superiors set a value upon it – it becomes the finest stuff in the world.'

On 12 September 1768 *Endeavour* reached Madeira, from which Amundsen was later to make his dramatic announcement regarding his real destination. Madeira was nothing but a re-victualling station to Cook, but a vital one. When he set sail from it, it was to begin the long haul south, round Cape Horn into the southern Pacific. Things had gone well so far, on the first leg of the journey. Morale was high. Punishments had been few. There had been no cases of scurvy. Life had settled into a comfortable – even easy-going – routine.

Below decks the seamen slept in incredibly cramped conditions, fourteen inches width was all that was allowed for each man's hammock; what little kit he had was stored in a canvas bag underneath it. For the men, every day of the week, every single moment of the day, was regulated. They were woken at six every morning by the bosun's pipes and a great shout of 'Whe-e-ugh, all hands on deck, aho-o-oy! Do you hear the news there below? Come, jump up, every man and mother's son of you!' Those who weren't out of their hammocks and on deck quickly enough for the bosun's liking were given a touch of his rattan cane. Bosun's 'starters' were part of Navy life. As far as he was concerned there was never an excuse for being late. There was no question of waiting for a man to find his shirt or breeches; they all slept in their clothes.

Until 7.10 am decks were scrubbed with sea-water and 'holystones' – sandstone or pumice blocks the size of a Bible. Then until breakfast was piped at 7.15 am hammocks were brought up to be aired in the nettings on the quarterdeck or maindeck. If the weather was rough, they were lashed up below. After breakfast the lower deck was cleaned and the brasswork polished.

At 9 am 'clear for divisions' was piped, and every man appeared ready for inspection when the drum beat. The only men excepted were the quartermaster at the wheel and the lookout on the top of the main mast. Cook attached great importance to the occasion, since cleanliness was something he insisted on. It was a necessary part of discipline, of course, but more important in his eyes it was essential if the ship was to be kept healthy. He insisted that every man wash at least once a week, using sea water and a pumice stone.

A sailor wearing the same clothes Cook issued to his men

Clothing had to be changed twice a week. There was no uniform in the modern sense, though Cook required a certain similarity of dress: off-white canvas blouses, blue baggy breeches, a round tarred hat. The men were clean-shaven, with their hair pulled back in a pigtail.

Cook introduced a number of refinements into the accepted techniques for keeping the ship clean. He used a method suggested by Lind for fumigating the lower deck – wood smoke. He then found that one of the problems caused by doing that was the lack of ventilation. Hatch covers were left open in good weather, but there was no way of completely evacuating stale air. Lind's technique helped. Cook found that by lowering buckets of burning wood and coals into the lower deck he could create sufficient up-draught of hot air to pull fresh cold air in from outside.

Lind had suggested the use of vinegar on all woodwork below decks to prevent the spread of disease. The process was known as 'curing'. Cook added gunpowder to the vinegar to produce a still more effective mixture, even though the smell was powerful. His concern for the health of the ship was certainly justified. During the whole three-year voyage of *Endeavour* not a single death resulted from the spread of infection within the ship. Even the few symptoms of scurvy that appeared were cured within days by draughts of the concentratrated orange and lemon juice that Cook provided.

After Cook's inspection of men and ship, the morning would be spent at stations. Men in the rigging checked halliards, sheets, yards, tackle; repaired sails. Then there were 'waisters', older or less skilful men who seldom went aloft and were given the job of 'worming' cables to prevent them chafing against rocks when the anchors were down. The 'idlers' – carpenters, sailmaker, cooper and the others who never went on watch – were constantly occupied in repairs. Even the Marines, whose job was to police the ship, were kept busy with musket practice and drill.

A drum was beaten for lunch at noon. And at 12.30 pm grog was served – half a pint of rum diluted with a quarter-pint of water. This was not the only ration of alcohol. A 'basic provision' was a pint of wine or a gallon of beer every day. The quantity of alcoholic drink carried on board at the beginning of the voyage gives some indication of the consumption that took place: 1200 gallons of beer, 1600 gallons of spirits, ten hogsheads, sixteen barrels and sixteen half-hogsheads of wine. There is little wonder that after the Christmas celebrations that took place off the eastern coast of South America Banks wrote in his journal:

'Christmas Day, all good Christians, that is to say all hands, got abominably drunk so that at night there was scarce a sober man on the ship. Wind, thank God, very moderate or the Lord knows what would have become of us.'

Cook, who had issued the traditional extra ration of grog, was characteristically more matter-of-fact: the crew 'were none of the soberest', he wrote.

During the afternoon, all hands except those on watch had time off. Some fished, others smoked and chatted on the quarterdeck. One or two played pipes and fiddles, some carved figureheads and miniature ships out of wood. The day finished at 8 pm when 'to hammocks' was piped. Chatting was allowed until 8.30 pm. After that, everyone below was silent – by order.

Even Cook's own day was similarly regulated. He inspected the men and the ship and issued any punishments he thought necessary. He was humane in this respect, rarely ordering floggings and even then usually keeping well below the maximum of twenty-four lashes that the regulations permitted for such crimes as theft, desertion and sleeping on watch.

The main activities for Cook and his officers – in particular Lieutenants Hicks and Gore, the second and third in command – revolved round the Great Cabin, set high in the stern, immediately aft of Cook's own quarters. It was here that the sightings taken were converted into geographical positions; here the store figures were checked; here the needs of the expedition were discussed, and plans made to meet them. Banks and his party also used the Great Cabin, to examine the specimens of fish they had already started to collect on a sheet of green baize laid out on the deck. Like the rest of *Endeavour*, conditions in the Great Cabin were cramped. The place was used as chartroom, mess, recreation room, library and writing room for twelve men. It contained a large table, two settees, lockers and bookcase, in a space 15ft by 20ft with less than 6ft headroom.

As they neared the Horn, Banks was full of enthusiasm. For five months he had been cooped up at sea. His own cabin measured 10ft by 6ft; the Great Cabin scarcely gave him more room. Even the decks were too cluttered with coiled ropes, ships, boats, guns – and chicken coops – for him to move about easily. He was anxious to go ashore, and indulge his interest in botany. *Endeavour* sailed right up to the Horn itself. The weather was, as always, bad, but not impossible: the notorious Cape Horn storms were stilled.

Cook anchored in the Le Maire Strait on the eastern side of Tierra del Fuego on 16 January 1769. His intention was to take on wood and water and whatever fresh meat and vegetables he could find. At once, Banks took advantage of the situation to set off inland with a small party to collect plants.

Cook soon had reason to be concerned about Banks, whom he had grown to like as a man, and for whose safety he was responsible. The weather had remained bad, with hail and snow. The place was inhospitable in the extreme. Even the natives were unappealing: red-skinned, heavily built and clumsy in their movements. Their huts were crude conical structures without any furnishings. They had nothing that might have been regarded as 'civilised' – no art, no musical instruments.

'Mr Banks and his party not returning this evening gave me great uneasiness,' Cook wrote.

The weather had caught Banks unprepared. His enthusiasm carried him some distance from the ship before he realised what he had committed his party to. The two black servants couldn't trek further so he left them in the care of

The natives of Tierra del Fuego, from a wash drawing by Buchan

a sailor. In the end he himself had to give up, but by then it was too late to get back to the ship or the others, so he took the rest of the party into the shelter of a wood and lit a fire. Everyone, including the two half-frozen greyhounds, huddled round it. 'Now might our situation be called terrible,' he wrote in his journal afterwards.

The storm continued through the night, then gradually abated. 'About six o'clock in the morning we immediately thought of sending to see whether the poor wretches we had been so anxious about last night were alive. Three of our people went but soon returned with the melancholy news of their both being dead.' According to Banks, the two black servants had opened the little rum barrel that had been intended for the whole party. It was his view that they had collapsed more with drink than exposure, and been frozen to death during the night.

'About noon they returned in no very comfortable condition,' wrote Cook after the rest of the party had returned safely to *Endeavour*. 'What was still worse, two Blacks – servants to Mr Banks – had perished in the night with cold.'

The ship sailed.

Beyond Tierra del Fuego, life on board *Endeavour* returned to its ordered routine. As well as the daily chores and watch keeping, there was exercise with the ship's guns and small arms on Monday; boat work on Tuesday; sail-handling on Wednesday. Thursday was a make-and-mend day; Friday spent restacking stores. On Saturday the whole ship was cleaned. Work was an automatic process that filled almost the whole of each day. Even Cook's new innovations had now become routine. The men had ceased to use the bilge for defecation which was the usual practice, and now used the two lavatories fitted with slop buckets.

On Sundays, Cook's usual captain's inspection was always followed by a religious service. Cook appeared on deck and the drum beat the retreat. Men fetched stools from below and brought chairs for the officers. The bell was tolled and the church pendant was hoisted at the gaff. Cook conducted the service on the quarterdeck, with a Bible and a prayer book in front of him, placed on a cloth draped over the compass box. A lesson was read, a hymn sung.

Then, always the final act, the British Admiralty's Articles of War were read to the company. Thus they were sternly reminded of their obligations to the Crown as well as to God. And the price of disobediance in this world was likely to be felt immediately – compared with the wait for reward in the next world.

Fifty-seven days after rounding the Horn, Peter Briscoe, Banks's footman, caught sight of land. 'At ten this morn my servant, Peter Briscoe, saw the land which we had almost passed by,' wrote Banks. 'A small island one-and-a-half to two miles in length.' It was one of the Tuamotas group, first discovered by Quiros in 1606. Another of them was described by Cook as being 'of an oval form with a lagoon in the middle for which I named it Lagoon Island'. He made a sighting and marked its position on the chart. It was one of those countless islands, bays and headlands all over the world to which Cook gave some sensible, down-to-earth name: Duskey Bay, Cape Farewell, Lookout Point, Double Island.

By the beginning of April a sense of anticipation could be felt throughout the ship. Their goal was approaching. Nearly every day they saw some new islands rising darkly against the blue waters of the Pacific. Then on the eleventh at 6 am: 'Saw King George's Island [Tahiti] extending W by S$\frac{1}{2}$S to W by N$\frac{1}{2}$N . . . very high and mountainous.'

Cook had already heard the remarkable tales of Tahitian hospitality and sexual licence that earlier visitors had brought back. Some of his present crew had been there two years earlier, when Wallis had visited the island in the *Dolphin*. They knew what to expect and the prospect appeared to please them well.

Cook had been warned by the Royal Society that the Tahitians might be treacherous, so he had drawn up a list of five rules for the conduct of his men on the island. They reveal much of his remarkable character: his concern for the safety and well-being of his men, and his regard for the natives they were about to meet. The rules also reveal a sternly practical concern for the ship's stores and equipment on which the future of the whole expedition depended. As they dropped anchor in the bay – 'The finest picture of Arcadia the imagination can form,' wrote Banks – Cook assembled the ship's company and read out his rules:

1. To endeavour by every fair means to cultivate a friendship with the Natives and to treat them with all imaginable humanity.

2. A proper person [it was to be Banks] or persons will be appointed to trade with the natives for all manner of provisions, fruit and other productions of the earth; and no officer or seaman, or other person belonging to the ship, excepting such as are so appointed, shall trade or offer to trade for any sort of provisions, fruit or other productions of the earth unless they have my leave so to do.

3. Every person emply'd on any duty whatsoever is strictly to attend to the same, and if by neglect he looseth any of his arms or working tools, or suffers them to be stole, the full value thereof will be charge' against his pay according to the custom of the Navy in such cases, and he shall receive such farther punishment as the nature of the offence may deserve.

4. The same penalty will be inflicted on every person who is found to embezzle, trade or offer to trade with any part of the ship's stores of what nature soever.

5. No sort of iron, or any thing that is made of iron, or any sort of cloth or other usefull or necessary articles are to be given in exchange for any thing but provisions.

On 14 April Cook wrote: 'This morning we had a great many canoes about the ship, the most of them came from the westward but brought nothing with them but a few coconuts, etc. Two that appeared to be chiefs we had on board together with several others for it was a hard matter to keep them out of the ship as they climbed like monkeys, but it was harder still to keep them from stealing but everything that came within their reach, and in this they are prodigious expert.'

The stealing was certainly a problem. If the seamen had done it they would have been flogged. And their comrades would have thought it right that they should have been. Yet no one punished the Tahitians. Cook's breadth of mind, the quality that set him apart from so many explorers as a man of infinite tolerance and understanding, was almost a dis-

1. Captain James Cook, played in the film by Dennis Burgess.

2. Cook and his officers planned their route to the unknown; while the dockyard men in Deptford continued to convert the Yorkshire collier which had been pressed into Royal Naval service for this dangerous voyage; a voyage with a double purpose.

3. *Endeavour*, round-bottomed, fat-sterned, overcrowded and, in Cook's words, 'ideally suited for her task . . . I could not have wished for better'. With *Endeavour* he charted and named so accurately that even today his navigation can barely be faulted.

4. In Tahiti they discovered that the natives had a particularly painful method of marking their skins, with dyes pushed into cuts which were made with sharp stones and cutters. Later, sailors all over the world were to adopt 'tattooing'.

5. A Tahitian feast in honour of Cook, his officers and the scientific party. The Tahitians were lavish with hospitality. But they had no moral code which embraced the concept of theft. It was at this banquet that Cook had to ask for, and have returned, snuff boxes and personal articles casually taken, or 'lifted', from his party by the Tahitians.

(continued p.177)

3

4

5

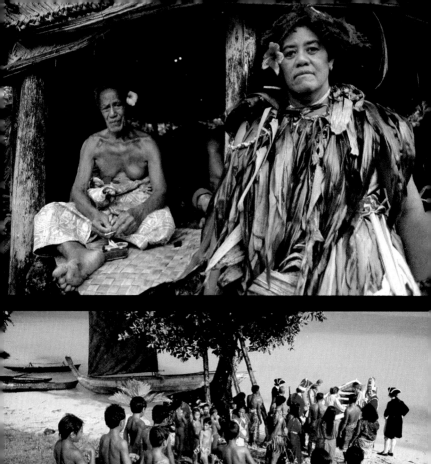

6. Little has changed since Cook and the men of _Endeavour_ landed. Cook's sailors used nails as an — illegal — trading commodity. Today this couple would undoubtedly not be bothered by travellers' cheques.

7. Cook guessed at, and feared for, the effects that would follow his discoveries and explorations. His compassion was not only for the men under his command, but for the people he found untouched – and undisturbed – by European ways.

The film was directed by John Irvin, and shot in London, the South Atlantic, the Pacific and Australia – in the footsteps of Cook.

advantage to him at such times. He could see how his men bridled at such dishonesty, uncorrected and unpunished. At the same time he could appreciate the Tahitian view. In a society where private property didn't exist, how then could the concept of theft exist?

That afternoon they went ashore. Chief Tubourai Tamaide entertained most of the ship's company in the great meeting house. 'Here the natives flocked around us in great numbers in as friendly a manner as we could wish, only that they showed a great inclination to pick our pockets,' wrote Cook. 'We were conducted to a chief who I shall call Lycurgus. This man entertained us with broiled fish, breadfruit, coconut etc. with great hospitality, and all the time took care to tell us to take care of our pockets, as a great number of people had crowded about us. Notwithstanding the care we took, Dr Solander and Dr Monkhouse [the surgeon] each had their pockets picked, the one of his spyglass the other of his snuff-box.'

There was considerable uproar. Cook protested to Chief Tubourai Tamaide. Eventually the stolen objects were located and returned. Cook dismissed the matter as of no particular significance: 'About six o'clock in the evening, we returned on board well satisfied with our little excursion.' Others were less magnanimous.

The very next day, 15 April, matters came to a head, predictably perhaps. Cook had set out to explore with a party of natives. 'We had but just crossed the river,' wrote Cook, 'when Mr Banks shot three ducks at one shot, which surprised them so much that most of them fell down as though they had been shot likewise. I was in hopes this would have had some good effect, but the event did not prove it, for we had not been gone long from the tent before the natives again began to gather about it, and one of them, more daring than the rest, pushed one of the sentinels down, snatched the musket out of his hand and made a push at him, and then made off, and with him, all the rest. Immediately upon this the officer ordered the party to fire and the man who took the musket was shot dead before he had got far off from the tent, but the musket was quite carried off. I had given strict orders that they should not be fired upon, even when detected in these attempts [of theft] for which I had many reasons; the common sentinels were by no means fit to be entrusted with a power of life and death, to be exacted whenever they should think fit. That thieves are hanged in England I thought no reason why they should be shot in Otaheite. They had no such law amongst themselves, and it did not appear to me that we had any right to make such a law for them.'

Even Cook himself was not immune to the attacks of the thieves: 'For my own part I had my stockings taken from under my head, and yet I am certain that I was not asleep the whole time.'

The thieving apart, there was a great deal that was attractive in the countryside and in the natives and their way of life. Buchan and Parkinson had endless scenes and specimens to paint and draw. Banks, Spöring and Solander collected plants, bringing them back in armfuls to the Great Cabin. There they were sorted, classified, placed between sheets of drying paper and pressed. Fish were caught with rod and line and stored in spirit in bottles. Animals and birds were shot with a gun and retrieved by the dogs, then preserved in wine casks of spirit.

The whole Tahitian way of life fascinated Banks. The range of canoes, from the great fighting Ivahahs more than 70ft long lashed together in pairs with a 'fighting platform' between them, to the little fishing Ivahahs with their single outriggers. The little individual houses of the ordinary people; the massive meeting-houses 200ft long that accommodated the 'principal' people. In particular Banks was fascinated by the strange custom of tattooing. Both sexes had intricate designs on their bodies, particularly on the buttocks. The tattooing process was immensely painful. A dye prepared from the smoke of the candlenut was driven below the skin by a series of blows from the toothed edge of a shell or bone. Each blow drew blood. Why the islanders underwent the rite was beyond Bank's comprehension.

But without question it was the Tahitian attitude to sex that was the chief preoccupation of the visitors. The European idea that sexual activity was something intensely private was quite alien to the Tahitian. The girls were amused to find the sailors insisted on taking them into the bushes before making love to them. To the Tahitian, everything was open.

According to Cook, the displays of dancing he witnessed, performed by young girls in groups of eight or ten, were uninhibited expressions of sex. There was in particular 'a very indecent dance which they called Timorodee, singing the most indecent songs and using most indecent actions in the practice of which they were brought up from the earliest childhood. In doing this they kept time to a great nicety.' Again: 'Both sexes express the most indecent ideas in conversation without the least emotion and they delight in such conversations beyond any other.'

Yet Cook was no prude. Despite the narrow background of his youth his outlook had a liberal tolerance. He could take a detached and sympathetic view of what he saw. If anything, far

Tattooing was not confined to the Tahitians. The son of a Maori chief.

from being shocked by Tahitian morals, he was amused and interested. 'Upon the whole these people seem to enjoy liberty in its fullest extent, every man seems to be the whole judge of his actions and to know no punishment but death, and this perhaps is never inflicted but upon a public enemy.'

Notwithstanding the thieving, Cook found

the Tahitians a most attractive and trustworthy people. He allowed some of his men to spend the night ashore, and some of the native women to come to the ship. There was never a moment's trouble as a result. In the widest sense, he endeavoured 'by every fair means to cultivate a friendship with the Natives and to treat them with all imaginable humanity'.

Tragedy, however, soon interrupted the tranquillity.

Buchan, the artist, was an epileptic, that much was known. What was uncertain was just how serious his condition was. When he collapsed into deep unconsciousness on 15 April, it came as a considerable shock. Two days later he was dead. At 9 am on 17 April his body was sewn in canvas, weighted with a dozen pieces of cannon shot, and buried at sea. Cook's epitaph was kindly: 'a gentleman well skilled in his pro-fession and one that will be greatly missed in the course of this voyage.' Banks's remarks, by comparison, seem callous: 'His loss to me is irretrievable, my airy dreams of entertaining my friends in England with the scenes that I am to see here are vanished. . . . Had providence spared him a month longer what an advantage would it have been to my undertaking, but I must submit.' Yet Banks was right. Buchan was the only member of the expedition able to record the magnificent landscapes of the South Seas. In modern terms his loss was comparable to the loss of the only photographer on an expedition.

The next day, work began on the building of Fort Venus, the defensive position from which the astronomical observations were to be made. The work took two weeks. In the meantime, Banks was put in charge of trading with the natives. 'Our traffic was carried on with as

Fort Venus, the stockade built to hold scientists and officers, during the observation of the transit of Venus

much order as in the best regulated market in Europe,' wrote Cook. 'Mr Banks took uncommon pains to secure every kind of refreshment that could be got. All sorts of fruit we purchased for beads – and nails.'

Other things could be purchased for nails, as the sailors quickly discovered. Three nails would buy a girl for an hour or two. The wild interest shown by the seamen in sex was natural enough, and it would have been difficult to control it when sex was such a blatant part of Tahitian life. To the natives, it was quite natural to take each other without shame or concealment. Cook records a scene that was by no means unique: 'The day closed with an odd scene at the gate of the fort where a young fellow about six feet high lay with a little girl about ten or twelve years of age, publicly before several of our people and a number of the natives. What makes me mention this is because it appeared to be done more from custom than lewdness, for there were several women present, particularly Obarea and several others of the better sort, and these were so far from showing the least disapprobation that they instructed the girl how she should act her part, who, young as she was, did not seem to want to.'

Such scenes didn't shock Cook. He saw it as part of a new culture. But what did shock him was the appearance of venereal disease, which he feared would 'spread itself over all the islands in the south seas to the eternal reproach of those who first brought it among them'. It was difficult to say where it had come from. A month before the ship arrived in Tahiti the crew had been given a clean bill of health. Yet now a third of them were suffering from the disease.

The observation of the transit of Venus across the sun took place on 3 June. The weather was fine, the temperature $119°$F. 'Not a cloud was to be seen the whole day,' wrote Cook. 'We had every advantage in observing the whole passage of the planet Venus over the sun's disc.' The readings, however, were far from satisfactory. 'We very distinctly saw an atmosphere or dusky shade round the body of the planet which very much disturbed the times of the contacts,' wrote Cook. 'We differed from one another in observing the times of the contacts much more than could be expected.' The difference between Green's reading and Cook's was twelve seconds. Originally, the Royal Society had hoped that from the transit observations the exact distance from the earth to the sun could be determined, but seventy years later it was realised that the wrong method had been used and all the calculations so painfully and carefully made in Tahiti were useless.

It was fortunate that there was a purpose behind the voyage other than the observation of the transit. As it turned out, it was to be by far the more important purpose.

Cook left Tahiti on 13 July, taking with him a chief called Tupia, who had begged to go along. 'Between eleven and twelve o'clock we got under sail and took our final leave of this people after a stay of just three months, the most part of which we have been on good terms with them.' Then he revealed to his officers, passengers and crew the secret orders that he had been given by the Admiralty a year earlier. *Endeavour* was not returning home.

If Terra Australis existed, she was going to discover it.

He set a course south-westerly. On 7 October they sighted land. It was, in fact, the unexplored east coast of New Zealand, although Banks was convinced it was the new land for which they were searching and recorded his certainty in his journal. More than a hundred years before, Tasman had discovered the west coast of New Zealand, but no one knew how far it extended. It might well have been part of that vast southern continent whose existence had yet to be proved: Terra Australis.

Two days later *Endeavour* dropped anchor. Cook took a party ashore in the pinnace and the yawl. His reception was as different from his welcome in Tahiti as can be imagined. Long war canoes with intricately carved sterns lay on the shore. Men with black hair and beads watched them from the trees. Four of them armed with long clubs ran towards the pinnace and tried to capture it. The coxswain fired a shot over their heads. They stopped, but only for a moment, then came on again. He fired again, with no effect. He fired a third time, this time killing one

Tahitian ceremonial and war canoes meeting *Endeavour*

of the attackers. The others turned and withdrew.

Next day Tupia, the Tahitian chief, found the Maoris understood his speech. He approached them and explained that Cook had no intention of harming them. Twenty or thirty of them gathered round the visitors and tried to snatch their weapons. One of them succeeded in grabbing Green's sword and making off with it. Again Cook had to defend himself. The man with the sword was shot and three others wounded.

It wasn't the end of the trouble. That same afternoon Cook tried to capture a canoe with seven natives in it. His intention was honest enough; he wanted to take the men aboard *Endeavour* and then, by treating them well, demonstrate his wish to be friendly. It was a disaster. The natives resisted violently. Three of them were killed and a fourth wounded. Banks wrote: 'Thus ended the most disagreeable day my life has yet seen; black be the mark for it.' Cook named the place 'Poverty Bay' – 'because it afforded us no one thing we wanted'.

Endeavour turned north, and for six months Cook charted every coastal feature of both islands: inlet, promontories, peninsulas. It was the work at which he was most skilled. He was fortunate, of course, in making the voyage when he did. A few years earlier there had been no accurate way for a navigator to determine longitude. Now a reliable sextant existed, and Neville Mashelyne, the Astronomer Royal, had produced his *Nautical Almanac and Natural Ephemerens*, whose mathematical tables saved hours of complicated calculations. Nonetheless, Cook's charting was a magnificent achievement. He made only two errors in the map of New Zealand, mistaking Banks Peninsula for an island and Stewart Island for a peninsula. In terms of position he was only three-quarters of a degree out in longitude. His charts could still be used by a ship's navigator today. Equally important – though personally disappointing to Cook – he had established that what Tasman had discovered was in fact two enormous islands. It could reasonably be assumed that Terra Australis did not exist.

Cook's intention despite his orders had been to return to England by way of the Horn if he believed it was best, and the Terra Australis problem had been solved. But after two years at sea, *Endeavour* was in no condition to face the weather they could expect there. The tropic seas had ravaged her hull. Even in Tahiti the anchor stocks had fallen off because they were so riddled with borer worm. Their only course was to continue westwards – on a circumnavigation of the earth.

He left New Zealand on 1 April 1770, and nineteen days later dropped anchor in a broad bay backed by woods on the east coast of New Holland. The natives showed no particular liking for them, throwing stones and waving boomerangs and spears, but they lacked that tenacious aggression of the Maoris and Cook took on wood and water without trouble. Later he wrote that it was possible to make excursions inland 'quite void of fear as our neighbours have turned out such rank cowards'.

For Banks the place was a botanical paradise. 'Our collection of plants had now grown so immensely large that it was necessary that some extraordinary care should be taken of them lest they should spoil in the books,' he wrote. Parkinson was kept busy every hour of daylight drawing the best specimens. Wrote Cook, 'The great collection of new plants Mr Banks and Dr Solander collected occasioned my giving it the name of Botany Bay.' Cook's interest in the plants was more practical than scientific. Could they be eaten he wondered. Would they help to prevent scurvy? They were important questions, not only for seamen but for the future colonists he saw living there. For he proposed claiming the territory for the English crown: 'During our stay I had caused the English colours to be displayed ashore every day.'

Endeavour moved slowly northwards, charting the coast in every detail, Cook taking the ship as close as possible to make certain of the accuracy of his readings. By 20 May he had passed the site of modern Brisbane and reached the southern limit of the Great Barrier Reef, the submerged cliff of coral that ran twelve hundred miles to the north. At low tide the ship rode beside the endless spears of coral. At high tide

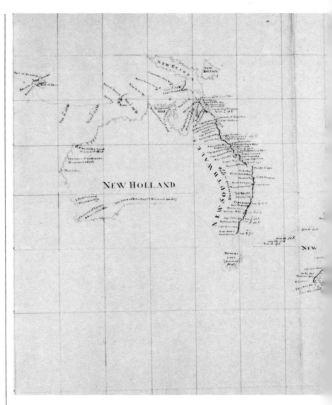

they disappeared from sight under six or eight feet of seething water. The work required great coolness and assurance.

And it was towards midnight on 11 June *Endeavour* ran her bows into them. It was the Barrier Reef that nearly ended it all. Only Cook's skill and inventiveness saved them.

Six days later, with the hole in her planks covered by the sail packed with oakum and dung, the ship was brought into the mouth of a river and anchored in the shallows. There, at low tide, they careened her for repairs. She was there for nearly seven weeks while John Satterly, the carpenter, and his mate Edward Terrell, carried out major repairs that normally would have required a dockyard. But they were successful.

It took a year, almost to the day, for Cook to reach England from the Great Barrier Reef, sailing by way of New Guinea and Batavia and round the Cape of Good Hope. He landed in Dover on Friday 12 July 1771, after a voyage of almost 42,000 miles which had taken three years. In retrospect, he found it a hard voyage: 'Was it not for the pleasure which naturally results to a man from being the first discoverer, even was it

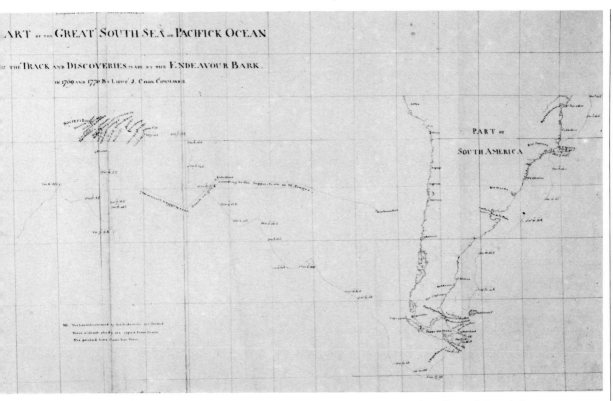

ART of the GREAT SOUTH SEA or PACIFICK OCEAN

of the TRACK and DISCOVERIES made by the ENDEAVOUR BARK.

in 1769 and 1770 By Lieut. J. Cook Commander

PART of

SOUTH AMERICA

Chart showing *Endeavour*'s route during the three-year circumnavigation of the globe

nothing more than sands and shoals, this service would be insupportable.'

The significance of Cook's achievement was at once obvious, though he was never a man to push himself into the limelight. He was made a commander by the Admiralty and retired happily into obscurity for a short time with his wife and family. But the British Government and the Admiralty were restless. It was time that the question of Terra Australis was settled once and for all – and the land, if it was there, claimed for the King. Cook was the man to do it.

In July 1772, with new orders, he sailed south again and circumnavigated the ice barriers of the Antarctic continent. When he returned after yet another three-year voyage, in July 1775, he had proved the fabled giant continent did not exist, thus solving the last of the mysteries of the southern seas, except for Antarctica itself.

Australia now appeared on the map.

Today, the main outlines of the southern globe are much as Cook left them.

But Cook had done more than just explode the myth of Terra Australis. He had conquered the sailing man's worst killer, scurvy. He had shown that long sea voyages need not mean a high death rate. In a thousand days, he had lost only one man out of 118.

Rewards came his way. He was raised to the rank of post-captain and appointed a captain in Greenwich Hospital. He was unanimously elected a member of the Royal Society, and given the Copley Gold Medal for the best experimental paper of the year.

In June 1776, he sailed on his final voyage. Its purpose was to settle the question of a northwest passage to the east, which had puzzled geographers from the time of Columbus. And this time he volunteered for the job.

He successfully took *Resolution* and *Discovery* through the Bering Straits and back to Hawaii. It was there, during a quite trivial incident with the natives, that he was stabbed to death.

'A plain sensible man with an uncommon attention to veracity,' Boswell called him. 'A grave, steady man and his wife, a decent plump Englishwoman.' Had he lived, he would probably have been given a knighthood. As it was,

The death of Captain Cook, killed by islanders in Hawaii

he received perhaps less than his just reward from his country, although a state pension was settled on his widow.

He was, without doubt, the peer of British maritime explorers. He opened up the whole southern region of the globe, and gave his country title to vast colonies in Australasia.

He was an explorer almost by accident. His first two voyages were at the command of his superiors, not out of any questing instinct of his own. He was, first and foremost, a superb practical seaman; meticulous, conscientious, professional.

Yet perhaps his greatest attribute was his concern for people, his compassion and understanding. It dominated his planning and his conduct at sea. He completely conquered scurvy, the principal cause of death at sea at that time, motivated not by any interest in the disease itself, but by an abiding concern for the men who suffered from it. He issued pipes and tobacco to the men who went with him in the *Endeavour* because he was concerned that they should be able to relax occasionally from the harsh life at sea.

His humanity and open-mindedness extended beyond the men under his command. It extended also to the native peoples with whom he came into contact.

His concern for their way of life, his desire to accept and understand it on their terms, is reminiscent of Mary Kingsley's. Cook could never escape a sense of deep personal responsibility for the destructive effect that contact with Europeans had brought about in the South Pacific. In 1773 he wrote in his journal:

'We debauch their morals already prone to vice and we introduce among them wants and perhaps diseases which they never before knew and which serve only to disturb that happy tranquillity they and their forefathers had enjoyed. If anyone denies the truth of this assertion let him tell what the natives of the whole extent of America have gained by the commerce they have had with Europeans.'

184

Francisco Pizarro 1471–1541

D. FRAN.ᶜᵒ PIZARRO.

Throughout history discovery has all too often been merely the prelude to bloody conquest.

There is, perhaps, no more extreme example than the career of Francisco Pizarro, the Spaniard who conquered Peru – and destroyed the Inca civilisation. In 1513, only twenty-one years after Columbus discovered the new world, a Spanish expedition hacked and fought its way across the Isthmus of Darien (Panama) until they came to a new sea. Vasco Nunez de Balboa promptly claimed, for the King of Spain, the world's largest ocean – the Pacific. In doing so he opened the way for the Conquistadors (as well as proving that Columbus had not, in fact, reached Asia).

With him on that journey was Pizarro. The illegitimate son of a Spanish army officer, he had fought as a mercenary all his life with but one ambition: to win enough gold, and booty, and honours, and respect, to retire in wealth. This driving ambition led him eventually to Peru, finally to the ambush and betrayal of Atahualpa, the Inca God-King.

In the name of Christ and Spain, Pizarro and the Conquistadors imposed on Peru a cruel regime motivated almost totally by a search for wealth and gold. In doing so they destroyed a culture.

But, whatever his motive, he brought to the world a knowledge of peoples and a country that would otherwise have escaped discovery for centuries.

Late afternoon, and still no movement from the vast Inca army camped outside the walls of Cajamarca. Francisco Pizarro stood in the shadow of a doorway and looked across the great empty square.

Opposite was the entrance through which the Lord Inca, Atahualpa, must come.

To the right lay Hernando Pizarro with half the Spanish cavalry. To the left lay De Soto with the rest. The infantry were hidden in the stone houses that flanked the open square, ready to move out at Pizarro's signal. On one of the two temples, Pedro de Candia had set up the two cannon and the half-dozen arquebuses.

There was nothing for it but to go on waiting. All day the tension had mounted. Messengers had come from the Lord Inca to say he was on his way. Pizarro had gone round his men, rousing the fight in them, trying to stiffen their morale with some of his own unquenchable drive. The horses had grown fretful, the little bells that had been hung on their harnesses tinkling with every movement they made. Then more messengers had come, to say the Lord Inca had changed his mind. There was no wonder Spanish nerves had reached breaking point. 'We prayed to Our Lord to spread His Holy shield over us, His soldiers, fighting to extend His Holy empire,' said Pizarro.

Then as the sun began to fall towards the western peaks of the Andes, a sound reached the waiting Spaniards; high-pitched, penetrating, filling the air above the walled square. To the 170 men under Pizarro's command it sounded like 'the songs of hell'. The Lord Inca was moving at last, supported by 40,000 of his men. The sentries could hardly believe what they saw: 'So much gold and silver they blazed like the Sun itself.'

'The men were full of fear for we were so deep in a land where we could not be reinforced,' said Pizarro. He looked at the handful of conquistadors who stood behind them. They were the toughest fighting men Europe had ever produced. For years they had fought the Moors and most of them had been in the Italian wars. Some had been with Pizarro since those days almost twenty years earlier when he had cut his way across the Darien Isthmus and stood with Balboa looking on the Pacific for the first time. Yet now they were pale. Their hands trembled. Some of them were actually urinating with terror at the prospect of what seemed certain to happen when that great glittering Inca horde swept into the empty square.

Pizarro tried to rally them. It was their only hope. 'I told them to take courage and trust in God, though there might be five hundred Incas to every Christian. When they received their orders they must act together coolly and quickly. If it proved to be necessary they should fight fiercely but fight steadily. If they charged, they must not let the horses collide. There must be no confusion. All that, if it came to a fight.'

The high-pitched chanting grew in strength. Sentries reported movements beyond the city as the great column approached. Then the first of the Indians appeared, coming into the square from the far end. They wore black and white livery with red yokes and they walked half-bent, brushing the path clear of stones before the approaching Lord Inca. Behind them came musicians with drums and pipes, and then groups of chanting men. The sound reverberated from the high stone walls, filled the square. Some of Hernando Pizarro's horses waiting out of sight beyond the walls became difficult to control.

Behind the musicians came the Orejones, court officials in brilliant costumes carrying staffs of office. They wore discs of burnished gold on their breasts and massive plugs of gold pushed through the lobes of their ears. Even Pizarro, who had heard tales of such riches throughout the twenty-odd years he had been in the Americas, could scarcely believe his eyes. Such an ostentatious display was no bad thing: he could sense the fear that had been crippling his men gradually giving way to the voracious greed that had always been their principal motivation.

Yet even Pizarro was unprepared for the appearance of Atahualpa himself.

The effect was 'like the Sun'. Pedro Pizarro, Pizarro's young cousin of sixteen, saw the Lord Inca borne on a vast litter by eighty chiefs in rich blue livery. He wore a collar of emeralds round his neck.

According to Francisco de Xeres, one of Pizarro's secretaries, the litter was 'lined with plumes of Macaws feathers, of many colours and adorned with plates of gold and silver. Many indians carried it on their shoulders on high. Next came two other litters and two hammocks in which were some principal chiefs; and lastly several squadron of indians with crowns of gold and silver.'

The litter was carried to the centre of the square before the bearers came to a halt. The Orejones and musicians formed up on either side of it. Behind it, several hundred selected warriors sealed the exit from the square.

Atahualpa raised a hand. At once the music and the chanting ceased. From high above the heads of his subjects, he looked round for the men he had come to see. He called out in Quechua, 'Where are the strangers?' After a moment, two men appeared from one of the openings into the square and began to approach him. One was the Dominican friar Valverde, carrying a crucifix and a breviary. The other was Felipillo the interpreter.

Pizarro watched, concealed in his doorway. There was no doubt now that it would come to a fight. Atahualpa had walked into the trap prepared for him. The confined space of the square made it impossible for him to deploy more than a thousand unarmed soldiers. Friar Valverde walked steadily across the open space between the Spanish positions and the litter. It wasn't so much an act of bravery as the action of a man wholly 'contemptuously' convinced of the superiority of his own God over this glittering heathen. He called: 'The Governor invites you to enter his house to talk and dine with him.' Felipillo translated the Spanish into Quechua.

It was an extraordinary piece of arrogance. Cajamarca was, in fact, Atahualpa's city. He had 40,000 soldiers camped outside its walls. Yet here was this stranger in the long black gown and white tunic inviting him to dine.

He said, 'I will not move forward until your Governor has returned every object you have stolen or consumed since your arrival in my lands.'

'I am a Minister of the Christian Church.' cried Valverde in reply. 'I am sent by the Em-peror to reveal the one true religion to you and your people. We summon you to abjure the errors of your own faith and to embrace Christianity.' He held up the breviary. 'This is my authority,' he said.

Atahualpa took the book, turned it over in his hands and finally opened it. It meant nothing to him. What authority did it have that could match the power of the Lord Inca, the child of Inti the Sun God? He threw it to the ground and responded, 'That says nothing!'

Valverde was incensed. God himself had been insulted by the heathen. He turned and ran back towards the Spanish positions, the crucifix held in front of him. He cried to the hidden conquistadors: 'Christians, avenge this insult to our Faith! Fall upon him! I absolve you!' The Inca troops began to stir.

Atahualpa called out to the Orejones.

This was the moment and Pizarro knew it. He lifted the white scarf that he had in his hand, then let it drop.

Candia, standing on the wall of the tower, put the glowing wick to the touch-hole of the cannon beside him. It fired with a great reverberating roar, spewing out broken iron and stone at the packed Indian forces below. A moment later the second cannon fired, then the arquebuses. Crossbow bolts struck half a dozen of the litter bearers. The whole scene broke in confusion.

Pizarro himself made for the royal litter with a commando of twenty swordsmen.

The battle-cry went up, 'Santiago y cierra España!' It was returned by the cavalry under Hernando Pizarro and De Soto. 'Santiago!' The terrible horses appeared. With their mounts they must have looked to the Indians like centaurs: their nostrils splayed, foam tossing from their mouths, their bodies covered in quilted armour. The horsemen charged hard into the milling mass of brown bodies and brilliant costumes and glittering gold decorations, cutting and pointing with the double-edged Toledo blades that chopped through the Indian cane helmets and fabric armour as if they scarcely existed.

Again the cannon sounded. Among the Incas panic broke out. The sweepers who had led the procession tried to get clear of the square, only to come face to face with the Spanish infantry with their swords and pikes cutting down everything that got in their way. 'Santiago!' they cried, forcing their way towards the Lord Inca still sitting in the litter. The Orejones were closing their ranks before him, trying to defend themselves with their bare hands, hanging on to the flying legs of the horses until they were tossed clear. Some grabbed hold of the horsemen, knowing them to be separate beings from the horses they rode, but they were cut down by the scything blades.

Pizarro and some of his men had cut through to the litter. He tried to pull Atahualpa out of it. If he could capture the Lord Inca he would have a tremendous hold over the Indians. It was the key to the future. But a Spanish infantryman, wild with battle fever, lunged at the Inca, forgetting Pizarro's earlier order: 'Let no one who values his life strike at the Inca.' Pizarro leaped to intercede, thrusting his arm forward and parrying the man's blade with his left hand. Blood poured from the deep cut he received.

The Orejones began to collapse before the weight of the cavalry that bored and thrust into them. The litter bearers fell. Blood spurted from severed limbs, chopped faces; ran over the flanks of the horses, and soaked into the dusty floor of the square. The air was oppressive with cries and screams from the Indians, and the triumphant, repeated yells of 'Santiago!' from the Spaniards.

At last there weren't enough bearers left to support the litter. It slid sideways, began to fall. Horsemen came up and heaved it over. As it hit the ground, Pizarro seized Atahualpa and dragged him clear into the shelter of a near-by house.

When the Indians saw the man-god they worshipped lying defenceless on the ground, their last resistance broke. Those who could still move

Pizarro seizing Atahualpa, Inca of Peru, by J. E. Millais, R.A. Painted at sixteen.

tried to get clear, escape the town that stank of ambush, betrayal and death. But they were followed by the Spanish infantry, and the cavalry even pursued them far beyond the town, cutting, hacking, killing.

In thirty minutes the destruction of an empire became a certainty.

The whole Inca civilisation lay at the mercy of one sixty-year-old man, Francisco Pizarro.

Under his command, 170 Spaniards had defeated an army of 40,000 men and taken their leader, the god-king Atahualpa, prisoner. The Spaniards had suffered no casualties. The only injury was to Pizarro when he had saved the Inca's life from the thrust of an over-zealous swordsman. By contrast, the Indians had 5000 dead. A further 5000 had retreated under the Inca captain Ruminavi. The rest had simply scattered, for their lives, into the high peaks of the Andes or towards Quito.

Even to Pizarro, a fighting man all his life, it seemed incredible that Atahualpa should have let himself be trapped in that confined square. Atahualpa was far from being an inexperienced leader. Only six months earlier he had defeated his own brother in a massive three-day battle, finally securing the throne – and the power – for himself.

That evening, as Pizarro entertained the Lord Inca at supper, he was asked by Atahualpa for an explanation: 'Do not be sorrowful,' Pizarro said, with Felipillo beside him to translate. 'Every prince who has ever resisted us has met with similar defeat. Take heart and confide in us. We Spanish are a generous people.'

Atahualpa said, 'It is the fortune of war to conquer or to be conquered. Yet I have known of your progress from the moment you landed. I had thought you too small in number to be any threat against me. I had intended to capture *you* – to take *your* horses, to put *your* men to service in *my* household.'

He was no more than mildly curious about his own fate. 'Will you now kill me?' he said.

'I will not,' said Pizarro. 'Christians kill with impetuosity, but not afterwards. We show grace to all who submit.'

The statement had a noble ring. In the event it was to prove false. And that in many ways sums up Pizarro's character – always aiming at nobility, without the real will to achieve it. In any situation where conflict arose, it was invariably expedience that triumphed over principle. It is not hard to see why. From birth Pizarro had had to fight for a place in the world. If he had bothered too much with honour and principle he might never have survived. . . .

He was born at Trujillo in the Spanish province of Estramadura in 1471, according to the most reliable sources. His father was either an infantry colonel or a minor nobleman; his mother was probably a serving woman. He himself was illegitimate. Though a story of his being abandoned and suckled by a sow is almost certainly a fabrication, there is no doubt that childhood left him with a deep sense of deprivation that shadowed the rest of his life.

He was illiterate the whole of his life, and his lack of education was something about which he was always sensitive. Estramadura, itself, left its mark on him. It was one of the poorest of the Spanish provinces. The only escape from Estramadura was through war and conquest. By fighting, even the meanest peasant stood a chance of amassing a fortune and returning home to build a castle, even to boast his own coat of arms.

From his earliest days, Pizarro was marked out by circumstances – and his own determination – for the life of a Conquistador.

As a young man he fought in the Italian wars, then in 1502 he made his first visit to the Indies. He went quite deliberately 'with a cloak and sword' to make his fortune in whatever ways he found open to him. From that time onwards, most of his life was spent as an armed adventurer in the Americas. In 1510 he was part of the Hojeda expedition to Hispaniola, and three years later he crossed the Darien Isthmus and saw Balboa claim the whole Pacific ocean in the name of the King of Spain.

By the time he was fifty he had acquired a modest estate near Panama, but none of those boundless riches of which he dreamed as a boy. There was no question of his returning home to brag of the wealth he had accumulated. 189

It began to look as if the vast treasure-house he had always expected to find didn't exist after all. Then Cortes discovered the riches of the Aztec civilisation in Mexico. Pizarro's dream was re-vivified.

He sailed south down the west coast of South America in 1524 and made his first contact with the coastal Indians of Peru. It was through them that he first heard of the rich lands of the interior and saw the first gold artefacts. He was fifty-three years old, and it seemed that at last the wealth he had always dreamed of was within his grasp.

He returned to Panama to make arrangements for a more substantial expedition. In march 1526 he signed a contract with two associates – the conquistador Diego de Almagro, and the priest Father Luque – to share all the riches of Peru between them. Father Luque was to provide the necessary finance for expeditions which Pizarro and Almagro were to command as joint leaders.

Later that same year Pizarro and Almagro sailed south again, to make a more determined search for the treasures of the Incas.

In the spring of 1527, Almagro returned to Panama, leaving Pizarro to push inland from what is now Buenaventura in Colombia. In the meantime, the ship supplying the expedition had reached as far south as Esmeraldas in Ecuador. Bartholomew Ruiz, commanding the vessel, was waiting for Pizarro to catch up with him when an extraordinary craft appeared on the horizon. It had a double-pole mast placed centrally and carrying a large square sail. When Ruiz bore down on it he could see it was a raft made out of whole tree trunks more than fifty feet long. A small thatched cabin at its centre carried some twenty Indians wearing finely-textured clothes. But what held Ruiz's attention, indeed riveted it, were the jewels they wore, set in solid gold.

When Ruiz drew alongside, some of the Indians panicked and jumped into the water. The other remained on board as the Spaniards secured the raft to the ship. Nine of them were Inca nobles, one of them a princess. They were dressed in tunics and garments of the finest wool, brilliantly coloured. Fear made them co-operative. Ruiz took three of them on board together with the treasure they carried, before releasing the others.

For Ruiz there was no doubt about it: none of the stories of a treasure hoard beyond the mountains seemed exaggerated now. He had in his possession riches the like of which he had never dreamed. There were crowns, diadems, belts, bracelets, leg armour, breastplates – all in gold. There were strings and clusters of beads and rubies, mirrors of silver, gold and silver cups. There were cloths of cotton and fine wool, dyed in crimson, blue and yellow, covered in ornate embroidered figures of birds, animals, fish and trees. There were pieces of crystal and bags of emeralds, chalcedonies and other jewels.

Two of the Indians were from Tumbez in northern Peru. They confirmed that what Ruiz saw before him was the merest sample from the treasure-houses that lay to the south and beyond the mountain wall.

Faced with such splendours, it was clear to Pizarro – when he and Ruiz met up again – that the enterprise was to be bigger than ever he had suspected. It would require more than local Panama support. It needed the support of Spain, of the King himself.

Details of the treasures taken from the raft were sent to Charles I, and in 1528 Pizarro himself went to the court. At first he seemed out of place, a rough conquistador wearing unfashionable clothes. He was unprepossessing: thin, wiry and bearded, abstemious as far as the 'good things' of life were concerned. Yet he impressed the court with his zeal and forthrightness. And in Estramadura he was able to recruit the men he wanted, young men of violent ambition, with nothing to lose but their lives.

On 26 July 1529 a royal Capitulation was promulgated. Pizarro was made a Knight of Santiago and granted his father's coat of arms. More important for the expedition that lay ahead, since it countermanded the contract made in Panama that gave Almagro co-leadership status, Pizarro was named governor and captain general of the future Peruvian colony of New Castille. He returned to Panama in the autumn of 1529, with the King's authority to command an expedition in his name. In return, Pizarro was to send one fifth of all the treasures he found to the crown, and convert the inhabitants of the territories to Christianity.

Pizarro wins support from the King

Almagro was furious when he heard of the arrangement. He believed that Pizarro had deliberately broken the contract between them by asking the King for supreme command. For the moment there was nothing he could do but submit. But it was the start of open conflict between the two men and their supporters that was to lead, in the end, to both their deaths. Nevertheless, at that stage there was too much at stake for Almagro to break openly with Pizarro. For the moment he set aside his growing hatred of the man in order to secure his share of the riches of New Castile.

The expedition left Panama at the beginning of 1531 and landed at San Mateo Bay in Ecuador. Pizarro's immediate objective was Tumbez, the town from which two of the Indians picked up by Ruiz had come. He had their word for it that somewhere near Tumbez lay the city of gold which was the source of the treasures.

He had with him 180 men and 67 horses. The odds against him were great and he knew it.

Some of the coastal Indians gave him trouble, but when he turned against them they were no match for his conquistadors. The conquistadors were, after all, the finest warriors the world had ever seen. They carried the best weapons in Europe: two cannon, eight or nine arquebuses, crossbows, lances, and above all those magnificent Spanish swords with the finest double-edged blades Toledo could produce. Additionally Pizarro carried the authority of the greatest monarch in Christendom. And, of course, the blessing of God Almighty.

More important, he had horses with him. If necessary he could cover ground quickly. The Indians had nothing to match them. Even the wheel was unknown to them. But Pizarro was quick to see that for the Indians the horses represented something more than efficient means of warlike transport. They were almost gods. At first the man and horse combination seemed to be one complex being able to divide itself into two separate creatures whenever it chose. Later, when the Indians grasped the fact that the horse was a separate beast, it became the target of their spears and arrows – rather than the man on its back. The supreme enemy became the horses, not the Spaniards they carried.

The journey south proved more difficult than they had anticipated. Apart from the attacks by Indians, diseases began to affect the men. Boils appeared like a plague, making it difficult to wear armour or ride the horses. A coastal disease called verruga produced great warty growths on the face and neck that had to be lanced and cauterised. But the men were immensely tough. There was little in the way of hardship that was new to them. They formed a tight-knit group that would close ranks instantly in the face of difficulty or danger. In many cases, whole families of brothers and cousins from Estramadura had joined Pizarro. He had five of his own relations with him: Gonzalo and Juan Pizarro and Francisco Martin de Alcantara were his illegitimate half-brothers; Hernando Pizarro was another half-brother, the only legitimate member of the family; Pedro Pizarro was a young cousin, who served as Pizarro's page.

It took a year of steady marching – and fighting – to reach Tumbez. Hernando had been injured by a spear thrust some weeks earlier in an engagement with the natives of the coast. His leg was badly affected by poison, and he rested it whenever he could. But the incident had, at least, produced prisoners and from them Pizarro learned something of the political situation existing in the Inca kingdom he had now entered.

He discovered that the old Lord Inca, Huayna Capac, had died six years earlier and left his kingdom to be ruled jointly by his two sons Atahualpa and Huascar. For five years the arrangement had worked – more or less. But only recently the 'war of the two brothers' had broken out and thousands of the best Inca warriors had been killed in the civil war that followed. Politically the country was still in total disarray. For the moment Atahualpa was in control, having captured his brother at the three-day battle of Cuzco.

And that, to Pizarro, seemed the most extraordinary piece of good luck. The forces against him were divided.

Pizarro consolidated his position on the coast, establishing settlements at Paita and San Miguel

Huascar the Inca held captive by troops of his half brother, Atahualpa

1. Francisco Pizarro, played in the film by Francisco Cordova.

2. The Conquistadors were Europe's toughest mercenary soldiers. In the name of Christ and in search of gold for Spain, they destroyed an entire civilisation.

3. Atahualpa, borne on his golden litter, was escorted into the square of Camarca. Pizarro and his Conquistadors lay in ambush. After that brief, bloody and unequal battle the Inca civilisation was never properly to recover.

4. Atahualpa agreed, to save his life, that a large chamber, more than the height of a man, would be filled with gold. This, the Conquistadors promised him, would be the ransom for his freedom. He agreed also that two smaller chambers would be filled with silver. The Inca and his people kept their bargain. The Spaniards did not.

5. In the end, deceived by Spanish promises, Atahualpa was garrotted, while his subjects lay prone before him, weeping. At the very end he had been 'converted' to Christianity. He agreed to it only in order to avoid death by burning. The Incas believed death by fire destroyed their spirit.

6. Atahualpa's General, Chalcuchima, refused to
(continued p.193)

4

5

6

convert to Christianity. Instead of garrotting, he was burned at the stake.

7. The Inca civilisation, possibly no less cruel than that of the conquering Spaniards, failed to survive.

The film was directed by Fred Burnley, and shot in the Peruvian Andes, among the remains of Inca strongholds destroyed by the Conquistadors.

at the mouth of the Piura river. Then in September 1532 the news he was waiting for reached him. Atahualpa was at Cajamarca, three hundred miles to the south. He turned his men up the river valley and began to climb into the mountains. The weather was hot, the landscape dry, the hooves of the horses threw up a cloud of choking dust.

Some of the men began to complain. The villages they passed contained none of the treasures they had been expecting to discover.

By Tambo Grande it became clear to Pizarro that unless he did something the expedition might disintegrate. He formed up the men in the village square and addressed them:

'A crisis has now been reached in our affairs. We must meet it with courage. If any man is unsure of this expedition, it is not too late to turn back to our settlement at San Miguel. No man should go forward who has the least doubt of our success. I want no man who does not bring a whole heart. And those who choose to take their chances with me, I shall lead to the very end. With however many or few, I shall go forward and conquer.'

It had the required effect. Four foot soldiers and five horsemen left the parade. The rest declared their support for Pizarro. The disaffection was quelled.

The doubts in the minds of the men were understandable. They, like Pizarro, were well aware that they were the first Europeans ever to climb the great wall of the Andes. There was no telling what lay beyond. They had nothing to go on but tales and rumours from the Indians they encountered. At Zaran, on the coastal plain, the route to Cajamarca turned south. Pizarro had already sent De Soto on to Cajas with a detachment, to check any threat that might exist to the north.

The Indian way of life they encountered was spartan. The houses were stone-built with pitched roofs thatched with grasses. There were no chimneys, and smoke from the fires inside simply filtered its way through the thatch. The day's work began at daybreak. After a drink of aka (known also as chicha) a mildly alcoholic malt brew, the family went into the fields. Except for meal breaks, they stayed there until

The Inca way of life was spartan

darkness. Their tools were primitive, a pointed stake for tilling the ground, a rake for breaking up the clods.

Corn was the principal food. It was cooked with chili peppers and herbs, or ground into a rough flour and made into bread. Potatoes were dehydrated to form 'chuñu', which was the basis of a stew called 'Locro'. As for the occasional meal of meat, most of it came from the llama, though guinea pigs were raised for food.

Aka was made by the woman of the household. She boiled corn, then chewed it. The resulting mash was then fermented in a large pot.

When De Soto finally returned he had with him an ambassador from the Lord Inca whom he had met in Cajas. De Soto was suspicious. He had seen another side of Inca life besides the one his companions had seen in Zaran. He had seen the bloated bodies of soldiers hanging by the feet from trees, a reminder of the savagery of the civil war. The ambassador had assured him that the Lord Inca welcomed the strangers to his country and wished them to visit him in peace. But the presents he offered De Soto seemed like a warning – two drinking vessels shaped like fortresses, and two skinned and stuffed ducks.

To Pizarro, the ambassador's curiosity about the size of his expedition and the nature of the arms it carried, made him seem more a spy than a man of peace:

'The envoy told us that the Inca king at the head of his army was waiting for us at a town called Cajamarca seven days' march away. Then he went about examining everything in the camp, as casually as if he had been brought up all his life among Spaniards. His clerk, who followed him everywhere, made a tally of our numbers in knots, because the Incas had no writing. This envoy had never seen modern weapons and armour like ours before: he hadn't even seen a full beard.'

To the ambassador Pizarro said: 'My Lord, tell your master the Inca that we come in the name of a powerful Emperor who dwells far across the seas. If Atahualpa Inca desires my friendship and will receive me in peace, then I will visit him as a friend and brother. I and the Christians of my company will gladly arm him against his enemies.'

The road to Cajamarca ran into the Sechura desert. The river petered out. The greenery of Zaran gave way to scrub and finally to sand and bare rock.

The horses had to be hauled through sand drifts and protected from the scorching heat whenever possible. They were the most precious pieces of equipment the expedition possessed. They carried no supplies that might have tired them; those were carried by hired porters – or by the men themselves.

On one occasion, on a particularly difficult stretch of the route, the porters actually carried the horses rather than let them wear themselves out in the oppressive heat.

For three days the column marched through the sandy wilderness without a single drop of water. It was hardly surprising that when they reached the river Leche on the far side, there was scarcely a man who didn't immerse himself over his head in its soothing waters.

The great barrier of the high Andes was now in full view, the massive peaks covered in snow. Condors turned and wheeled overhead, black silhouettes against the clear sky. It grew cold, colder even than on the high plateau of Castille.

At night they put up cotton tents, lit fires and huddled together to keep warm. There was certainly nothing easy about reaching this treasure-house – assuming it existed at all. Everyone was aware, too, that they were being watched by Inca scouts. From time to time they spotted fortified posts on the hillsides above them. Pizarro said, 'Let none of you lose heart. In the greatest extremity God fights for us. He will humble the pride of these heathen and bring them to the true faith. That is the great object of our conquest.'

He was in direct touch now with Atahualpa through the messengers he had sent ahead.

As the column climbed higher and into the Nancho Gorge, prolonged exposure to the rarefied atmosphere began to affect the Spaniards. The porters were thick-set men with well-developed chests adapted to breathing the thin air. But the Spaniards wheezed, like asthmatics, and found all exertion painful. The altitude produced sickness and lassitude. In some cases the men's lungs began to fill with fluid, causing bronchial pneumonia.

They were at a height of 12,000 feet, the first Europeans ever to scale the coastal mountains and reach the heart of the Andes.

It was not this achievement that was uppermost in Spanish minds, but the possibility of ambush. Hernando Pizarro said, 'The road was so bad that they could very easily have taken us there or at another pass which we found between here and Cajamarca. For we could not use the horses on the roads even with skill, and off the road we could take neither horses nor foot soldiers.'

But ambush never came. Beyond the gorge, the country opened into a broad plain covered in dried yellow grass.

Another envoy from Atahualpa was waiting for them. 'My Lord,' he said, 'the Inca Atahualpa sends greetings. He wishes to know on what day you will arrive in Cajamarca?' Cajamarca, it seemed, had been evacuated to receive the Spaniards, and Atahualpa was camped outside it.

Pizarro replied, 'I will come as quickly as I can, you may tell my brother Atahualpa. And I come in peace to bring knowledge of God to the inhabitants of these lands.' Then, in case the envoy mistook the statement for weakness, he added, 'If he prefers war, I will fight him. Yet tell him I neither fight nor molest anyone unless I am attacked.'

On the morning of the next day, Friday 15 November 1532 – Pizarro's force reached the heights overlooking Cajamarca. The scene before them struck awe into every man present. Below was a wide fertile valley knee-high in rich grass and wild spring flowers. Through it ran the great Inca road that linked Quito and Cuzco, more than a thousand miles apart. It was wide enough to take six horsemen riding abreast and it led to the main gate of the town. Behind the town rose the mountains, their peaks capped in snow.

And in the meadows that sloped towards them lay Atahualpa's army: row upon row of white tents. Amongst them fires burned, standards flew, men paraded. There were, according to Jerez, 30,000 soldiers. Others thought there were more. Pizarro said, 'We never thought the Incas could maintain such a proud estate. . . . We were truly filled with a great apprehension. . . . Was this an ambush we were being enticed into?'

It seemed very likely that it was an ambush, but there was nothing Pizarro could do about it. 'It was unwise to show any fear, far less to turn back. We had to go into the town. So with a show of good spirits we descended into the valley. . . . I knew that if they had sensed any weakness, our own native porters we had recruited on the way there would have turned upon us. The most sensible course was to make as bold an appearance as possible and continue openly without any apparent fear or regard for the Incas' divisions we were passing.'

The troops formed up three deep and in three divisions and then, 'with the bravest possible show' they marched towards Cajamarca.

The town was surrounded by a brown adobe wall. Jerez, Pizarro's secretary, was impressed by what he found inside:

'The houses are more than 200 paces in length and very well built, being surrounded by a strong wall three times the height of a man. The roofs are covered with straw and wood, resting on the walls. The interiors are divided into 8 rooms, much better built than any we had seen before. Their walls are of very well cut stones and each lodging is surrounded by its masonry wall with doorways, and has its fountain of water in an open court conveyed from a distance by pipes, for the supply of the house. In front of the plaza, towards the open country, a stone fortress is connected with it by a staircase leading from the square to the fort. Towards the open country there is another small door with a narrow staircase, all within the outer wall of the plaza.'

It was the plaza that interested Pizarro. Atahualpa had told the truth when he said the town was empty. There wasn't a trace of life; no smoke rose through the thatch of any of the houses. If the Spaniards could occupy the square and the buildings surrounding it, they could hamper the Incan army for some considerable time.

Again, the arms that Pizarro had seen carried by the Inca soldiers didn't begin to match the weapons his own men carried. The crude spears, with wooden points hardened by fire, were toys in comparison with the steel-tipped lances of his horsemen. The Incas used clubs of heavy palm wood and axes of cast bronze. Neither could match the European broadsword that could lop off a wrist or cleave a head with a single stroke. What interested Pizarro more were the slings made of fine wool and the projectiles the size of small cannon balls. He was curious too about an arrangement of balls and ropes that he had seen used to entangle a man. But still he had no doubt that any man of his could match ten that Atahualpa might produce, if only there was some way of producing favourable odds.

'My first task was to post guards and secure the town against surprise attack,' said Pizarro. He sent De Soto and Hernando Pizarro with a small cavalry detachment to visit Atahualpa. Ostensibly they were to offer greetings and invite the Inca to visit Pizarro in the plaza. The real intention was to put the horses through their paces before the Inca army and so achieve some psychological superiority.

By the time they returned with Atahualpa's promise to come to Cajamarca the next day, Pizarro had the outlines of a plan in his head.

Atahualpa would be lured into the plaza and ambushed.

The cavalry was to be divided between De Soto and Hernando Pizarro and hidden in the hills surrounding the square until they were needed. The infantry were to be hidden in another hall with access into the plaza through the many doorways that opened onto it. The artillery and the arquebusiers under Pedro de Candia were to be placed in the fortress that commanded the plaza. Small detachments of foot and horse were to be held ready to close the exits from the square when the Inca and his attendants were inside. Finally, Pizarro and a detachment of twenty foot soldiers were to be ready to seize Atahualpa.

The signal to spring the ambush would be the discharge of one of de Candia's guns on a command from Pizarro himself. He, himself, would signal, by dropping a white scarf. The breastplates of the horses were to be fitted with bells to increase the noise and so add to the confusion.

That evening it rained and there was a hailstorm. It seemed a bad omen. The night was black, lit only by the hundreds of fires amongst the tents of the Inca army. No one slept much.

In the morning the weather had changed. The sun shone. Mass was celebrated. The conquistadors settled at their posts to wait.

The morning passed without movement from the Inca camp. Then in the afternoon conches began to sound and there was considerable activity. But still the Inca didn't come. Pizarro went round his men again, telling them to wait for the signal and to fight with courage when it came, assuring them that they were each worth five hundred of these Indians camped on the hillside. Above all, telling them that God was on their side. Then as the afternoon slipped past, Atahualpa began to approach.

And, as the sun was already settling over the mountains, the ambush was sprung.

Thirty minutes later, any future for the civilisation of the Incas had virtually ceased to exist. . . .

The next day, Inca captives dragged the dead out of the plaza, piled them in great heaps. De Soto took a detachment of cavalry into the Inca encampment and came back with 80,000 pesos of gold.

Pizarro shows cavalry to Atahualpa. The Inca executed Indians who flinched.

Atahualpa was still unsure whether the Spaniards intended to kill him or not. When he saw their reaction to the gold, he saw a possible way to safety. He said to Pizarro, 'If you set me free, I will cover the floor of this room with gold.' Pizarro looked round the room. It would be far better if the Inca's men brought the gold to him rather than his men having to search for it. Pizarro hesitated. Atahualpa said, 'I will not only cover the floor, I will fill this whole chamber with gold as high as I can reach. And another chamber I will fill twice with silver. All this shall be accomplished within two months.'

It was an offer beyond anything Pizarro had dreamed. The whole of Spain could hardly contain such wealth. He nodded and said, 'If you commit no treason and perform your promise, I shall restore you to liberty.'

During the whole of his captivity, Atahualpa preserved an extraordinary dignity. His court was very much what it had been before the arrival of the Spaniards. The Orejones approached him with bare feet and symbolic burdens on their backs. His food was still served by his principal wife, the Royal Coya, and a bevy of high-born young women. Dishes of gold and silver and pottery were placed before him on thin green rush mats, and he indicated what he wished to eat simply by pointing at it. The myth of his godhead continued to be preserved, amongst those who served him. The clothes he wore were burned when they were discarded and the ashes blown into the air. No one was allowed to touch anything that he had touched.

It was all done with Pizarro's approval: 'Though a prisoner, it suited me to let him control his empire thereby keeping the land at peace.'

Atahualpa was the seventh Inca since the empire was established under Manco Capac, in the thirteenth century. At the time of his capture, he was in his early thirties, a well-built man with a handsome face. He wore his hair short and decorated with gold ornaments. His eyes were bloodshot, giving him a deceptively fierce appearance. His left ear had been badly torn in battle and he had a habit of concealing it with his cloak. In formal relations with his own officers he preserved an icy detachment, but with the Spaniards who guarded him he unbent. 'Atahualpa was quick to learn our ways,' said Pizarro. 'Even to learn the language of Spain. We found ourselves liking this man.'

Spanish wasn't the only thing he learned. He learned chess from Hernando Pizarro and became very proficient. His rational ability was highly regarded by the Spaniards. Hernando Pizarro in particular grew very close to the Lord Inca, and perhaps it was this that led Pizarro to send Hernando into the countryside to speed up the gold collection. He might have felt that Atahualpa was using his popularity with the Spaniards for political ends, for to Pizarro's great annoyance the Lord Inca had ordered the death of his brother Huascar and so robbed Pizarro of a possible ally.

Hernando's search for gold was conducted in the characteristic conquistador way. At Pachacamac, a three-week ride south from Cajamarca, he smashed his way into the great temple only to find the gold had already been removed. In Jauja he was no more successful. The area had been a stronghold of support for Huascar, and was now under the control of Atahualpa's chief commander Chalcuchima. It seemed to the Spaniards that Chalcuchima was hiding Huascar's treasure from them. Hernando set out to lure him back to Cajamarca. He said, 'Your Lord Inca has repeatedly requested your presence at his side. And that you should bring all the gold and silver from this city. You must come with us.'

Chalcuchima hesitated. In any other society he would have crushed the invaders. He was chief commander of an army that was still extensive in men and supplies. He was the only man with the stature to bridge the differences between the two rival Inca factions. But the rigid autocracy of the Inca state prevented him taking the necessary action without the express command of Atahualpa, and Atahualpa refused such a command because it would have cost him his life. Instead of destroying Hernando Pizarro and his small force and marching on Cajamarca, Chalcuchima agreed to go peacefully to see the Inca.

Once inside Cajamarca, Chalcuchima was seized and tortured. Pizarro demanded, 'Now you will tell us where you have hidden the gold of Cuzco.'

Chalcuchima denied there was more gold. 'We have given it all to you,' he said.

De Soto was furious with him. He shouted, 'You are lying. Where is the gold you took from Huascar? You *will* tell us.'

The Inca commander was bound to a wooden stake in the centre of the plaza, straw and firewood stacked round him. Atahualpa was brought out to witness the scene. Soldiers threw blazing brands on the tinder. The straw caught at once and flamed up in a great circle round Chalcuchima. He kept his eyes on the Lord Inca, hoping for some indication from Atahualpa that he should tell the Spaniards what they wanted to know, and so save himself the fearful pain of death by burning. But the only signal from the Inca plainly indicated that Chalcuchima should keep silent – whatever they did to him.

The flames caught his clothes, scorched his hair, eyebrows and the lashes of his eyes. His legs were burning where the blazing firewood rested against them. Pizarro shouted, 'Where is the gold?'

The pain was more than he could bear. He cried out, 'Please. Take away my Lord! Please!'

Atahualpa was hustled away, the fire put out with water. Chalcuchima, in agony, cried, 'I do not have the gold of Cuzco. It is still there.' He told himself that it was too late to save anything from these barbarians who were sacking the state. Everything was lost now. As they cut him down from the stake he said bitterly 'On several occasions I have come with a large force against you. It is the Lord Inca who ordered me to withdraw, for fear you would kill him.'

When Almagro arrived from Panama with reinforcements, he could scarcely believe what he saw. A large chamber in the Inca palace was filled to a height of more than six feet with ornaments of pure gold. Two other rooms were filled with silver. His share, according to the terms of the contract made so many years earlier in Panama, would be the same as Pizarro's. But that wasn't how Piazarro saw it. Almagro hadn't been present at the taking of Cajamarca. He hadn't risked his life, as Pizarro and the rest of them had, to capture the Inca and subdue his army. If Almagro was to have any share at all, it could only be a token one. That unilateral decision hardly improved the relationship between them.

By now, the Inca had fulfilled his promise. Eleven tons of 22-carat gold had been collected as his ransom. But still Pizarro refused to release him. Instead, furnaces were built – and the whole priceless treasure of the Inca culture was melted down into convenient ingots. Each man was given his share according to a system of distribution that had been worked out long before. There wasn't a Spaniard who wasn't rich beyond his dreams. Pizarro's share was 800 pounds in weight of pure gold, to say nothing of the silver and emeralds. The share due to the crown was 2700 pounds of gold. And Hernando Pizarro was ordered to escort it back to Spain.

The departure of Hernando marked a turning point in the fortunes of the Lord Inca. Hernando had become attached to him. He had taken his side on occasions, even against Pizarro. He had always assured Atahualpa that however ruthless the Spaniards were in their search for treasure, they were basically honourable men. If Pizarro had given his word that the Lord Inca would be released, then Atahualpa could rely on it. As long as Hernando was there to reassure him, Atahualpa retained some confidence in Pizarro's word. But when Hernando left for Spain, the Inca's hopes began to fade.

Pizarro was in a difficult position. He wanted to honour his promise to the Lord Inca. His brothers supported him. Yet if he released Atahualpa, would any of the Conquistadors manage to get out of the country alive?

Again, the Church was bitterly opposed to releasing such a heathen. Valverde made the position quite clear. But there was more telling opposition from the Royal Notary, 'who warned that an account of these proceedings would be sent to Spain. With the authority of the Crown, he too condemned the Inca because while alive he was a constant threat to the safety of our expedition.'

Fortuitously, it seems, one of the Orejones came to Pizarro with a tale of Atahualpa's treachery. 'He has sent orders that Ruminavi should attack your camp by night,' said the Inca. 'The first person they will try to kill will be you. Then they will release their Lord Atahualpa from prison.'

Pizarro confronted Atahualpa: 'I am told you have sent orders to your army to attack this camp and kill me,' he said.

Atahualpa denied the accusation: 'Why do you mock me?' he said. 'You are always mocking me. I am in your power. If these reports were true, you could kill me. You little know my people, if you think my armies will move without my permission. If I do not wish it, no bird will fly, and no leaf remain on the trees, throughout my land.'

Pizarro was unconvinced. It became more certain that Atahualpa's death would, at the very least, remove a source of worry. Almagro, the Royal Notary, and Friar Valverde constantly pressed for it.

Finally, despite the protests of his brothers, Pizarro agreed. Atahualpa would be burned. Atahualpa received the news calmly, but he made a request that some other form of death be considered. 'According to the belief of these people,' said Pizarro, 'if Atahualpa's body were burned, he would not be able to pass into another life. A matter of some concern to him.'

So, at the stake, Atahualpa was offered an alternative. Friar Valverde said, 'If you will become a Christian and be baptised, your body will not be burned. Will you become a Christian? Will you be baptised?'

Atahualpa agreed. The 'alternative' may have suited his beliefs, but could hardly have seemed attractive: he was to be garrotted instead of burned. Valverde read the articles of Holy Faith in Latin and performed the baptism. The new name of the Lord Inca was to be Don Francisco Atahualpa. As it was pronounced, the executioner put the garrotte round his throat and drew it tight.

And, later, despite Valverde's promises, the body was burned. The date was 26 July 1533.

Now Pizarro turned his attention towards Cuzco, the Inca capital, a thousand miles to the south. At first the going was not too difficult. 'This mountainous region would have been almost impassable but for the Inca's own roads,' he said. 'Nowhere in Christendom could such magnificent roads be seen in country as rough as this.'

He had with him the Inca commander Chalcuchima, carried as a hostage in a litter. But as they progressed, it became clear that Inca resistance in the south was stiffening, and Pizarro began to suspect that Chalcuchima, far from protecting the party, was somehow getting information to the enemy.

On several occasions, Inca forces blocked the great Royal Road of the Incas ahead of the Spaniards, but each time they were driven off by quick cavalry thrusts.

Then on 8 November, De Soto was caught with a detachment in the steep Vilcaconga Pass. He had stopped to feed the horses and let the men rest from their wearing exertions in the thin air, when a barrage of stones was fired from slings from the top of the cliffs above. They caused utter confusion amongst horses and men, and before the Spaniards could recover scores of Inca soldiers ran down the hillside towards them, armed with bronze axes and maces and spiked clubs. The Spaniards broke and fell back. Many were beaten to death. Some of the horses were killed. For the first time, the Incas had defeated the enemy – and proved, too, that the dreaded horses were far from indestructible.

The Battle of the Vilcaconga Pass could have been a disaster. It raised the morale of the Incas as nothing else could have done. But before the Inca resistance could be properly organised, Pizarro met Manco Capac, half-brother to the dead Huascar. He was unquestionably the rightful heir to the throne. More important, he was perfectly content to collaborate with the Spaniards. His first action was to denounce his enemy Chalcuchima. In the plaza of Jaquijahuana, towards evening on 13 November, Chalcuchima was tied to a stake. Valverde offered him baptism, but Chalcuchima had seen what conversion to Christianity meant when Atahualpa had been murdered. Manco himself set fire to the pyre. Chalcuchima cried out, 'Viracocha! Huanacauri! Let my brother Quisquis avenge me!' According to Pizarro, 'he died with Pagan vengeance in his heart'.

Two days later, Pizarro rode into Cuzco.

It was, for him, the moment of supreme triumph. The banner of Castille and the standard of Pizarro were carried at the head of the procession through the streets. Trumpets sounded. Indians watched in the plaza, the magnificent stone walls of coursed masonry rising up twenty feet behind them. 'The greatest and finest city ever seen anywhere in the Indies,' it was called. 'It is so beautiful and has such fine buildings that it would be remarkable even in Spain.'

A contemporary drawing shows Pizarro entering Cuzco violently. In fact there was no fight.

In December 1533 Pizarro placed the royal fringe on Manco's forehead and pronounced him the Lord Inca. The crowd cheered. They had been taken into the empire of Spain without as yet knowing what that meant. They were also called upon to renounce the religion of their fathers and embrace Christianity. The Royal Requirement was read out: 'In the name of God and the Emperor, it is required that all must submit to the law of our Lord Jesus Christ and the service of His Majesty. All must Acknowledge our Holy Mother the Church and His Holiness the Pope. The Emperor of Spain who rules on behalf of His Holiness, brings to all native populations the one true religion. . . .'

The final outcome was inevitable. Despite Pizarro's orders that the newly-crowned Inca founded Lima as his capital city. But he never resolved his quarrel with Almagro and eventually he had him executed

But Almagro had friends with long memories.

The matter was not allowed to rest. On 26 June 1541 Pizarro, in his palace in Lima, had just finished lunch and was sitting talking with friends when a dozen armed Almagrists under the command of Juan de Herrada ran into the courtyard.

A Peruvian servant who tried to give the alarm was killed. Martin de Alcantara rushed into the room to warn his brother. Most of the guests ran for safety, but those who were armed stood beside Pizarro.

Pizarro carried a sword and buckler. He always did. He also fought as he had always done,

A map of North and South America drawn in 1592, less than 100 years after Columbus

and his subjects were to be treated with respect, everything of worth in Cuzco was taken. In some cases, the inhabitants were treated abominably.

Later, even the modicum of fairness shown to them disappeared. They were exploited, beaten, starved, worked to death. The most sacred relics of their religion were stolen, their wives and daughters taken from them, and even the Lord Inca, the central figure of their beliefs, was horribly abused. In the end, Manco – after two heroic rebellions – like Atahualpa before him was murdered by the Spanish invaders.

Even amongst the Spaniards themselves, the treasure they had found brought trouble. Pizarro was created a Marquis in 1535 and with courage, with unquenchable determination, without giving – or expecting – any quarter. He fought as befitted a conquistador. The odds were against him, but that was nothing new. What failed him, at last, was his luck. Martin fell with a thrust from Herrada. The Almagrists drove the others back into the room. In the end, no one but Pizarro was left standing. Eight men opposed him, yet it wasn't in his make-up to ask for mercy. He was overwhelmed by the sheer weight of numbers, falling to the floor with half a dozen sword blades through him. His last gesture was to make the sign of the cross with his own blood. His last utterance was a surprising 'God have mercy . . .'.

Almagro, executed by Pizarro at Cuzco. But Almagro had friends with long memories.

The relationship between the Viceroyalty of New Castille and Spain lasted almost 300 years. It was, however, never an easy one. Even in the early days there was the problem of the disillusioned Manco who had withdrawn into the high sierras, where from Vilcabamba and the magnificent stronghold of Macchu Picchu – a city the Spaniards never found – he conducted a guerrilla campaign until his eventual murder.

His kingdom, as it had been known under his father, had perished in all but one respect – its violence. It is easy to forget, in assessing Pizarro and his achievement, that the Inca civilisation he destroyed was, in fact, no less violent than the Spanish civilisation that replaced it.

Atahualpa himself was arguably no less guilty of torture and brutality than Pizarro. The Inca system was militaristic and highly organised and, admittedly, fed a large population. But still, if anything, the common peasant of Inca Peru was even worse off than his European counterpart. Mutilation, burning alive, hanging and quartering were common facts of life. Though Pizarro and the conquistadors who marched with him show badly against the standards of the twentieth century, in their own time they were neither better nor worse than the rest.

If their humanity is open to question, if their motives are seen to be only of conquest and of greed, there can be no doubt about their courage, their drive and their audacity.

Often, what they discovered they then destroyed. But their search for riches produced explorations and journeys as remarkable and significant as many travels undertaken only in the spirit of curiosity.

Christopher Columbus 1451–1506

Most schoolboys know that Columbus *didn't* discover America.

Christopher Columbus died believing he had discovered another route to Cathay (China). In fact, he had landed only in Cuba and the Bahamas; hadn't even found the 'new world' beyond. The riches, the jewels, the silks, the gold and the spices that he expected would crown his discovery didn't exist – where he landed.

The early colonies he set up for the King and Queen of Spain, financed by the Royal Exchequer in expectation of a rich reward, were miserable, impoverished failures.

At one stage Columbus was even brought back to Spain in chains, to face trial for his failure. He talked his way out of that.

Still his name, and his achievement, have never ceased to catch the imagination. He so nearly succeeded in discovering a land of fabled riches. Further north he would have come upon Mexico where later the Conquistadors were to loot and pillage. Further south were the fabled treasures of the Incas.

But Columbus did open up an era of discovery and exploration that was to last for centuries. He became a talisman, a model, for those who, through the centuries, were to suffer and strive to follow – and to discover.

CRISTO: COLOMBO

The prisoner sat, slumped, on the bare planking, his back against the rough oak timbers. He heard the caravel creak as the stiff wind thrust her through the water. Bare feet ran across the deck above him; in the distance someone bellowed an order.

He felt old and exhausted. He looked at the great shackles on his hands and feet. He wanted to weep.

He was the Admiral of the Ocean Seas, 'Viceroy and Governor-General in all the said Islands or Mainlands which he may discover in the said seas'.

Yet they were taking him back to Spain in chains, to face charges of 'misconduct and incompetence in the administration of their Majesties' colonies'.

The great dream of 'Gold, God and Cathay' was over. His enemies had brought him to his knees.

How different, he thought, from that first time. The spring of 1493 – 20 April. He had ridden into the great city of Barcelona, at the left hand of King Ferdinand, wearing a damask gown and red silk doublet, displaying the honours that their Majesties had bestowed on him. The city had gone wild with delight to see the Indians, the strange animals and birds he had brought back. No one had whispered against him then. No one had doubted that he had penetrated westwards into the fabled empire of the Great Khan of Cathay. The air had been full of falling rose petals, showered from windows and balconies, and thunderous shouts of 'Cristoval!'. . . .

He looked up to find Alonso Vallejo, captain of the caravel, standing in the entrance to the hold. Vallejo called him 'Admiral' and asked to be allowed to remove the chains. Cristoval shook his head. His face was drawn, his hair white. 'No', he said. He would wear them until their Majesties in person ordered them to be struck off. Even then he would keep them beside him 'as relics and as memorials'. They would remind

Columbus returning to Spain, in chains, to face charges of incompetence

him of the way Spain had rewarded him for the dedicated service he had given her.

He was as good as his word. Years later his son Fernando said that he 'saw them always hanging in his cabinet, and he requested that when he died they might be buried with him'.

Yet as he looked at Vallejo, he began to feel a glimmer of hope. He asked for pen and paper and began to write a letter to the Queen:

'The captain of the vessel that takes me to Spain says I may remove my chains. I have told him to leave them – I will wear them till your Highness pardons me.

'I came to serve you at the age of 28 and now I have not a hair on me that is not white, and my body is infirm and exhausted. All that was left me, and my brothers, has been taken away and sold, to my great dishonour, even to the cloak that I wore, without hearing or trial. Hitherto I have wept for others: now, Heaven have pity on me, and Earth, weep for me. Weep for me, Cristoval Colon. Whoever has truth and justice and charity – weep!'

If it reached Isabella, he knew very well the effect it would have.

It wasn't the first time he had used the technique. All his life he had felt himself forced to fight and wheedle to achieve what he wanted. And he had never been above using theatricality to achieve his ends.

From birth he had been driven by an insatiable ambition for wealth and glory. He never let anything stand in the way of it. . . .

He was born in Genoa in 1451, the son of a weaver. We know him as Christopher Columbus, though it wasn't the name he later gave himself. His early years are obscure. According to his son, Ferdinand, he studied astronomy, geometry and cosmography at the University of Pavia. According to his own account, he went to sea when he was fourteen. Certainly in his early twenties he was sailing the Mediterranean, and at twenty-five he was aboard a Genoese ship when she was attacked and sunk off Cape St Vincent by the Franco-Portuguese fleet. He was fortunate to escape drowning. He reached the Portuguese mainland and settled in Lisbon.

At the time, Lisbon was the centre of a large colony of Genoese merchants and seamen. Its cosmopolitan atmosphere suited Columbus. In 1477 he joined a voyage to the north visiting Bristol and possibly Ireland and Iceland. It might well have been this voyage and what he learned on it that helped to crystallise the ideas that had been forming in his mind.

Ambition began to press him. He had the drive for power, riches and status that characterised Pizarro and so many other Renaissance Europeans. He set up a map-making business in the Portuguese capital with Bartholomew, a brother ten years his junior.

Then at the age of twenty-eight he married. It was a surprising match, giving him a taste of that status he craved. He was an attractive young man, tall, blond and blue-eyed, and with his drive and sense of purpose any young woman might have been taken by him. Nevertheless, he was hardly in the same social stratum as Felipa Perestrella de Moniz. Her father had been governor of Porto Santo, one of the Portuguese possessions in the Atlantic, and her family had connections with Prince Henry the Navigator. Yet she married him, despite his background, and introduced him to a world of ideas and culture which he found greatly to his taste. A year later she gave him a son, Diego.

The marriage served as yet another spur to his ambition. He wanted not the modest wealth he might have earned from map-making, but great riches. Two voyages to West Africa had shown him that gold could be had for the taking – if one knew where to look for it. He conceived the idea that since it existed in Africa it must exist elsewhere in tropical climates. Marco Polo, years before, had written about the vast wealth of the east. He had painted a lavish picture of Cathay, the land known to us as China. Marco Polo had talked of Japan – Cipangu, he called it – as an island of silks, spices, ivories, gems and golden temples.

But the talk amongst the most ambitious of the merchants and seafarers in Lisbon wasn't of Africa or the east. The east was owned by the Grand Khan. The voyage there was long and difficult. Africa, what was known of it, was already largely under the control of Portugal.

What the visionaries talked of lay to the west, beyond the vast Atlantic. Despite the popular belief of the day, most mariners had little doubt that the earth was round, not flat. The classical geographers had also believed that there was only a short ocean distance between Spain and India. Between them, to the west, there might be unknown lands full of gold and treasure beyond imagination. If not, they calculated a voyage would establish a direct sea route to the eastern seaboards of Cipangu and Cathay and the spice islands of the Indies.

The idea caught the imagination of Columbus. And there was another aspect to it now. Besides gold, he sought glory. If he sailed westwards and discovered new lands, if he penetrated the great empire of the Khan, he could carry with him the gospel of Christ and convert millions of heathen to the one true religion. Where Pizarro was later in history to see himself as a conquerer, who had made a business arrangement with the state, Columbus saw himself as the very instrument of God. He wrote later: 'In the New Heaven and Earth which our Lord made He made me Cristoval Colon the messenger and showed me where to go.'

He began to prepare for the enterprise. He read widely and made a particular study of geography. He needed a sponsor, and the sponsor would require facts and convincing arguments before he would provide the ships and stores that Columbus required.

Sixteen hundred years earlier, Eratosthenes had made a very accurate calculation of the size of the earth. Since then, cosmographers had gradually reduced that size. Medieval mapmakers had gone even further, pulling the eastern extremity of Asia increasingly to the west. It seemed to Columbus that contemporary mapmakers bore out his growing belief that the way to the riches of the Indies lay to the west. His own calculations not only confirmed this but showed the route to be very much shorter than anyone had dreamed. On one of his voyages to West Africa he estimated that a degree of longitude was $45\frac{2}{3}$ miles. Using that figure as the basis of his calculations, he concluded that Japan lay just beyond the Azores. The discovery was immensely exciting. It was also immensely in-

accurate. He calculated that Japan lay a mere 2400 nautical miles west of the Canaries, and China no more than 3550. In fact the distances are 10,600 and 11,766 respectively.

At this time, Columbus' wife, Felipa, died and left him with a young son to bring up. He took it calmly. It made little difference to his plans. The dream of 'gold, God and Cathay' dominated his mind. All his efforts were directed to making it a reality. He managed to examine the correspondence of Paola da Toscanelli, a Florentine scientist who had approached King Alfonso V of Portugal with a similar project twenty-five years earlier. He saw a copy of the map that Toscanelli had made. It tallied very much with his own view of the world. His study of Toscanelli simply reinforced the vision that Columbus already had. He put his project to Alfonso's successor, King John II of Portugal. It was rejected by a committee of experts. Quite simply they couldn't accept Columbus' estimate of the distance to the Indies by the western route he proposed. More importantly, King John was committed to the idea of the route via the Cape.

But Columbus had the kind of personality that is stiffened by rejection. His determination to mount an expedition that would reach the Indies from the west grew stronger. His conviction that Cathay lay at the far side of the Atlantic became unshakeable. If King John's committee had doubts about his calculations they were fools. He turned from Portugal to Spain.

It wasn't easy. From 1485 to 1489 Columbus spent his time building influential friendships, sounding court opinion, finding individual backers. He took a mistress, Beatriz Enriquez, who bore him a son, Ferdinand. He sent his brother Bartholomew to sound out the French and English courts, but the young man had no success.

Increasingly Columbus was becoming the butt of court ridicule. 'From the age of twenty-eight, I served in the enterprise and conquest of the said Indies,' he wrote. He was now thirty-eight. For ten years he had peddled his scheme in all the centres of European influence, without success.

Then in 1489 the sovereigns of Spain, Ferdinand and Isabella, agreed to see him.

Columbus pleads his cause with Ferdinand and Isabella. The Queen finally agreed.

Again his hopes rose. Again they were shattered. Their Majesties wouldn't – couldn't – support him. The Moors in Granada were being crushed. It was an expensive business. Even if the sovereigns had wished to back him, there was no money to do it.

For Columbus it was another setback. But it wasn't the end. His single-mindedness became little less than obsession. The vision of the Indies grew and strengthened, the more he was frustrated and ridiculed.

Isabella, actually, liked the scheme. In particular she liked the missionary aspect that Columbus had taken care to stress. It would give her great satisfaction to think that, through her, millions had been saved from darkness – shepherded into the bosom of the true church. She didn't forget. In 1492, when the last stronghold of Islam had been crushed in Granada, Columbus was recalled to court. Ferdinand and Isabella agreed that a small expedition of three ships could sail west in search of the Indies.

But the terms Columbus wanted for himself were unacceptable. He asked for the hereditary title of Admiral of the Ocean Seas. He wanted to be made Viceroy and Governor-General of all territories he claimed in their Majesties' names. He wanted a tenth of the profits from the expedition, and to be a major investor in any subsequent expeditions. It was too much. Columbus was adamant. He hadn't waited thirteen years to give way now. Reluctantly, the sovereigns withdrew their offer.

Columbus knew he was right, though it didn't take the edge off his disappointment. It began to seem that the whole thing was going to remain a dream for ever. Then suddenly the Queen's confidante told him that Isabella had changed her mind. She and Ferdinand would accept all his conditions. He couldn't believe that it had finally happened, after the long years of ridicule and disappointment. He could only conclude that God himself had interceded on his servant's behalf. He wrote:

'When there was incredulity among all men, He gave the Queen, my Lady, the spirit of understanding and great courage. I went to take possession of the New World in her Royal Name. The rest of them sought to cover their ignorance, concealing their small knowledge by harping upon obstacles and the expense. But Her Highness on the contrary approved the Enterprise and supported it the best she could.'

By 17 April, the agreement between the sovereigns and Columbus had been completed and signed. His terms were accepted. He was given a letter of introduction from the Spanish court to the Grand Khan of Cathay. By the middle of May he was in Palos, near Cadiz, awaiting the arrival of the ships and stores. The town was to provide two of the vessels in payment of a debt it owed the Crown. Columbus carried a letter addressed to one of the town dignitaries, Diego Rodriguez Prieto, from Ferdinand and Isabella:

'Know ye that whereas for certain things done and committed by you to our disservice you were condemned and obligated by our Council to provide us for a twelvemonth with two equipped caravels at your own proper charge and expense . . . we command that within ten days of receiving this our letter . . . you have all ready . . . to depart.'

Ten days was to prove far too optimistic as an estimate of the amount of time necessary to provide the vessels. In the event it took ten weeks. The time wasn't wasted. There was a great deal for Columbus to do. A third ship had to be found, lists of stores and equipment drawn up and assembled, a crew sworn in. The Crown, now the decision to mount an expedition had been taken, was unstinting in putting its whole authority behind the enterprise. Apart from the letter to the town of Palos, three other royal letters were issued. They instructed all timber merchants, carpenters, ship's chandlers, bakers and provision merchants in Andalusia to provide Columbus with everything he needed at reason-

1. **Christopher Columbus,** played in the film by Carlos Ballesteros.

2. *Santa Maria*, **the flagship commissioned and financed by King Ferdinand and Queen Isabella to extend the boundaries of the Spanish Empire, and also to discover the quick route to the west across the sea to Cathay (China) and – most of all – sent to exploit that fabled land.**

3. **Wherever they explored, natives greeted them. Some wore gold ornaments. It was enough for Columbus. He died still believing that he and his men had in fact reached Cathay.**

4. **Columbus returned triumphantly to the Royal Palace in Barcelona from his first exploration. He was showered with rose petals, cheered by the crowd, honoured by the King and Queen.**

5. **He displayed gold trophies and curios. Not many, but it was sufficient to excite the royal curiosity, and the royal greed. They agreed to finance another expedition.**

6. **Columbus returned to Navidad, the colony he left on the shores of what he thought was China, but was, in fact, Cuba. At once he knew something was wrong. The garrison had been slaughtered, the fort was ransacked.**

(*continued p.209*)

4

2

3

5

7. When their search for gold finally became desperate and unrewarding, they discovered and then exploited a new trade — slaves.

8. The end of a dream. Columbus, stripped of his office, is returned to Spain in chains, hauled away to face charges of incompetence.

The film was directed by Lawrence Gordon Clark, and shot in Spain, the Atlantic and the Caribbean.

able prices. The articles he bought were to be free from local taxes. In addition, if anyone who agreed to sail with Columbus had a civil or criminal action pending against him, such action was to be suspended.

The two ships eventually provided by Palos were caravels, a type of vessel that had already been used for the successful exploration of the West African coast. They were single-decked craft with a low forecastle for stowage of cables and sails. The raised quarter-deck had a toldilla on it, a construction that housed the captain's and master's cabins. They drew about six feet of water and had a hold some nine feet deep. The overall length was seventy feet and the beam a little over twenty. Their names were *Pinta* and *Niña*.

The third ship, when she arrived, was a não. Her name was *Santa Maria*, and she was a disappointment to Columbus. He had asked for three caravels. Instead, for his flagship, he had to make do with this heavier, slower, more rounded vessel, that was rarely seen outside the Mediterranean. She drew no more water than the caravels, though she weighed almost ninety tons against their sixty. The one thing in her favour was the great size of her hold.

The fleet left Palos on 3 August 1492. There was modest rejoicing at the departure, though Palos itself was in a state of some confusion: Spain had decided to expel its Jewish population and the quayside was full of wretched emigrants.

The *Santa Maria* turned south-westerly and began to run down the African coast, the *Niña* and *Pinta* holding station behind her.

Despite the support that Ferdinand and Isabella had given Columbus, their actual financial involvement in the expedition was slight. Most of the funds came from friends of Columbus at court and from Genoese financiers operating in Spain. Additionally, many of the men on board the three ships had investments in the enterprise. The three owners of the ships were present, Juan de La Cosa of the *Santa Maria*, Cristobal Quintero of the *Pinta* and Juan Nino of the *Niña*. La Cosa and Nino were also masters of their vessels.

Despite the official position held by Columbus as Captain of the *Santa Maria* and overall leader of the expedition, most men felt their involvement to be an individual one rather than a co-operative one as a member of a team. Family loyalties amongst the crew posed a particular problem. They cut across loyalties to superiors and in particular to Columbus. The Pinzons were a case in point. Martin Alonso Pinzon, an experienced sailor in his late forties, was captain of the *Pinta*. His brother, Vincente Yanez Pinzon, was captain of the *Niña*. A third Pinzon, Francisco Martin, was master of the *Pinta*. These tight blood relationships were not the only ones to cause disunity. Regional loyalties were intense. Most amongst the crews were from Andalusia. But there were sufficient Basques and Galicians to form a northern faction under the control of the *Santa Maria*'s master and owner, Juan de La Cosa. With a strong overall commander, such rivalries would have been held in check. But Columbus was not that. He was as individual as any man under his command in his aspirations, and not used to welding men to common purpose.

The *Santa Maria* with her crew of forty put into Gomera in the Canaries on 12 August. She was followed by the *Niña* with twenty-two men on board. The twenty-six man crew of the *Pinta* were left to take their vessel into Las Palmas to have a defective rudder repaired. Spirits were high. The voyage so far had gone almost exactly to plan. The intention now was to turn westwards into the open Atlantic, in the hope of picking up a favourable north-east trade wind that would carry them all the way to Cathay. In the meantime there were last-minute repairs and adjustments to be carried out, and the final load of stores to be taken aboard. It was vital to carry all the provisions necessary to meet every eventuality.

It was usual at that time to carry fresh meat in the form of live pigs and chickens, in pens and coops on deck. The rest of the food was carried in barrels. There was salted meat and sardines, flour, rice and biscuits, chick-peas, lentils, beans, almonds, raisins, honey, cheese and vinegar. Wine and water were carried in casks, olive oil in great earthenware jars.

A ship at sea, in the midst of an unknown ocean, had to be totally self-sufficient. If planks were sprung in a storm they had to be replaced or repaired. If sails ripped or rotted, there had to be stores from which new ones could be made, and sailmakers to make them. Apart from food and drink, stores had to include wood, bolts, nails, pitch, whale oil, tallow and sulphur. There had to be supplies of sailcloth, yarn, ropes, cord, and sheets of copper and iron, together with the tools for using them.

Apart from Columbus' own inspired, but totally inaccurate calculations, there was no way of knowing how long the journey west might take, nor what strange monsters or human enemies might be met with on the way. No one aboard seriously thought they might sail off the edge of the earth and fall into the bottomless pit. But there were few without some lingering fear of running into seas of boiling water, or coming face to face with three-legged men and one-eyed fiends.

Each ship was armed. There were iron cannon and falconets. The cannon were mounted on wooden carriages with wheels, and fired through ports in the ships' sides. They weighed half a ton each and could throw a 4-pound stone ball up to 1000 yards. The falconets were mounted on the bulwarks on swivels. They had a calibre of a little under two inches, and were more usually loaded with pieces of iron scrap than with ball. In case of a boarding attempt, the artillery could be backed up by arquebuses carried by some of the crew.

The armament required its own specialist stores. There were stone balls for the cannon, scrap for the falconets and barrels of powder. There was wadding and matches for the artillery and arquebuses, bolts for the crossbows, arrows for the bows. Bucklers, swords and lances had to be carried for use by the crew.

The range of additional stores necessary to make the expedition self-sufficient was enormous. There were copper cauldrons, three-legged iron cooking pots, copper ladles, measuring vessels, bowls, candles and snuffers, lamps and oil and wicks to go with them. There was tinder and firewood for the cooking stove, and steel and flint to fire it. There were boat-hooks, sweeps, wooden buckets and tubs, mats, baskets, fish hooks, lines, sinkers, nets and harpoons. In case of mutiny there were manacles and leg irons, and for trading with the subjects of the Great Khan there were brass hawks' bells, tambourines and strings of coloured glass beads. Each ship was a microcosm of late-fifteenth-century Spain.

On 6 September the fleet left the Canaries. Three days later, land finally disappeared from view. The weather remained calm, the sea was a magnificent greeny blue, full of leaping flying fish. The men worked together well enough, but even then Columbus could sense an underlying discord. He wrote in his journal: 'I decided at this point to reckon less than I made, so that if the voyage were a long one the people would not be frightened and dismayed.' He was making, in fact, an average of 110 miles a day.

What added to Columbus' problems was the frequent hint that land lay just beyond the horizon. The men knew well enough what was involved in the voyage. For the most part they were experienced sailors. They would have put up with a hard trip and long days of empty sea if it hadn't been for constant signs of nearby land and the no less constant disappointment of not finding it. They were no more than a week out from the Canaries when the first of the signs reached them: '. . . many bunches of very green weed which had a short time been torn from land; whereby all judged they were near some land'. Columbus knew they were wrong. Even his most optimistic assessment of the Atlantic's width hadn't put Cathay as close as this. 'I make the mainland further on,' he wrote.

The expedition had in fact reached the eastern extremity of the Sargasso Sea. Next day – the 17th – more weed appeared. Someone found a little live crab in it, no bigger than a thumbnail. It sent spirits and expectations soaring. Yet still there was no land to gratify those expectations and the men showed the first signs of turning sour. Columbus was concerned about the thickening weed. If it continued to become more dense, there was a possibility that the ships might stick fast in it. The prospect was terrifying. To be wrecked on a reef was one thing. There was always a chance of scrambling on to dry land. But to be marooned, for ever, in a swamp of black seaweed in the middle of an unknown ocean – that was something quite different.

The weed wasn't the only disturbing phenomenon. That same day the position of the pole star, always considered to be fixed, appeared to have moved a full seven degrees. The cause was a combination of the comparatively small movement that the star actually makes, and a large westerly magnetic variation. To Columbus and the two other captains, it was an awesome discovery. It challenged their view of the universe. If the pole star could leave its appointed place in the heavens and move about at will, what other terrors might lie ahead?

From the 20th, things grew worse. They were out of the trade winds. What wind there was was unpredictable. For days on end they were becalmed in the endless weed. At times they covered no more than twenty-five miles in an entire day. The men were less concerned now with finding Cathay than with finding a wind that would carry them safely home again. Still there were the signs of land, constantly playing with their hopes. Birds settled in the rigging. Some of them sang. But the lookout aloft saw nothing but the sea of weed running to the horizons. There was talk of throwing Columbus overboard and returning to Spain.

On the 25th, Martin Alonso Pinzon rushed to the poop of the *Pinta* and shouted across to the *Santa Maria* and the *Niña*, 'Tierra, Tierra!' He claimed the reward offered by the sovereigns to the first man who sighted land – an annuity of 10,000 maravedis, equal to ten months of an able seaman's pay. But investigation showed nothing. On 7 October it was Vincente Yanez Pinzon's turn to raise a flag at *Niña*'s masthead. Land, he declared, lay dead ahead. Once more it was a false alarm.

On the 10th, mutiny broke out on the *Santa Maria*. The men refused to go any farther. 'I calculate landfall at Cathay at any hour,' said Columbus. 'But the men fear we have sailed too far South and missed Asia altogether.' There were disagreements between Columbus and the Pinzon brothers as to whether they should proceed or return. Columbus promised the crews that if the Indies weren't sighted within the next two or three days he would turn back. In his journal there is no hint of a compromise: 'I will continue until I find them,' he wrote.

That night a gale sprang up, and blew all next day. The weed had disappeared. The *Niña* picked up a branch from the water with a flower on it resembling the wild rose of Castille. The *Pinta* found lengths of cane and a land plant. Expectancy grew. 'Everybody breathed more freely and grew cheerful.' No one was anxious to go below. Men stood on deck looking westwards to where the outline of a coast was expected at any moment. Columbus thought he saw a light in the darkness ahead, but it proved to be nothing.

Then, at 2 am on Friday 12 October 1492 Rodrigo de Triana, lookout on the *Pinta's* forecastle, saw the New World.

Columbus had covered 3066 miles in thirty-three days. As far as he was concerned, the island that lay revealed ahead of them when the sun rose was part of the Great Khan's Cathay. It was a view he held until his death. He landed that same afternoon, dressed in his scarlet doublet and carrying the royal standard. Once on the beach, with the natives watching from the shelter of palm groves, he knelt and prayed:

'O Lord, Almighty and Everlasting God, Thou hast created the Heaven and the Earth, and the Sea, blessed and glorified by Thy Name, and praised be Thy Majesty which hath used Thy Humble servants, that Thy Holy Name may be proclaimed in this second part of the Earth.'

Columbus named the place San Salvador and claimed it in the name of Spain. Then he turned to the task of finding the court of the Great Khan. He had with him a 'converso', a converted Jew by the name of Luis de Torres. De Torres spoke Hebrew and Arabic and was to act as interpreter for the expedition. It was believed that through one or other of the two languages,

First landing of Christopher Columbus, painted by Frederick Kemmelmeyer about 1800

de Torres would be able to communicate with the Khan's representatives.

De Torres called to the natives in Arabic, then Hebrew. The Indians – Arawaks of the Taino tribe – came forward tentatively, showing curiosity and no sign of aggression. Neither did they show any understanding of what de Torres was saying. Columbus gave them trinkets, 'so that these people might be well disposed towards us – to be delivered and converted to our Holy Faith by love rather than by force'. Later he described them in detail:

'They go quite naked as their mothers bore them; and also the women, although I didn't see more than one really young girl. All that I saw were young men, none of them more than 30 years old, very well-made, of very handsome bodies and very good faces; the hair coarse almost as the hair of a horse's tail and short: the hair they wear over their eyebrows except for a hank behind that they wear long and never cut. Some of them paint themselves black, and some paint themselves white, and others red, and others with what they have. Some paint their faces and others their whole body, others the eyes only, others only the nose.'

Columbus concluded that he had landed on one of the islands in the archipelago that was known to lie east of Japan. It was understandable that the Indians there should be so poor. Many that he saw bore the scars of battle, yet none seemed warlike. The most reasonable explanation to Columbus was that the Khan's warriors made periodic raids, stole the Indians' gold and took them away as slaves.

'They ought to be good servants and of good skill,' he wrote, 'for I see that they repeat very quickly all that is said to them; and I believe that they would easily be made Christians, because it seemed to me that they belonged to no religion.'

There were just enough signs of gold in San Salvador to whet the expedition's appetite. A Taino with a gold ornament in his nose pointed southwards when he was questioned about it. It simply confirmed what Columbus was already thinking. The mainland, with the vast treasure houses, lay in that direction. Taino guides agreed to show him the way. He wrote:

'I here propose to leave to circumnavigate this island until I may have speech with this King and see if I can obtain from him the gold that I heard he has, and afterwards to depart for another much larger island which I believe must be Japan according to the description of these Indians whom I carry, and which they call Colba, in which they say that there are ships and sailors both many and great; and beyond this is another island which they call Bofio, which also they say is very big; and the others which are between we shall see as we pass, and according as I shall find a collection of gold or spicery, I shall decide what I have to do. But in any case I am determined to go to the mainland and to the city of Quinsay, and to present your Highness's letters to the Grand Khan, and to beg a reply and come home with it.'

Colba turned out to be Cuba not Japan, though Columbus was never aware of it. He dropped anchor in the large bay of Puerto Gibara, which he called Rio de Mares, at the end of October. The pressure on him to find gold was increasing. The Pinzons in particular were becoming restive. They had travelled 3000 miles to see the fabled city of Quinsay, which Marco Polo had described as being built of gold. So far they had seen nothing but empty beaches and naked Indians.

Columbus' tragedy was his inability to shift his view when confronted by seriously conflicting facts. He took a sighting of the star beta cephei, mistaking it for the pole star. It gave him a reading of 42°N, the latitude of Cape Cod. He was in fact at 21°06′N. A navigator like Cook would have questioned the reading. To Columbus it merely convinced him he was in China. The vision that had sustained him through thirteen long years of ridicule and disappointment had become an *idée fixe*.

Cuba was beautiful. 'I never beheld so fair a thing,' said Columbus. Yet still there was no gold. He wondered how much further he had to go to find the treasures Marco Polo had seen. The men had become troublesome, accusing him of having misled them. For a moment he had a vision of himself returning to Spain empty-handed. It was unthinkable. Then he heard the words he had been waiting for so long.

A naked Taino was standing before him and pointing south. He was saying 'Cubanacan'; it was the name of an inland village. Columbus mistook it for 'El Gran Khan'.

An expedition was mounted at once. De Torres collected his impressive credentials bearing the signatures of the sovereigns of Spain. He was to 'carry gifts and letters of credence from your Highnesses to the mighty Emperor of that city where seven palaces are roofed entirely with gold'. The prospect filled de Torres with apprehension. He expected a scene of such monumental magnificence he wondered if he could handle it.

Cubanacan turned out to be a bitter disappointment. It was a village of fifty thatched huts, a few large and rectangular, most small and circular. The inhabitants, Taino Indians, were little more than subsistence farmers, living on manioc, corn and potatoes and smoking rolled tobacco through their nostrils. De Torres couldn't make himself understood in either Arabic or Hebrew. The few trinkets of gold that the Tainos wore hardly matched Marco Polo's description of Cathay. Taino Caciques, the provincial ruler, was kind and courteous to the visitors; his subjects kissed their hands and feet, believing them to have come from heaven. But the conquerors from Andalusia had expected gold. Obeisance was not a satisfactory substitute.

The news that de Torres carried back to Rio de Mares depressed everyone. The expedition split into factions, each one with its own plans and opinions.

Columbus seemed unaware of the dangerous currents that were strengthening around him. On 21 November Martin Alonso Pinzon sailed away in the *Pinta* and disappeared. Columbus wrote, 'Martin Pinzon of the Pinta deserted this night. I believe he has gone to seek gold in an island to the south. He has always been a rebellious and avaricious man. I trust your Highnesses will not forget his treason.'

Columbus raised anchor once again and turned south with the *Santa Maria* and the *Niña*. A new and splendid vision was forming in his mind. He wrote: 'I intend to make a new chart of navigation, upon which I shall place the whole sea and lands of the Ocean Sea in their proper positions under their bearings, and further, to compose a book, and set down everything as in a real picture, by latitude north of the equator and longitude west; and above all it is very important that I forget sleep and labour much at navigation, because it is necessary and the which will be a great task.'

The crew had more mundane things to occupy them. Most of them were aged between twenty and thirty, except for the 'gromets' – the ship's boys who were anywhere from twelve to eighteen. The day was broken into six watches, set at 3, 7 and 11 am and pm. There were no ship's clocks and the passage of time was kept by the 'ampolleta'. The ampolleta was a waisted glass containing sand. It took the sand exactly thirty minutes to run from the upper compartment to the lower, at which point a gromet reversed it.

Shipboard life was dominated by religious ritual. At dawn, the gromet on the ampolleta duty sang:

> *Bendita sea la luz*
> *y la Santa veracruz . . .*
> *Blessed be the light of day*
> *and the Holy Cross, we say;*
> *and the Lord of Veritie*
> *and the Holy Trinity.*
> *Blessed be th'immortal soul*
> *and the Lord who keeps it whole*
> *blessed be the light of day*
> *and he who sends the night away.*

He then recited the Pater Noster and Ave Maria, then said: 'Dios nos de bueno dias . . . God give us good days, good voyage, good passage to the ship, sir captain and master and good company, so let there be, let there be a good voyage, many good days. May God grant your graces, gentlemen of the afterguard and gentlemen forward.'

The watch came on duty and were given a meal of cheese and biscuits, with wine and perhaps a few salted sardines. They had spent the night fully dressed, sleeping on mats and old sailcloth under the forecastle or in some corner of the deck. Their first task was to scrub the deck with besoms and salt water pulled up from the sea in buckets. Lookouts were posted forward and aloft, rigging was continually adjusted, empty store barrels were taken below and fresh supplies brought up. A gromet would prepare meat for the midday meal by treading it for an hour in a barrel of water. This removed some of the salt from the tissues and made it more edible.

Sailing a ship like the *Santa Maria* or the *Niña* was a continuous occupation. What little free time there was was spent playing cards or dice, fishing with a line trailed behind the ship, mending clothing. In calm weather, some of the men swam, leaping into the warm sea and splashing about for a moment, then catching hold of a rope trailing from the ship's waist.

Before the first night watch was set, all hands were called to prayer. The process was complex. It began with a gromet trimming the binnacle lamp and chanting: 'Amen, and God give us a good night and good sailing; may the ship make a good passage, Sir captain and master and good company.' All hands then chanted *La doctrina Christiana*, followed by the Pater Noster, Ave Maria and Credo. Finally they sang the Salve Regina. Throughout the night, a prayer was offered to God every half-hour by the gromet on the ampolleta:

One glass is gone and now the second floweth;
more shall run down if my God willeth.
To my God let's pray
to give us a good voyage;
And through his blessed Mother,
our advocate on high,
protect us from the waterspout
and send no tempest nigh.

Columbus' own accommodation in the toldilla on the poop was little more than a cell. It contained a small desk, table and chair, bed and washstand. A trunk carried his personal belongings. Like the rest of the crew and officers, there was plenty to occupy him:

'I sleep very little when I am commanding the ship. I have to plot the course and take the speed and see that everything is properly recorded. . . . I do not trust anyone else to do these things properly. The smallest error can be disastrous. I watch everything all the time.'

The need for such constant watch became apparent on 24 December. Columbus had reached

Columbus' own sketch map of the coast of the New World

the north coast of Hispaniola – today Haiti and the Dominican Republic. In his view there were encouraging signs of gold, though the crews of the *Santa Maria* and *Niña* were becoming increasingly disillusioned about the prospect of ever finding it. The Indians were helpful and extremely friendly. Their chief, Guarcanagari, showered Columbus with presents and entertained him and his men. Columbus would have stayed there for the Christmas festival, but a conviction grew in him that Cipangu – Japan – lay only a few miles away. There was no basis for the conviction, beyond a simple misunderstanding of something Guarcanagari said, but Columbus put to sea at once and headed eastwards.

At eleven o'clock that night, Columbus handed over the watch to Juan de la Cosa and retired. An hour later the *Santa Maria* was on a reef. La Cosa had handed the tiller to an inexperienced gromet and gone to sleep. The damage to the ship at that point wasn't substantial. Columbus ordered La Cosa into the ship's boat with the kedge anchor; he was to let it go clear of the reef so that the *Santa Maria* could be hauled off. But La Cosa panicked. He was certain the ship was going down, and he pulled for the *Niña* to save himself.

By the time La Cosa was persuaded to return, it was too late. The *Santa Maria* had come beam on to the sea and the jagged coral tore her to pieces. The crew were safe, but the expedition that had started so full of hope from Spain was now reduced to one ship. The prospect of returning home loaded with the treasures of the Indies seemed increasingly remote. Yet even then Columbus could see the benevolent hand of God in the disaster: 'In truth, the shipwreck was no disaster but great fortune. If we had not run aground, we should never have found this place. It is certain there is much gold here. God must have ordained our shipwreck so that we should find a settlement on this shore.'

The place was called Navidad. With the help of Guacanagari and his Indians, Columbus carried the timbers of the *Santa Maria* ashore and set to work on a stockade. 'I have given orders to build a fortress,' he wrote. 'Thirty-nine seamen have volunteered to man it. I will leave them with provisions for a year so that they are free to find the gold mines. The Indians here are cowardly beyond hope but this great tower will show them the might of your Highnesses and turn them more readily to God.'

Columbus left Hispaniola in the *Niña* on the morning of 16 January 1493, for Spain. He carried a few Indians with him and a little gold. His intention was to return as soon as possible with reinforcements. Gold lay somewhere at the back of Hispaniola, he was convinced. He would have it whatever the cost. It had become the driving passion of his life: 'O most excellent gold! Who has gold has a treasure which gives him power to get what he desires, it lets him impose his will on the world and even helps souls into paradise.' He set back for Spain.

He anchored in the Rio Tinto at Palos on 15 March. The *Pinta* was already there, just ahead of him. He was furious with her captain, Martin Alonso Pinzon, for leaving the expedition as he had, but before he could confront the man Pinzon had landed and taken himself off to his estate. He was sick, and died within a week.

Columbus' reception in Barcelona, where the court was sitting, was ecstatic. The town went wild about the hero who had reached Cathay and claimed so much of it for Spain. He pointed to the group of Taino Indians and the pile of gold

Columbus returned to the court with Indian captives and gold artefacts

216

artefacts he had brought, and said: 'The humble gifts which I bring to your Highnesses will give you some idea of the wealth of these regions. Doubters may say I exaggerate the amount of gold and spices to be found, and, in truth, we have only yet seen a hundredth of the splendour of these kingdoms. . . . I know that huge mines of gold will be found if your Highnesses allow me to return.' (It was not known then that as well as the 'humble gifts' he was displaying to their Catholic Majesties, his expedition was carrying syphilis from the New World and introducing it into Europe for the first time.)

His plea to Ferdinand and Isabella for continued support was successful. He was allowed to return to Hispaniola. This time it was to be no mere voyage of exploration, but a full-scale conquest. Seventeen ships and 1500 men went with him, including noblemen, courtiers and priests. The Indians were to be converted to Christianity, a trading colony was to be established, and Columbus was to explore Cuba and find out whether it was the mainland as he himself believed, or simply another island.

On 27 November Columbus reached Navidad. It was clear at once that something terrible had happened. The stockade was smashed and the garrison had disappeared. A search revealed the remains of eleven bodies. The chief Guacanagari told what had happened. The Spaniards had quarrelled amongst themselves; groups had gone off pillaging amongst the Indians, stealing gold dust, molesting women. Finally one of these groups under Pedro Gutierrez had run into the savage Carib Indians who inhabited the centre of the island. Caonabo, their chief, had killed the Spaniards and wiped out the garrison in the fort. Guacanagari had tried to help, but the Tainos were no match for the Caribs.

That winter, Columbus set up two forts on Hispaniola at Isabella and Santo Tomas, and put them under the command of two soldiers, Hojeda and Magarit. A certain amount of gold was found at Cibao in the hinterland, but none of the rich mines that Columbus had promised to Ferdinand and Isabella. He began to feel desperation. With the massive investment that had now been made in the enterprise, he had to show some substantial results.

He wrote: 'I have been ill with a high fever and delirium. My eyes also trouble me. My desire to find Cathay for your Highnesses' glory makes me work ever harder.'

He set off for Cuba, determined to establish that it was the mainland. It was a difficult voyage. He met his first serious opposition from the Indians since the Navidad massacre. He wrote: 'Were it for my own sake alone, I would no longer endure these torments and dangers. For not a day passes but that we see death staring us in the face.' He sailed along the southern coast, through the maze of islands that he called the Garden of the Queen, to within a hundred miles of the western extremity of the island. Then suddenly he abandoned the project. He knew he was right. It was the mainland. It might even be the east coast of the Malayan peninsula. He drew up a document to the effect that Cuba was the mainland of Cathay. The crew were forced to sign it, or face the prospect of never seeing Spain again. Any man who later recanted would be fined 10,000 Maravedis and have his tongue cut out.

Columbus returned to Hispaniola in July 1494. He was exhausted and ill. He suffered a high fever, with delirium and lapses into coma. In fact, he was going through what in modern terms would be called a severe nervous breakdown. Throughout the summer and autumn he lay in a stupor, hardly fit to issue an order. Not till December was he sufficiently recovered to review the situation on the island. It was not encouraging. Magarit had met severe opposition from the Indians after raping their women and stealing their food and gold dust. He had suppressed them with cavalry. In the end he had sailed back to Spain with one of the priests, Fray Buil, and other malcontents.

And there, he set about slandering Columbus at court.

The dissatisfaction of Ferdinand and Isabella with Columbus became apparent in their dispatches to him. It was clear that he would have to produce a good deal more wealth for them than he had been able to do so far, if he was to find his way back into their favour. He decided on a threefold plan: the capture of Caonabo, whose Caribs had caused so much trouble, the introduction of a slave trade, and more effective ways of extracting gold from the island.

Caonabo was taken by a ruse, lured into putting manacles on his hands and feet by being told that that was what the great sovereigns of Spain did on important occasions. Columbus described it to Ferdinand and Isabella:

'We captured Caonabo, the king who destroyed the garrison at Navidad. He led a warlike tribe in the north of this island of Haiti. They carry bows and spears and are very fierce. I will send him to your Highnesses in chains. We caught him by a trick. Since all Indians have a great love for bells we told him we wished to give him the great bell at Isabella. We made him believe that shackles were worn on all state occasions by your Majesties so it would be a great honour for *him* to put them on.'

Caonabo never reached Spain. He was one of the hundreds who died at sea and were tossed into the waves.

As early as February 1494, Columbus had drawn up a memorandum on the establishment of a trade in slaves between Hispaniola and Spain, but the sovereigns had not welcomed the idea. Now he returned to the plan. He sent an expedition into the interior to capture Caribs and bring them back to Isabella. De Cuneo, who had come out with Columbus on the second expedition, wrote:

'We gathered together in our settlement 1600 people male and female of those Indians, of whom, among the best males and females, we embarked on our caravel on 17th February 1495, 550 souls. Of the rest who were left the announcement went around that whoever wanted them could take as many as he pleased; and this was done. And when everybody had been supplied there were some 400 of them left to whom permission was granted to go wherever they wanted. Among them there were many women who had infants at the breast. They, in order the better to escape us, since they were afraid we would turn to catch them again, left their infants anywhere on the ground and started to flee like desperate people; and some fled so far they were removed from our settlement of Isabella 7 or 8 days beyond mountains and across huge rivers; wherefore from now on scarcely any will be had.'

Slave trading in the New World, 1494

The Indians now began to resist. Under Guatiguana, a leader who had escaped from the Spaniards, they massed in the Vega Real. On 27 March 1495 Columbus and his brother Bartholomew marched against them with a force of two hundred foot soldiers, twenty cavalry and twenty dogs. The result was a massacre. In this confrontation Indian resistance was broken for ever.

Inevitably, the supply of Caribs shipped to Seville, for sale in the market there, ran out. Columbus turned his attention to the friendly Tainos, despite the fact that it was their leader Guacanagari who had helped to rescue stores from the wrecked *Santa Maria* and tried to save the defenders of Navidad from Caonabo's Caribs.

'. . . as many as might be in that village were punished with execution and torture'

And to fulfil his aim of increasing the supply of gold, Columbus introduced a system of tribute. Every Indian over fourteen was required to pay or be killed. The tribute exacted was one hawk's bell full of gold dust every three months. The alternative for those Indians living where no gold at all existed, was twenty-five pounds of spun or woven cotton. When payment was made, the Indian was given a stamped token of copper or brass to wear round his neck.

The system was brutal and barbaric. There was little gold on Hispaniola. The Indians worked ceaselessly to meet the tribute. Many couldn't pay it at all. Las Casas, who knew Columbus personally, described the system as 'irrational, most burdensome, impossible, intolerable, and abominable'. Even when Columbus was persuaded to reduce his demands by half, they remained exorbitant. Las Casas wrote:

'Some complied, and for others it was impossible; and so, falling into the most wretched way of living, some took refuge in the mountains while others, since the violence and provocation and injuries on the part of the Christians never ceased, killed some Christian for special damages and tortures that they suffered. Then straightaway against them was taken the vengeance which the Christians called punishment; not only the murderers, but as many as might be in that village or region were punished with execution and torture, not respecting the human and divine justice and natural law under whose authority they did it.'

Thousands of Indians took poison or chose suicide rather than face being taken alive

Those who ran into the mountains were hunted by dogs. Thousands took cassava poison, rather than face the horrors of being taken alive.

When Columbus reached Hispaniola in 1492 it had an estimated population of 300,000. Fifteen years later, 240,000 had been killed or sold into slavery.

Columbus returned to Spain in the summer of 1496 to answer charges of incompetence. He was astute enough to remove his decorations and finery before landing, and cover himself in the contrite habit of a Franciscan. Despite the work of his detractors, the Crown remained loyal to him. He was well received at court and given a new fleet of eight ships to take back to His-

paniola. The terms of his business contract were improved. He was to receive one eighth of the gross and one tenth of the net profits of each subsequent voyage, for a period of three years. He was granted the right of creating a *mayorazgo*, by which his titles and estates were entailed in perpetuity.

He was in Spain for two years before returning to Hispaniola by way of the Cape Verde Islands and the mouth of the Orinoco. 'If this Earthly river does not come from the Earthly Paradise,' he wrote, 'then it must come from an immense land in the South, about which we yet know nothing.' He made no attempt to discover what land that was. He was old and ill. Much of the fire and drive had gone out of him, though the old vision of gold and glory remained.

For two years he managed to survive in the chaos and strife of Hispaniola, resorting to excesses of brutality to keep order. Finally the sovereigns sent Francisco Bobadilla to examine

It was the end of Columbus' governorship, but not of his travels. Cathay still beckoned. On 9 May 1502 he sailed westwards again with four caravels and 150 men. Still ignorant of the continent to the west, he wanted to penetrate into Portuguese Asia. For a year he sailed round

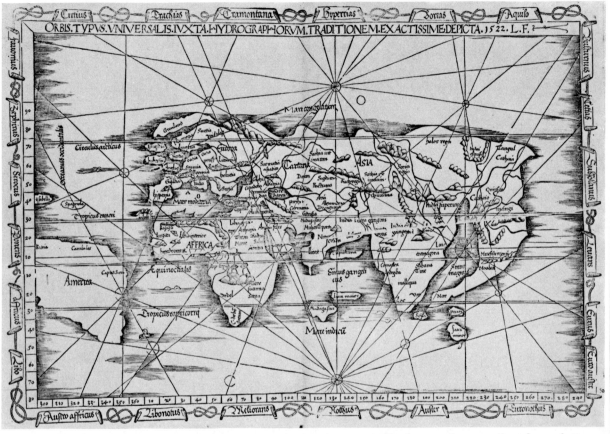

Sixteen years after Columbus' death, a map of 1522 shows not Cathay to the west, but America

the truth behind the stream of reports of mismanagement that were reaching them. Almost the first sight that met him when he reached the settlement at Isabella, on 23 August 1500, was a scaffold with seven Spanish corpses hanging from it. He sent Columbus back to Spain in irons. . . .

But Isabella was moved to tears.

Columbus' hair was white, his long face drawn. He was an old man, sick, worn out. Isabella repudiated everything that Bobadilla had done. Columbus was to be compensated for what had happened to him, and Bobadilla was to be replaced and impeached. Columbus had not, in the end, lost.

the Caribbean, discovering the mainland of Honduras and a number of islands. Then in the summer of 1503 he ran aground in Don Christopher's Cove in Jamaica. There his worm-riddled ships fell to pieces.

For a year he stayed in Jamaica waiting for a ship. It was not until the end of 1504 that he finally managed to get back to Spain.

It was clear to everyone that he would never go back to sea. He went with the court to Segovia and Valladolid. But he was failing fast. He made adjustments to his will, putting in a final codicil on 19 May 1506, bequeathing the *mayorazgo* to Diego. The next day he was dead.

In 1542 his body was removed from Seville

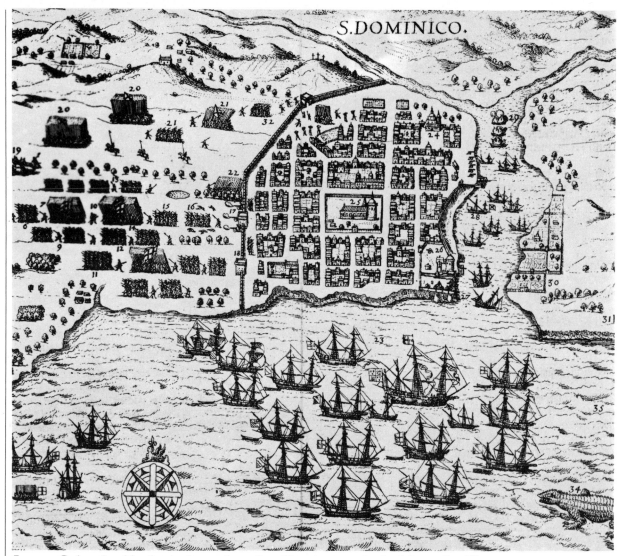

In 1542 Columbus' body was brought to San Domingo cathedral from Seville

and taken to the cathedral of San Domingo. Later it was placed in a tomb in the cathedral of Cuidad Trujillo.

Columbus has never ceased to catch the imagination. As recently as 1940 work started on a memorial lighthouse at the mouth of the Ozama river in the Dominican Republic.

Columbus failed to find Cathay.

He failed even to discover the vast continent that did lie beyond the Atlantic. He failed to find the gold that obsessed him. He introduced, to the new world, a system of colonial exploitation, a pattern of tyranny and violence, torture and slavery, the bitter results of which still surround us.

Yet he so nearly succeeded in his search for the great fabled riches.

Further north he would have found the treasures of Montezuma, that Cortes was to find a few years later. Further south lay the golden artefacts of the Incas, later to be plundered by Pizarro.

While his ambition burned fierce all the time and his persuasive powers seldom waned, his shortcomings – both as a man, as a leader of men, and even as an explorer – were considerable. But his contribution to our knowledge of the world is quite as great as that made by anyone.

For Columbus directed man's attention westwards, where the riches of the New World lay.

Further reading

These books, which are among those that helped most in the writing of this book, are suggested for further reading:

AMUNDSEN, R. *The South Pole*   J. Murray, 1912

BLEVINS, W. *Give your heart to the Hawks* Ballantine, 1974

BOTTING, D. *Humboldt and the cosmos*   M. Joseph, 1973; Sphere, 1973

CARRINGTON, H. *The life of Captain Cook* Sidgwick and Jackson, 1967

de VOTO, B. A. *Across the wide Missouri*   Houghton Mifflin, 1947; Eyre and Spottiswoode, 1948

DOUGHTY, C. M. *Travels in Arabia Deserta* C.U.P., 1888; Cape, 1936

GOULD, R. T. *Captain Cook*   Duckworth, 1935

GWYNN, S. L. *The life of Mary Kingsley* Macmillan, 1932

HALL, R. *Stanley: An adventurer explored*   Collins, 1974

HEMMING, J. *The conquest of the Incas*   Macmillan, 1970

HOLLOWAY, D. *Lewis and Clark and the crossing of North America*   Saturday Review Press, 1974

INNES, H. *The Conquistadors*   Collins, 1969

KINGSLEY, M. *Travels in West Africa*   Macmillan, 1897; F. Cass, 3rd edn 1965; C. Knight, n.e. 1972

MOOREHEAD, A. *Cooper's Creek*   H. Hamilton, 1968; White Lion Publishers, 1973

MORGAN, D. L. *Jedediah Smith and the opening of the west*   University of Nebraska Press, 1964

MORISON, S. E. *Christopher Columbus: Admiral of the ocean sea*   O.U.P., 1942

RUSSELL, C. *Firearms, traps and tools of the mountain men*   Knopf, 1967

STANLEY, H. M. *Through the dark continent*   Low, 2 vols 1878–9

SYMONS, A. J. *H. M. Stanley*   Duckworth, 1933; Falcon press, 1950

VILLIERS, A. *Captain Cook, the seaman's seaman* Hodder and Stoughton, 1967; Penguin Books, 1969

Picture Credits

Acknowledgement is due to the following for permission to reproduce illustrations. Figures refer to page numbers.

Radio Times Hulton Picture Library 7; Mansell Collection 8–9; Mansell Collection 10, back cover; Syndication International 11; Radio Times Hulton Picture Library 12; Aftenposten, Oslo 13; Emil Schulthess 18; Royal Geographical Society 19; Mansell Collection 26–7; Royal Geographical Society 28; Syndication International 29; Mrs Ruth M. Robbins front cover, 31; Popperfoto 32–3; Mrs Ruth M. Robbins 34, 37; Arabian American Oil Co. 39, 40; Popperfoto 42, 43, 47, 51; Fitzwilliam Museum, Cambridge 52; Mrs Ruth M. Robbins 53; Radio Times Hulton Picture Library 54, 55, back cover; Mansell Collection 56–7, 61, 62–3; Radio Times Hulton Picture Library 63; Mansell Collection 66, 67; Richard Stanley 68; Radio Times Hulton Picture Library 71; Mansell Collection 72; Illustrated London News 73; Bodleian Library, Oxford, courtesy Mrs J. Brown 74–5; Radio Times Hulton Picture Library 76; Richard Stanley 77; Radio Times Hulton Picture Library front cover, 78, 79 (left); State Library of Victoria, Melbourne front cover, 79 (right); National Gallery of Victoria, Melbourne (Gilbee Bequest, 1907) 81; State Library of Victoria, Melbourne 83, 84–5; John Carnemolla 86–7; Popperfoto 87; John Carnemolla 89; Mansell Collection 91; Radio Times Hulton Picture Library 93; National Library of Australia, Canberra 95 (left); State Library of Victoria, Melbourne 95; Mitchell Library, Sydney 98; Mansell Collection 99, back cover; Liverpool Public Library 101; Radio Times Hulton Picture Library 103 (left); Mansell Collection 103; L. F. Savage 105; Royal Geographical Society 106–7, 109; Barnaby's Picture Library (photo Hubertus Kanus) 111; Mission Evangelique, Paris 115; Derek Holt 120; Missouri Historical Society back cover, 121; Barnaby's Picture Library 122–3; Thomas Gilcrease Institute of American History of Art 124; Missouri Historical Society 125; The Bettmann Archive, New York 127; Museum of the American Indian, Heye

Foundation 130; Barnaby's Picture Library 131; Mary Evans Picture Library 133; History Division – Los Angeles County Museum of Natural History 134; Layne Library, Dakota Wesleyan University, South Dakota 136; Northern Natural Gas Company Collection, Joslyn Art Museum, Omaha, 137, 138; Bettmann Archive 139; Thomas Gilcrease Institute of American History of Art 141; National-Galerie, East Berlin front cover, 143; M. A. von Heinz, East Berlin 145 (bottom); Bildarchiv Preussischer Kulturbesitz, West Berlin 145 (top and bottom right); Deutsche Staatsbibliothek, East Berlin 146; Museum National d'Histoire Naturelle, Paris 147; Deutsche Akademie der Wissenschaften zu Berlin 149; Historia-Photo, Bad Sachsa 150; Bildarchiv Preussischer Kulturbesitz, West Berlin 154; British Museum (photo John Freeman) 158; M. A. von Heinz, East Berlin 162; Linnean Society (photo John Webb) 163; Mary Evans Picture Library front cover, 165; The British Library 166, 168; Mansell Collection 172; The British Library 174, 182–3; Mary Evans Picture Library 184; Foto Mas, Barcelona 185; Radio Times Hulton Picture Library 188, 191; Det Kongelige Bibliotek 192, 194, 197; Mary Evans Picture Library 200; Fotomas Index 201; Mary Evans Picture Library 202; Radio Times Hulton Picture Library 203; Mansell Collection 204; Radio Times Hulton Picture Library 207; National Gallery of Art, Washington 212; Fotomas Index 215; Radio Times Hulton Picture Library 216, 218; The British Library 219, 220; Fotomas Index 221, 222.

The colour photographs for Amundsen were taken by John Perkins, except 8 which was taken by Paul Bonner; for Doughty by Penny Tweedie; for Stanley by David Reed; for Burke and Wills by Penny Tweedie; for Kingsley by Mike Barnard, except 4 which is from Syndication International; for Smith by John Marmaras; for Humboldt by Michael Brennan; for Cook and Pizarro by Roger Jones; and for Columbus by John Perkins.